COMPUTER SIMULATION OF
LINEAR CIRCUITS AND SYSTEMS

THEODORE F. BOGART, Jr.
UNIVERSITY OF SOUTHERN MISSISSIPPI

JOHN WILEY & SONS
NEW YORK CHICHESTER BRISBANE TORONTO SINGAPORE

mw 4/15/85

PREFACE

COMPUTER SIMULATION OF LINEAR CIRCUITS AND SYSTEMS is intended to serve as an introduction to this topic, suitable for engineering and four-year engineering technology students. Users should have a knowledge of BASIC programming and the theory of Laplace transforms, though both of these topics are summarized in early chapters for reference and review purposes. At least one of these subjects could be studied concurrently with the material presented in the book, but for an in-depth coverage of transform theory a supplementary text would probably be desirable.

The ever increasing importance of computers, both as instructional tools and in the industrial environment, was the motivation for the preparation of this material. The widespread availability of computers, particularly with the advent of the microcomputer, makes it imperative that students, engineers, and technologists have the knowledge and experience that will enable them to capitalize on the power that is now so easily accessible to them. Although the emphasis in the book is on digital computer techniques, the last five chapters cover the theory and use of analog computers. These are still valuable instructional tools and have certain other advantages that are discussed in the book.

The principal areas in which computer applications are discussed are transient circuit analysis and control systems theory. Besides computational techniques, the theory behind these topics is explored, including prediction of responses, optimization of design, and interpretation of computer-generated results. Non-linear simulation is covered, but only in the context of a large software package (CSMP) and in analog computer simulation. This is not a textbook on numerical analysis or numerical methods of computation.

Each chapter after the third consists of discussion material that outlines a particular area of the theory and an appropriate computer technique, followed by a set of exercises. The exercises in a sense constitute experimental procedure: they require the writing of programs (or the construction of analog circuits) and an interpretation of the results obtained from their performance.

I would like to thank Mrs. Lenore Seidman for a highly professional job in typing the manual. I am grateful to Dr. Wesley Baldwin of the University of Southern Mississippi for his assistance in preparing the computer-generated plots of transient responses. Thanks also to Dr. Howard Heiden of the University of Southern Mississippi for providing departmental support and encouragement.

THEODORE F. BOGART, JR.

CONTENTS

COMPUTER SIMULATION OF LINEAR CIRCUITS AND SYSTEMS

1 Introduction

ANALYSIS, SYNTHESIS AND SIMULATION

When describing electronic devices or systems, it is conventional to use the word linear in a somewhat loose sense to mean, simply, non-digital. Examples include audio amplifiers, servomotors, tachometers, operational amplifiers, piezoelectric transducers, filters, position control systems, in short, any device or combination of devices whose output is directly proportional to its input. The equations that describe the behavior of these devices, that is, how outputs are functionally related to inputs, are therefore linear equations. The word continuous is also used to describe such components, though this broader category can include devices whose equations are non-linear. Examples are diodes, AM and FM modulators, electronic multipliers, and function generators. In either case, the adjectives linear and/or continuous are used when we wish to emphasize that we are referring to non-digital devices or systems. We thus exclude pulse code modulators, logic gates, flip-flops, shift registers, digital computers, and so forth. In this book, we will be primarily concerned with linear devices, circuits, and systems, though we will have the opportunity to study some continuous, non-linear systems.

Linear systems analysis is the mathematical modeling of linear systems and the procedures we must perform to solve the equations of that model in order to predict responses to excitations. A mathematical model is simply an equation or set of equations which completely describe the system. As a simple example, one model for a capacitor C could be the equation

$$v = \frac{1}{C} \int_0^t i\,dt \tag{1}$$

which relates the voltage v across it to the current i through it. This model is imperfect, since it does not relate the effect of leakage resistance on the voltage, but for many practical situations it is an adequate mathematical representation of the behavior of a capacitor. If a more sophisticated model is required, then a correspondingly more sophisticated equation would be needed to represent it. Whatever the model, the analysis process requires us to solve for the response given the excitation. In the present example, if we regard current as the response to a voltage excitation, then we would solve (1) to find

$$i = C\frac{dv}{dt} \tag{2}$$

Synthesis is concerned with the specification of system components, i.e., with its design, in such a way that it responds in a prescribed way to an excitation. In the previous example, if we wanted the AC current in the capacitor to have a peak value of 1 ampere when the voltage across it is 10 volts at a frequency of 1 kHz, then we would synthesize the circuit by choosing C to be 15.91 μF. Synthesis of complex systems is often a trial and error process involving repeated changes in parameter values followed by repeated analysis.

For example, one way to determine the value of the capacitor required in the example would be to solve equation (2) repeatedly using a 10 volt sine wave for v and different values for C until we found the value of C that resulted in a one ampere peak current. (Of course, in this simple example, that would not be the most efficient way to find C.)

A computer simulation of a linear system is nothing more than the use of a computer to obtain a solution for the equations that model the system. A computer used in this way can be a significant benefit to investigators involved in either the analysis or the synthesis of a system. Whether the simulation is performed on a digital or an analog computer, a principal feature of this approach is the ease with which the user can alter parameter values. The investigator concerned with analysis can specify the parameter values that are appropriate for a particular system and then obtain a fast, reliable result from a simulation run. The system designer can alter parameter values at will until the simulation produces desired results. In each case, he or she is spared the time and labor required for hand computations, as well as the potential for error associated with such computations, and is thus better equipped to focus on the implications of results and the underlying theory.

In our study of simulation using a digital computer, our first approach will be to write programs that produce solutions based on our previous knowledge of the response of a system of a particular type to a particular excitation. Thus we will apply the appropriate theory to analyze a system in general terms, and then implement the solution by programming the computer to evaluate it for user-specified parameter values. We will limit ourselves initially to relatively simple electrical networks which can be solved by straight-forward Laplace transform techniques. For example, we will analyze an RLC circuit to obtain a mathematical expression for the current $i(t)$ that flows after a DC source is switched into it. The form of this expression and its value at any time t will of course depend on the parameter values R, L, and C. We will then write a program that computes current as a function of time and use that program to study the nature of the current as one or more of the values of R, L, and C are varied. A similar approach will be used to simulate simple position control systems, both in the time and frequency (s) domains.

For more complex systems, we will use a program package (CSMP) that will allow us to obtain a time-domain response without first having to find a general form of its equation. Typical of several large software packages available today for simulating a linear system, CSMP allows the programmer to define the individual components of the system using FORTRAN-like statements; the computer then performs all the analysis required. The advantages of a program package such as CSMP are obvious. Disadvantages include the need for a large, fast computer with a substantial memory capacity and the fact that the program software must be purchased.

ANALOG VERSUS DIGITAL SIMULATION

Digital computer simulation necessarily produces discrete values of the solution it derives from the mathematical model of a system. Continuing our capacitor example, the result of a digital computer simulation designed to find $i(t)$ given $v(t)$ would typically be a set of values of the current in the capacitor at specific instants of time, for example, i = 1.0 A at t = 0, i = 0.81 A at t = .1 ms, i = 0.31 A at t = .2 ms, and so forth. The resolution of a digital computer simulation is determined by the programmer's specification of the interval between such computations. Because the modern digital computer can represent extremely small numbers, such as 10^{-73}, the resolution can be as good or better than we would normally require for most practical linear system simulations. However, since each computation of a solution value requires a certain amount of computer time, the greater the resolution, the longer the time required to generate the set of values occurring in a fixed time interval.

The accuracy of the values produced by a digital computer simulation is also better than we need for most practical simulations, since the number of significant digits available to represent a solution value results in a computational accuracy that is usually much better than the accuracy of the mathematical model. This exceptional accuracy is valuable when parameter values are such that numbers nearly equal in value are subtracted or divided. If, for example, the mathematical model requires the computation of the value of $V = 10^5 - 10^5(V_2/V_1)$, and $V_1 = 1.0007$ while $V_2 = 1.0004$, then $V_2/V_1 = .99970021 \simeq 1$. However, $10^5 - 10^5(V_1/V_2) = 29.979$, a value which in the context of the model may be significantly greater than the approximation $10^5 - (1)(10^5) = 0$.

We conclude that high accuracy and good resolution are important advantages of digital computer simulation. Another advantage is the fact that simulations can be performed by users who have no knowledge whatsoever of digital computer hardware. In contrast with analog computer simulation, the programmer need not be concerned with voltage levels, instrument accuracies, scaling, or any other aspects of the mechanisms by which solutions are generated in the computer. These advantages, and the fact that digital computers are now widely accessible, are the reasons that digital computers have largely supplanted their analog counterparts in the simulation of linear systems.

An analog computer employs operational amplifiers and passive components (resistors, capacitors, and potentiometers) that are patched together by a user to simulate a linear system. Non-linear components such as multipliers and function generators are also available for simulating non-linearities in a system. In contrast with the digital computer, the solution produced by an analog computer is <u>continuous</u>. That is, it generates a time-varying voltage whose value at any instant of time is proportional to the value of the solution at that time. The solution therefore has infinite resolution. The accuracy of the solution depends on the accuracy of the hardware components, including the amplifiers, and the accuracy with which the solution voltage can be measured. Also in contrast with the digital computer, the solution from an analog computer is produced in <u>real time</u>. (As we shall see in a later chapter, solutions can also be time-scaled so that they occur in either "fast time" or "slow time.") By real time, we mean that the solution voltage varies with time in precisely the same way that the quantity being simulated would vary with time. The digital computer requires a certain amount of time to calculate each solution value, so, as we have already mentioned, the total time increases with increasing resolution. For this reason, analog computers are used in applications where real-time solutions are a requirement, as, for example, where instantaneous adjustments must be made to continually maintain certain performance criteria. This real-time capability of an analog simulation can be particularly important when the mathematical model is quite complex, as for example when a large number of differential equations must be solved simultaneously. When speed of computation is the primary consideration in such large simulations, the analog computer has a distinct advantage.

Another advantage of analog simulation is the fact that the user is not required to analyze the system model mathematically and produce an explicit expression for the solution. It is only necessary to patch together components that affect voltage levels in the same way that the variables are affected in the mathematical model of a system, apply power, and observe the result.

Analog computers are better than digital computers from the standpoint of affording the investigator immediate insight to the effects of parameter changes. This is especially true when the computer is used in its fast-time, repetitive operation (rep-op) mode. By simply varying potentiometer settings, the user can observe instantaneously the effect that parameter changes have on the shape of the complete solution voltage displayed on an oscilloscope. Synthesis of system components to achieve optimum performance is greatly facilitated in this way. Also, the behavior of other variables in the simulated system can be similarly viewed in real or fast time, giving the investigator a better understanding of overall system performance.

The principal disadvantage of analog computation is that the user must be reasonably well acquainted with the computer hardware for a maximally effective simulation. He or she must be aware of amplifier limitations, noise sources, frequency response, and the capabilities and operation of output display devices. Also, analog computers capable of simulating large, complex systems are expensive and not widely accessible. With the advent of the microcomputer, powerful digital computer capabilities are, in contrast, available to virtually everyone.

2 A Summary of Laplace Transform Theory

INTRODUCTION

When analyzing electrical and electronic circuits, it is frequently necessary to express relationships between electrical variables as mathematical functions of time, and to manipulate these functions to obtain equations that reveal how quantities of interest (voltage, current) change with time. A common example is the equation for the voltage across a capacitor C in an RC network after a DC voltage E is switched into it:

$$v(t) = E(1 - e^{-t/RC})V$$

As we shall see, this equation is the solution to an equation which expresses Kirchhoff's voltage law applied to the circuit when each voltage drop is itself expressed as a time-varying quantity. The importance of time as a variable in network analysis and the time-dependency of current and voltage in most practical networks stems from the fact that the voltage across and current through reactive elements (inductors and capacitors) depend on the rate at which one of the variables is changing. These relations are expressed mathematically by the two fundamental equations:

$$e = L\frac{di}{dt} \tag{1}$$

and

$$i = C\frac{dv}{dt} \tag{2}$$

Equation (1) expresses the fact that the voltage across an inductor is directly proportional to the rate-of-change of the current through it(L, the inductance, being a constant) and equation (2) states that the current through a capacitor is directly proportional to the rate-of-change of the voltage across it. If, for example, the current in an inductor L is sinusoidal, $i = A\sin\omega t$, then the voltage across it is

$$e = L \frac{d(A\sin\omega t)}{dt} = LA\omega\cos\omega t \; V$$

Of course, the time dependence of voltage and current in a network may also be due to the time-varying nature of the voltage or current that is applied to the network, the excitation. A sinusoidal AC voltage source is an example of a time-varying excitation that is often found in practical networks. The voltage or current that is developed in the network due to the excitation is called the response.

As might be supposed from equations (1) and (2), the mathematical functions that we write to describe voltage and current relations in networks are often differential equations, equations that contain derivatives. A solution to a differential equation is a function (of time) that satisfies the differential equation. To illustrate, consider the R-L network shown in Figure 1. We will apply Kirchhoff's voltage law to this network after the switch is closed at t = 0.

5

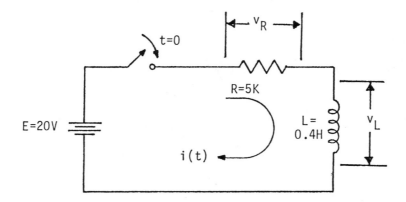

Figure 1. A series RL network whose differential equation
is $20 = i(5 \times 10^3) + .4\, di/dt$.

At each instant of time after the switch is closed, Kirchhoff's voltage law states that

$$E = v_R + v_L$$

In terms of the current i(t) that follows in the circuit, this equation may be written

$$E = iR + L\frac{di}{dt}$$

or,

$$20 = i(5 \times 10^3) + .4\frac{di}{dt} \tag{3}$$

Equation (3) is a differential equation whose "unknown" is the current i, actually the function i(t). It can be shown that the solution is

$$i(t) = \frac{E}{R}\left[1 - e^{-t/(L/R)}\right] A$$

$$= 4 \times 10^{-3}\left[1 - e^{-t/80 \times 10^{-6}}\right] A \tag{4}$$

EXERCISES

1. Write the mathematical expression for the voltage across a 20 mH inductor when the current through it is $i = 50\sin 100t$ A.

2. Write the mathematical expression for the current through a .05 μF capacitor when the voltage across it is $v = 4\sin(10^6 t - 30°)$ V.

3. Write the mathematical expression for the voltage across a 0.5 H inductor when a DC current of 250 mA flows in it.

4. Write the mathematical expression for the voltage across a 25 μF capacitor when the current through it is $i = 40\cos 10^5 t$ A. (Hint: integrate both sides of equation (2) to obtain a general expression for v in terms of the integral of i.)

5. By substituting equation (4) (and its derivative) into equation (3), verify that (4) is a solution to (3).

6. Show that $v = \sin\omega t$ is a solution to the differential equation

$$\frac{d^2v}{dt^2} + \omega^2 v = 0.$$

THE LAPLACE TRANSFORM

There are a number of standard mathematical techniques available for solving differential equations, many of which require a thorough knowledge of calculus and considerable insight. The method of Laplace transforms, on the other hand, provides us with a technique for solving differential equations that is purely algebraic. Using a <u>table</u> of Laplace transforms, we convert, or transform, time varying quantities to another "domain," in which we may find a solution to a differential equation by strictly algebraic manipulations. The solution obtained in this way is then inverse-transformed, again by use of the table, to produce the desired solution as a function of time. When dealing with variables that are expressed as functions of time, we say that we are in the "time-domain."

The Laplace transform of a time-domain function f(t) is written F(s) and is defined by the following equation:

$$F(s) = \int_0^\infty f(t)e^{-st}dt \tag{5}$$

Equation (5) states that f(t) is transformed by multiplying it by e^{-st} and then integrating the result between the limits t = 0 and t = ∞. Note that the result of this integration will never have the variable t appearing in it, since the integration is with respect to t (t is "integrated out"). As far as the integration is concerned, s is treated as a constant. Therefore, the result of the integration <u>will</u> contain s, and will in fact be a function of s, F(s). As an example, we will apply equation (4) to find the Laplace transform of $f(t) = e^{-at}$, where a is a constant.

$$F(s) = \int_0^\infty e^{-at} e^{-st} dt$$

$$= \int_0^\infty e^{-(s + a)t} dt$$

$$= -\frac{1}{s + a} e^{-(s + a)t} \Big]_{t = 0}^{t = \infty}$$

$$= -\frac{1}{s + a} (0-1) = \frac{1}{s + a}$$

(Note that we require (s + a) > 0, in order that $e^{-(s + a)t}$ be zero when evaluated at t = ∞. This is a mathematical restriction which need not concern us in the practical problems that follow. In practice, the constant a in e^{-at} will always be a positive number.) Thus, the Laplace transform of, say, $f(t) = e^{-3t}$ is F(s) = 1/(s + 3). The transformation is often expressed by the symbol $\mathcal{L}$. We write

$$\mathscr{L}\{f(t)\} = F(s)$$

In the example above,

$$\mathscr{L}(e^{-3t}) = \frac{1}{s+3}$$

Note that is <u>not</u> correct to write $e^{-3t} = \frac{1}{s+3}$, a common error.

A very useful function in network analysis is the <u>unit step</u> function u(t). This function is defined by

$$u(t) = 0 \text{ for } t < 0 \tag{6}$$

$$= 1 \text{ for } t \geq 0$$

Note that u(t) has value zero for all time up to t = 0, where it changes value instantaneously to 1 and retains that value for all positive time. The unit step is sketched in Figure 2.

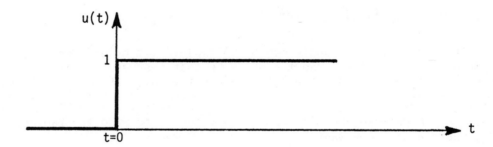

Figure 2. The unit step function.

The unit step function is often multiplied by the function representing an excitation to express the fact that the excitation is applied, or switched into, a circuit at t = 0. Since the step function is zero for t < 0, the value of its product with the excitation is also zero for t < 0. For t > 0, the product is identical to the excitation, since u(t) = 1 for t ≥ 0. For example, the function

$$5\cos(100t)u(t) \tag{7}$$

has value zero for all t ≤ 0 and value 5 for t = 0. For t ≥ 0, (7) has exactly the same values as 5cos100t.

A step function may have value other than unity for t ≥ 0. A K-unit step function is defined by

$$Ku(t) = 0 \text{ for } t < 0$$

$$= K \text{ for } t \geq 0$$

Note that K may be any real number, positive or negative. The switching of a DC current or voltage source into a network at t = 0 may be expressed using this type of step function. For example, the 10 volt step 10u(t) represents a + 10 V DC source switched into a network at t = 0.

The Laplace transform of a K-unit step may be found from the definition as follows:

$$\mathscr{L}\{Ku(t)\} = \int_0^\infty Ku(t)e^{-st}\,dt$$

$$= K\int_0^\infty e^{-st}\,dt$$

$$= K\left[-\frac{1}{s}e^{-st}\right]_0^\infty$$

$$= K\{0 - (\frac{-1}{s})\} = \frac{K}{s}$$

Another widely used time-domain function is the Dirac delta function, also known as an impulse function. The Greek letter δ is used to symbolize this function, which has the unusual property that it is equal to zero for all t except t = 0. In conventional integral calculus, a function which is zero everywhere except at a single point must have an integral equal to zero (since it has zero width, it must have zero area). But the integral of the impulse function δ(t), over any interval that includes t = 0, is equal to 1! By definition,

$$\delta(t) = 0,\ t \neq 0$$

and

$$\int_{-\infty}^\infty \delta(t)dt = 1$$

We can think of this function as having all of its "area" (1) concentrated at a single point, where the function has zero width and infinite height. More rigorously, think of the impulse function as being the limit of a rectangle whose area keeps the value 1 while we allow its width to shrink to zero. Clearly, the height of the rectangle must grow, and in the limit approach infinity, if the area is kept constant while the width shrinks. Similarly, the function Kδ(t) has area, or "weight", as is frequently said, equal to K.

On a graph, Kδ(t) is shown by a single arrow, drawn upward for positive K and downward for negative K. See Figure 3.

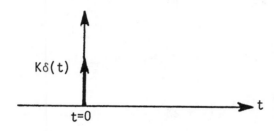

Figure 3. An impulse function having
weight K.

To find the Laplace transform of the impulse function, we write

$$\mathscr{L}\, K\delta(t) = \int_0^\infty K\delta(t)e^{-st}dt = K$$

This result follows from the fact that $\delta(t) = 0$ for all t except t = 0, which means the product $\delta(t)e^{-st}$ must be zero for all t except t = 0; and at t = 0, $e^{-st} = e^0 = 1$.

The Laplace transform is a <u>linear</u> operator, that is,

$$\mathscr{L}\{Kf(t)\} = K\,\mathscr{L}\{f(t)\}$$

where K is any constant, and

$$\mathscr{L}\{f_1(t) \pm f_2(t)\} = \mathscr{L}\{f_1(t)\} \pm \mathscr{L}\{f_2(t)\}$$

The linearity property follows from the fact that the transform is defined by an integration (equation 4), and integration is a linear operation in the same sense. ("The integral of a sum is the sum of the integrals," for example.) The linearity property for the Laplace transform may be paraphrased by stating that the transform of a sum of time-domain functions is the sum of the transforms of those functions, and the transform of a constant times a function is the constant times the transform of the function. Following are examples:

$$\mathscr{L}\{10e^{-2t}\} = 10\,\mathscr{L}(e^{-2t}) = \frac{10}{s+2}$$

$$\mathscr{L}\{u(t) + \delta(t)\} = \mathscr{L}\{u(t)\} + \mathscr{L}\{\delta(t)\} = \frac{1}{s} + 1$$

$$\mathscr{L}\{5e^{-.5t} - 2u(t)\} = \frac{5}{s+.5} - \frac{2}{s}$$

Note that it is NOT true that the transform of a product is the product of the transforms. In other words,

$$\mathscr{L}\{f_1(t)f_2(t)\} \neq \mathscr{L}\{f_1(t)\}\,\mathscr{L}\{f_2(t)\}$$

EXERCISES

7. By direct application of the definition of the Laplace transform (equation 5), verify that

$$\mathscr{L}\{\tfrac{1}{a}(1-e^{-at})\} = \frac{1}{s(s+a)}$$

8. By direct application of the definition of the Laplace transform (equation 5), verify that

$$\mathscr{L}(t) = \frac{1}{s^2}.$$

(Hint: you will need to apply integration by parts, i.e.,

$$\int u\,dv \ = \ uv \ -\int v\,du.)$$

9. Using the Laplace transforms already derived, including those in exercises 7 and 8, use the linearity property to find the Laplace transform of each of the following:

(a) $10^3\delta(t) - \dfrac{u(t)}{2}$

(b) $.5(1 - e^{-.5t}) + \dfrac{t}{4}$

(c) $50t - 4 + e^{-4t}$

(d) $20(1 - e^{-5t})$

(e) $\delta(t) + u(t) - t$

10. The <u>ramp</u> voltage $v(t) = 12t$ is switched into a network at $t = 0$. Express this excitation mathematically and sketch it versus time. What is the value of the excitation at $t = 40$ ms?

11. What is the derivative of $100u(t)$? What is the integral of $0.5\delta(t)$?

12. Using the definition of the Laplace transform, prove the linearity property.

INVERSE TRANSFORMATION

The process of obtaining the time-domain function that corresponds to a given Laplace transform is called <u>inverse</u> transformation. Thus if $\mathscr{L}\{f(t)\} = F(s)$, then $f(t)$ is the inverse transform of $\overline{F(s)}$ and we write

$$\mathscr{L}^{-1}F(s) \ = \ f(t).$$

For example,

$$\mathscr{L}^{-1}(\frac{4}{s + 3}) \ = \ 4e^{-3t}$$

and

$$\mathscr{L}^{-1}\{5 - \frac{2}{s}\} \ = \ 5\delta(t) - 2u(t)$$

(Note that $\mathscr{L}\,5\delta(t) = 5$, so $\mathscr{L}^{-1}(5) = 5\delta(t)$.)

Inverse transformation is linear in the same sense that we discussed earlier.

A table that contains time-domain functions and their corresponding transforms (that is, a table of transforms and inverse transforms) is called a table of <u>Laplace transform pairs</u> and is extremely useful when solving practical problems using transform techniques. Following is a table containing many commonly used transform pairs that have been derived by investigators.

TABLE OF LAPLACE TRANSFORM PAIRS

$f(t)$	$F(s)$
1. $\delta(t)$ unit impulse	1
2. 1 or unit step $u(t)$	$\dfrac{1}{s}$
3. t	$\dfrac{1}{s^2}$
4. $\dfrac{1}{(n-1)!}\, t^{n-1}$	$\dfrac{1}{s^n}$
5. e^{-at}	$\dfrac{1}{s+a}$
6. $\dfrac{1}{(n-1)!}\, t^{n-1} e^{-at}$	$\dfrac{1}{(s+a)^n}$
7. $\dfrac{1}{a}(1 - e^{-at})$	$\dfrac{1}{s(s+a)}$
8. $\dfrac{1}{ab}\left[1 - \left(\dfrac{b}{b-a}\right)e^{-at} + \left(\dfrac{a}{b-a}\right)e^{-bt}\right]$	$\dfrac{1}{s(s+a)(s+b)}$
9. $\dfrac{1}{ab}\left\{\alpha - \left[\dfrac{b(\alpha-a)}{b-a}\right]e^{-at} + \left[\dfrac{a(\alpha-b)}{b-a}\right]e^{-bt}\right\}$	$\dfrac{s+\alpha}{s(s+a)(s+b)}$
10. $\dfrac{1}{b-a}(e^{-at} - e^{-bt})$	$\dfrac{1}{(s+a)(s+b)}$
11. $\dfrac{1}{a-b}(ae^{-at} - be^{-bt})$	$\dfrac{s}{(s+a)(s+b)}$
12. $\dfrac{1}{b-a}\left[(\alpha-a)e^{-at} - (\alpha-b)e^{-bt}\right]$	$\dfrac{s+\alpha}{(s+a)(s+b)}$
13. $\sin \omega t$	$\dfrac{\omega}{s^2+\omega^2}$
14. $\cos \omega t$	$\dfrac{s}{s^2+\omega^2}$
15. $\dfrac{\sqrt{\alpha^2+\omega^2}}{\omega}\sin(\omega t + \theta)$ where $\theta = \arctan\dfrac{\omega}{\alpha}$	$\dfrac{s+\alpha}{s^2+\omega^2}$
16. $\dfrac{1}{\omega^2}(1 - \cos \omega t)$	$\dfrac{1}{s(s^2+\omega^2)}$
17. $\dfrac{\alpha}{\omega^2} - \dfrac{\sqrt{\alpha^2-\omega^2}}{\omega^2}\cos(\omega t + \theta)$ where $\theta = \arctan\dfrac{\omega}{\alpha}$	$\dfrac{s+\alpha}{s(s^2+\omega^2)}$
18. $\dfrac{1}{b}e^{-at}\sin bt$	$\dfrac{1}{(s+a)^2+b^2}$
19. $e^{-at}\cos bt$	$\dfrac{s+a}{(s+a)^2+b^2}$
20. For $\zeta < 1$, $\dfrac{1}{\omega_n\sqrt{1-\zeta^2}}e^{-\zeta\omega_n t}\sin(\omega_n\sqrt{1-\zeta^2}\,t)$	$\dfrac{1}{s^2+2\zeta\omega_n s+\omega_n^2}$

21. $\dfrac{1}{a^2}(at - 1 + e^{-at})$ $\qquad$ $\dfrac{1}{s^2(s + a)}$

22. $\dfrac{1}{a^2}(1 - e^{-at} - ate^{-at})$ $\qquad$ $\dfrac{1}{s(s + a)^2}$

23. $\dfrac{\sqrt{(\alpha - a)^2 + b^2}}{b}\,e^{-at}\sin(bt + \theta)$ $\qquad$ $\dfrac{s + \alpha}{(s + a)^2 + b^2}$

$\qquad$ where $\theta = \arctan\dfrac{b}{\alpha - a}$

24. $\dfrac{e^{-at}}{a^2 + \omega^2} + \dfrac{\sin(\omega t - \theta)}{\omega\sqrt{(a^2 + \omega^2)}}$ $\qquad$ $\dfrac{1}{(s + a)(s^2 + \omega^2)}$

$\qquad$ where $\theta = \arctan(\omega/a)$

25. $\dfrac{e^{-at}}{\omega^2 + a^2 - \zeta a\omega} + e^{-\zeta\omega t}\sin(\omega\sqrt{1 - \zeta^2}\,t - \theta)$ $\qquad$ $\dfrac{1}{(s + a)(s^2 + 2\zeta\omega s + \omega^2)}$

$\qquad$ where $\theta = \arctan\left(\dfrac{\omega\sqrt{1 - \zeta^2}}{a - \zeta\omega}\right)$

26. $\dfrac{-ae^{-at}}{\omega^2 + a^2} + \dfrac{\cos(\omega t - \theta)}{\sqrt{(\omega^2 + a^2)}}$ $\qquad$ $\dfrac{s}{(s + a)(s^2 + \omega^2)}$

$\qquad$ where $\theta = \arctan(\omega/a)$

27. $\dfrac{-ae^{-at}}{a^2\omega^2 - 2\zeta a\omega + \omega^2} + \dfrac{e^{-\zeta\omega t}\sin(\omega\sqrt{1 - \zeta^2}\,t - \theta)}{\sqrt{(1 - \zeta^2)(a^2\omega^2 - 2\zeta a\omega + \omega^2)}}$ $\qquad$ $\dfrac{s}{(s + a)(s^2 + 2\zeta\omega s + \omega^2)}$

$\qquad$ where $\theta = \arctan\left(\dfrac{\omega\sqrt{1 - \zeta^2}}{a - \zeta\omega}\right) - \arctan\left(\dfrac{\sqrt{1 - \zeta^2}}{-\zeta}\right)$

28. $\dfrac{1}{2\zeta\omega^2}\sin\omega t - \dfrac{e^{-\zeta\omega t}}{2\zeta\omega^2\sqrt{1 - \zeta^2}}\sin\omega\sqrt{1 - \zeta^2}\,t$ $\qquad$ $\dfrac{s}{(s^2 + \omega^2)(s^2 + 2\zeta\omega s + \omega^2)}$

29. $\dfrac{(a - b)e^{-bt}}{\omega^2 + b^2} + \dfrac{1}{\omega}\left(\dfrac{\omega^2 + a^2}{\omega^2 + b^2}\right)\sin(\omega t + \theta)$ $\qquad$ $\dfrac{s + a}{(s + b)(s^2 + \omega^2)}$

$\qquad$ where $\theta = \arctan(\omega/a) - \arctan(\omega/b)$

More extensive tables are available in the literature. See, for example, Gardner and Barnes, Transients in Linear Systems (Wiley, 1956) or Nixon, Handbook of Laplace Transformation (Prentice-Hall, 1960).

14

Typically, when using the table to solve a problem using Laplace transforms, we look up the transforms of the time-domain quantities that occur in the problem, manipulate these transforms to obtain another transform, and then use the table again to find the inverse transform of the latter. However, it is usually the case that the transforms and inverse transforms arising in a practical problem do not appear in precisely the same form as those listed in the table, and we must therefore modify our functions algebraically to obtain the forms shown in the table. As a simple example, suppose we wished to find the inverse transform of

$$F(s) = \frac{2}{2s + 4}$$

There is no transform in the table that fits this particular expression, but if we divide numerator and denominator by 2, we obtain the equivalent transform

$$F(s) = \frac{1}{s + 2}$$

whose inverse transform is, from pair (5), $f(t) = e^{-2t}$. As another example, suppose we wish to use the table to find the transform of $f(t) = t^3 e^{-10t}$. According to pair (6) in the table,

$$\mathscr{L}\,\frac{1}{(n-1)!}\,t^{n-1}e^{-at} = \frac{1}{(s + a)^n}$$

By virtue of the linearity property, this is equivalent to

$$\mathscr{L}\{t^{n-1}e^{-at}\} = \frac{(n-1)!}{(s + a)^n} \tag{8}$$

Since we wish to find the transform of $t^3 e^{-10t}$, we must set n = 4 and a = 10 to make $t^3 e^{-10t}$ fit the form of the left side of (8). Thus,

$$\mathscr{L}\{t^3 e^{-10t}\} = \frac{4!}{(s + 10)^4} = \frac{24}{(s + 10)^4}$$

Note that pair (6) in the table is equivalent to

$$\mathscr{L}\{\frac{1}{n!}t^n e^{-at}\} = \frac{1}{(s + a)^{n + 1}}$$

and also to

$$\mathscr{L}\{t^n e^{-at}\} = \frac{n!}{(s + a)^{n + 1}}$$

As another example, suppose we wish to find the inverse transform of $F(s) = \frac{10^6}{s^2 + 25}$. By rewriting F(s) in the equivalent form

$$F(s) = (2 \times 10^5)\left(\frac{5}{s^2 + 5^2}\right)$$

we see from pair (13) in the table that

$$\mathscr{L} f(t) = 2 \times 10^5 \sin 5t$$

As a final example, suppose we wish to find the Laplace transform of $10\sin(\omega t + 30^0)$. One approach to this problem is first to express the function as the sum of sine and cosine terms with zero phase angles. Recall that $A\sin(\omega t + \theta) = A\sin\theta\cos\omega t + A\cos\theta\sin\omega t$. Thus, $10\sin(\omega t + 30^0) = 10\sin30^0 \cos\omega t + 10\cos30^0\sin\omega t = 5\cos\omega t + 8.67\sin\omega t$. Then using pairs (13) and (14) and applying the linearity property,

$$F(s) = \frac{5s}{s^2 + \omega^2} + \frac{8.67}{s^2 + \omega^2}$$

EXERCISES

13. Using the table of Laplace transform pairs, find the Laplace transform of each of the following:

    (a) $30t^4 e^{-7t}$

    (b) $.04\cos75t$

    (c) $\dfrac{e^{-t/2}}{0.2}$

    (d) $e^{-.05t}\sin100t$

    (e) $600(1 - \cos t)$

    (f) $50\sin(10^3 t - 60^0)$

    (g) $.025\cos(25t + 45^0)$

14. Using the table of Laplace transform pairs, find the inverse transform of each of the following:

    (a) $\dfrac{4 \times 10^6}{50s + 200}$

    (b) $\dfrac{100}{12s(2.5s + 1)}$

    (c) $\dfrac{1}{s^2 + 10^4}$

    (d) $\dfrac{s}{(.2s + 1)(.5s + 1)}$

    (e) $\dfrac{s + 10^3}{4s(10s + 1)(s + 10)}$

    (f) $\dfrac{10^5}{(s + 5)^3}$

(g) $\dfrac{10}{s^2 + 8s + 9}$ (Hint: Complete the square in the denominator and use pair 18.)

DIFFERENTIATION AND INTEGRATION

We have already discussed the significance of derivatives in the study and analysis of electrical circuits. Equations (1) and (2) reveal the importance of the derivatives of current and voltage in inductors and capacitors. By integrating both sides of each of equations (1) and (2) between the limits 0 and t, we may derive the following equally important relations:

$$i = \frac{1}{L} \int_0^t v\,dt \tag{9}$$

$$v = \frac{1}{C} \int_0^t i\,dt \tag{10}$$

Since both derivatives and integrals are likely to occur in the analysis of a circuit, we must be able to transform both the derivative and the integral of a time-domain function when using the transform method to solve the circuit. Given that the transform of a certain f(t) is F(s), i.e., given that $\mathscr{L}\{f(t)\} = F(s)$, then the transform of the derivative of f(t) may be found using the following relation:

$$\mathscr{L}\{f'(t)\} = sF(s) - f(0) \tag{11}$$

where f'(t) denotes the derivative of f with respect to time, and f(0) is f(t) evaluated at t = 0. The term f(0) is called the <u>initial condition</u>. For example, suppose f(t) = e^{-2t}. Then we know that F(s) = 1/(s + 2), and therefore

$$\mathscr{L}\{f'(t)\} = s\left(\frac{1}{s+2}\right) - e^0 = \frac{s}{s+2} - 1 = \frac{s-(s+2)}{s+2} = \frac{-2}{s+2}$$

Note that f'(t) = $-2e^{-2t}$ and $\mathscr{L}(-2e^{-2t}) = \dfrac{-2}{s+2}$, confirming the above result.

Again, if $\mathscr{L}\{f(t)\} = F(s)$, then the transform of f''(t), the second derivative of f(t), may be found from

$$\mathscr{L}\{f''(t)\} = s^2 F(s) - sf(0) - f'(0) \tag{12}$$

where f'(0) is the first derivative of f(t) evaluated at t = 0.

Given that $\mathscr{L}\{f(t)\} = F(s)$, the Laplace transform of the integral of f(t) may be found from

$$\mathscr{L}\left[\int_0^t f(t)\,dt\right] = \frac{F(s)}{s} \tag{13}$$

For example, if f(t) = 4t then F(s) = $\dfrac{4}{s^2}$ and

$$\mathscr{L}\left[\int_0^t 4t\,dt\right] = \dfrac{4}{s^2}\Big/s = \dfrac{4}{s^3}$$

Note that $\displaystyle\int_0^t 4t\,dt = 2t^2$ and $\mathscr{L}(2t^2) = \dfrac{4}{s^3}$, confirming the above result.

From equation (1)

$$v = L\dfrac{di}{dt}$$

Taking the Laplace transform of each side, and assuming i(0) = 0, we have

$$V(s) = LsI(s) \qquad\qquad (14)$$

The assumption that i(0) = 0 means that we are assuming there is no initial current in the inductor. Dividing both sides of (14) by I(s), we obtain

$$\dfrac{V(s)}{I(s)} = Ls \qquad\qquad (15)$$

Since the ratio of voltage to current is <u>impedance</u>, equation (15) gives us the transform of the impedance of an inductor L, namely Ls.

Similarly. from equation (10),

$$v = \dfrac{1}{C}\int_0^t i\,dt$$

Transforming, we obtain

$$V(s) = \dfrac{I(s)}{Cs} \qquad\qquad (16)$$

from which we obtain the transform of the impedance of a capacitor C,

$$\dfrac{V(s)}{I(s)} = \dfrac{1}{Cs} \qquad\qquad (17)$$

EXERCISES

15. Given that f(t) = 2t−u(t) and $\mathscr{L}\{f(t)\} = \dfrac{2}{s^2} - \dfrac{1}{s}$, use equation (11) to find $\mathscr{L}\{f'(t)\}$.

16. Use equation (12) to find $\mathscr{L}\{f''(t)\}$ given that f(t) = $10e^{-5t}$ and $\mathscr{L}\{f(t)\}$ = 10/(s + 5). Now differentiate f(t) twice and find the Laplace transform of the result, using the table. Show that the transform obtained this way is the same as the transform found by using equation (12).

17. Given that f(t) = $8e^{-t/2}$ and F(s) = 8/(s + .5), use equation (13) to find

$$\mathcal{L}\left[\int_0^t f(t)dt\right]$$

Now integrate f(t) between 0 and t and find the Laplace transform of the result, using the table. Show that the transform obtained this way is the same as the transform found by using equation (13).

18. Given pair (3) in the table of transform pairs, using equation (11) to derive pair (2).

19. Given pair (13) in the table of transform pairs, use equation (11) to derive pair (14).

20. Given pair (2) of the table of transform pairs, use equation (13) to derive pair (3).

21. Find the transform of the impedance of

    (a) a .02 µF capacitor

    (b) a 40 mH inductor

SOLVING DIFFERENTIAL EQUATIONS

To solve a differential equation using Laplace transforms, we first transform each term in the equation and then solve for the "unknown" function in terms of s. It is conventional to use capital letters to represent transformed functions. Thus, the transform of a function i(t) would be written I(s). To illustrate, suppose we wish to solve the differential equation

$$\frac{di}{dt} + 4i = 8u(t)$$

Writing the transform of each term and assuming zero initial condition, i.e. i(0) = 0, we obtain

$$sI(s) + 4I(s) = \frac{8}{s}$$

Solving for I(s),

$$I(s)(s + 4) = \frac{8}{s}$$

$$I(s) = \frac{8}{s(s + 4)}$$

Finally, we obtain the solution i(t) by finding the inverse transform of I(s). From pair (7) of the table,

$$i(t) = 8\{\tfrac{1}{4}(1 - e^{-4t})\}$$

$$= 2 - 2e^{-4t}$$

As another example, suppose

$$\frac{d^2v}{dt^2} + 6\frac{dv}{dt} + 8v = 12u(t)$$

with initial conditions $v(0) = 0$, $v'(0) = 4$. Transforming, we obtain

$$s^2V(s) - sv(0) - v'(0) + 6\{sV(s) - v(0)\} + 8V(s) = 12/s$$

$$s^2V(s) - 0 - 4 + 6sV(s) - 0 + 8V(s) = 12/s$$

$$V(s)(s^2 + 6s + 8) = 12/s + 4$$

$$V(s) = \frac{12}{s(s + 2)(s + 4)} + \frac{4}{(s + 2)(s + 4)}$$

Using pairs (8) and (10) from the table, we find

$$v(t) = \frac{12}{8}(1 - 2e^{-2t} + e^{-4t}) + \frac{4}{2}(e^{-2t} - e^{-4t})$$

$$= 1.5 - e^{-2t} - .5e^{-4t}$$

Note that this solution satisfies the initial conditions that were specified, $v(0) = 0$, and $v'(0) = 4$. As an exercise, substitute the solution into the original differential equation and verify that it is a solution.

As a final example, suppose

$$6\frac{di}{dt} + 12i = \sin 6t$$

Assuming $i(0) = 0$, we transform the equation and obtain

$$6sI(s) + 12I(s) = \frac{6}{s^2 + 36}$$

Then

$$I(s)(6s + 12) = \frac{6}{s^2 + 36}$$

$$I(s) = \frac{6}{6(s + 2)(s^2 + 36)} = \frac{1}{(s + 2)(s^2 + 36)}$$

and from pair (24)

$$i(t) = \frac{e^{-2t}}{40} + \frac{1}{6\sqrt{40}} \sin(6t - \theta)$$

where $\theta = \arctan(6/2) = 71.56°$.

EXERCISES

22. Use Laplace transforms to solve each of the following differential equations, subject to the initial conditions given. In each case, verify that your solution satisfies the initial conditions, and verify that it satisfies the differential equation.

(a) $\dfrac{di}{dt} + 20i = 0$; $i(0) = 5$

(b) $0.5\dfrac{dv}{dt} + 0.1v = 4.5u(t);\quad v(0) = 0$

(c) $10^3\dfrac{di}{dt} + 500i = 100u(t);\quad i(0) = 1$

(d) $\dfrac{d^2v}{dt^2} + 11\dfrac{dv}{dt} + 10v = 10^5u(t);\quad v(0) = 0,\ v'(0) = 0$

(e) $\dfrac{d^2i}{dt^2} + 8\dfrac{di}{dt} + 16i = 12u(t);\quad i(0) = 0,\ i'(0) = 0$

(f) $\dfrac{dv}{dt} + 8v = \cos t;\quad v(0) = 0$

PARTIAL FRACTIONS

It is often the case that the transform of the solution to a problem cannot be found in a table of transform pairs. However, by using the method known as partial fractions the transform can frequently be expressed as a sum of transforms that can be found in the table, and it is therefore possible to determine its inverse. To apply the method, the transform whose inverse is desired must be written with its denominator expressed as a product of factors of the form (s + a), (s + b), ..., where any of a, b, ..., may be zero. In other words, F(s) must be written in the form

$$F(s) = \frac{P(s)}{(s + a)(s + b) \ldots (s + z)}$$

where P(s) is a polynomial in s and any of a, b, ..., may be zero. We will discuss first the case where a, b, ..., are all distinct values, i.e., we assume there are no terms of the form $(s + a)^2$ or $(s + a)^3$, etc.

The first step in the procedure is to equate F(s) to a sum of terms with unknown co-efficients A, B, C, ..., where each term has a denominator equal to one of the factors of F(s). There must be one term for each factor in the denominator of F(s). Thus we write

$$F(s) = \frac{P(s)}{(s + a)(s + b)\ldots(s + z)} = \frac{A}{(s + a)} + \frac{B}{(s + b)} + \ldots + \frac{Z}{s + z}$$

For example,

$$F(s) = \frac{s^2 + 1}{(s + 1)(s + 2)(s + 10)} = \frac{A}{(s + 1)} + \frac{B}{(s + 2)} + \frac{C}{(s + 10)}$$

The next step is to find the values of the coefficients A, B, C, ..., in such a way that the equality we have assumed will hold. The proper values of the coefficients may be found by performing the following computations:

$$A = (s + a)F(s)\Big|_{s = -a}$$

$$B = (s + b)F(s)\Big|_{s = -b}$$

In our example,

$$A = (s + 1) \frac{(s^2 + 1)}{(s + 1)(s + 2)(s + 10)}\bigg|_{s = -1} = \frac{(-1)^2 + 1}{(-1 + 2)(-1 + 10)} = \frac{2}{9}$$

$$B = (s + 2) \frac{(s^2 + 1)}{(s + 1)(s + 2)(s + 10)}\bigg|_{s = -2} = \frac{(-2)^2 + 1}{(-2 + 1)(-2 + 10)} = \frac{-5}{8}$$

$$C = (s + 10) \frac{(s^2 + 1)}{(s + 1)(s + 2)(s + 10)}\bigg|_{s = -10} = \frac{(-10)^2 + 1}{(-10 + 1)(-10 + 2)} = \frac{101}{72}$$

Note in each case the cancellation of one of the factors in the denominator of F(s). The factor that cancels is the one corresponding to the term whose coefficient is being evaluated.

Having determined the values of A, B, and C, we can write

$$F(s) = \frac{s^2 + 1}{(s + 1)(s + 2)(s + 10)} = \frac{2/9}{s + 1} - \frac{5/8}{s + 2} + \frac{101/72}{s + 10}$$

The inverse of F(s) is now easily found to be

$$f(t) = \frac{2}{9} e^{-t} - \frac{5}{8} e^{-2t} + \frac{101}{72} e^{-10t}$$

As another example, suppose we wish to find the inverse of

$$F(s) = \frac{s + 8}{s(s^2 + 16s + 48)}$$

We first express the denominator as a product of factors:

$$F(s) = \frac{s + 8}{s(s + 4)(s + 12)}$$

Then

$$F(s) = \frac{s + 8}{s(s + 4)(s + 12)} = \frac{A}{s} + \frac{B}{s + 4} + \frac{C}{s + 12}$$

Note in this case that a = 0. Finding A, B, and C as before,

$$A = \frac{s(s + 8)}{s(s + 4)(s + 12)}\bigg|_{s = 0} = \frac{8}{(4)(12)} = \frac{1}{6}$$

$$B = \frac{(s + 4)(s + 8)}{s(s + 4)(s + 12)}\bigg|_{s = -4} = \frac{4}{-4(8)} = \frac{-1}{8}$$

$$C = \frac{(s + 12)(s + 8)}{s(s + 4)(s + 12)}\Bigg|_{s = -12} = \frac{-4}{-12(-8)} = \frac{1}{24}$$

Therefore,

$$F(s) = \frac{s + 8}{s(s + 4)(s + 12)} = \frac{1/6}{s} - \frac{1/8}{s + 4} - \frac{1/24}{s + 12}$$

It is a good idea to check one's work at this point by combining the right hand side over a least common denominator, collecting terms in the resulting numerator, and verifying that the result is indeed equal to the left hand side. If this is not the case, then an error has been made in the evaluation of the coefficients A, B, C. Once the check has been made, the inverse transform in this example is seen to be

$$f(t) = \frac{1}{6} u(t) - \frac{1}{8} e^{-4t} - \frac{1}{24} e^{-12t}$$

The values $s = -a$, $s = -b$, ..., that are used to evaluate the coefficients A, B, C,..., are called the <u>poles</u> of F(s). Note that when F(s) is evaluated at a pole, the magnitude of F(s) becomes infinite. In the preceding example, F(s) has poles at $s = 0$, $s = 4$, and $s = -12$. A value of s that causes F(s) to equal zero is called a <u>zero</u> of F(s). In the preceding example, $s = -8$ is a zero of F(s).

When the denominator of F(s) contains one or more terms of the form $(s + a)^n$, where $n > 1$, the method of partial fractions described above must be modified. A denominator term of the form $(s + a)^n$ is called a pole of <u>order n</u>, or a repeated pole. We will discuss only poles of order two. When F(s) has one or more poles of order two, the expansion of F(s) into a sum of terms must include one term for each pole itself and one term for each repeated pole. To illustrate, suppose

$$F(s) = \frac{s + 1}{s(s + 4)^2}$$

This F(s) has a pole at $s = 0$ and a repeated pole of order two at $s = -4$. We therefore expand it in partial fractions as follows

$$F(s) = \frac{s + 1}{s(s + 4)^2} = \frac{A}{s} + \frac{B}{(s + 4)} + \frac{C}{(s + 4)^2}$$

The coefficients A and C are evaluated in a similar way to that previously described. Thus

$$A = \frac{s(s + 1)}{s(s + 4)^2}\Bigg|_{s = 0} = \frac{1}{16}$$

$$C = \frac{(s + 4)^2(s + 1)}{s(s + 4)^2}\Bigg|_{s = -4} = \frac{3}{4}$$

However, to determine the coefficient B of the term containing $(s + 4)$ in the denominator we must perform the following computation:

$$B = \left[\frac{d}{ds} (s + b)^2 F(s)\right]_{s = -b}$$

$$= \left[\frac{d}{ds} (s + 4)^2 \frac{(s + 1)}{s(s + 4)^2} \right]_{s \ = \ -4}$$

$$= \left[\frac{d}{ds} (1 + 1/s) \right]_{s \ = \ -4}$$

$$= \left. \frac{-1}{s^2} \right|_{s \ = \ -4} = \frac{-1}{16}$$

Thus

$$F(s) = \frac{1/16}{s} - \frac{1/16}{s + 4} + \frac{3/4}{(s + 4)^2}$$

and using the table of transform pairs,

$$f(t) = \frac{1}{16} u(t) - \frac{-1}{16} e^{-4t} + \frac{3}{4} + e^{-4t}$$

As a final example, suppose

$$F(s) = \frac{s-3}{s^2(s + 1)}$$

Then

$$F(s) = \frac{s - 3}{s^2(s + 1)} = \frac{A}{s} + \frac{B}{s^2} + \frac{C}{s + 1}$$

$$A = \left. \frac{d}{ds} \frac{s^2(s - 3)}{s^2(s + 1)} \right|_{s \ = \ 0} = \left. \frac{(s + 1) - (s - 3)}{(s + 1)^2} \right|_{s \ = \ 0} = 4$$

$$B = \left. \frac{s^2(s - 3)}{s^2(s + 1)} \right|_{s \ = \ 0} = -3$$

$$C = \left. \frac{(s + 1)(s - 3)}{s^2(s + 1)} \right|_{s \ = \ -1} = -4$$

Thus

$$F(s) = \frac{4}{s} - \frac{3}{s^2} - \frac{4}{s + 1}$$

and $\qquad f(t) = 4u(t) - 3t^2 - 4e^{-t}$

EXERCISES

23. Use partial fractions to find the inverse of each of the following. In each case, check your partial fraction expansion to verify that it equals the original transform.

(a) $F(s) = \dfrac{s + 4}{s(s + 5)}$

(b) $I(s) = \dfrac{s^2 - 2}{s(s + 1)(s + 6)}$

(c) $V(s) = \dfrac{s}{s^2 + 10s + 16}$

(d) $F(s) = \dfrac{s^2 + 2s + 1}{s(s + 5)^2}$

(e) $I(s) = \dfrac{s - 1}{s^2(s^2 + 6s + 9)}$

INVERTING TRANSFORMS WITH COMPLEX POLES

In many practical problems, the denominator of a transform cannot be expressed as a product of factors containing real numbers; that is, all the poles of the transform may not be real poles. Consider, for example,

$$F(s) = \frac{s}{(s + 1)(s^2 + 4)}$$

In this example, $F(s)$ has one real pole at $s = -1$, and two complex conjugate poles at $s = 0 \pm j2$. (The complex poles are found by writing $s^2 + 4 = 0$ and solving for s.) As another example, consider

$$F(s) = \frac{1}{s^2 + 4s + 9}$$

By equating the denominator to zero and using the quadratic formula to solve for s, we find that the poles of $F(s)$ are the conjugate pair $s = -2 \pm j3$. Complex poles always occur in conjugate pairs.

There are several methods available for inverting a transform containing complex poles. One method is to use partial fractions, where the partial fraction expansion contains one term for each complex pole, as well as terms for any real poles that are present. The coefficients A, B, ..., are evaluated in the same way as described before, and it turns out that the coefficients corresponding to the complex poles are themselves complex numbers. This method involves a considerable amount of complex algebra and we will not discuss it further.

If the denominator consists <u>only</u> of a second-degree polynomial (a quadratic) and the numerator is of the appropriate form, then it may be possible to use one of pairs 18, 19, 20, or 23 from the table of transform pairs. Suppose, for example, that

$$F(s) = \frac{1}{s^2 + 6s + 25}$$

The transform should first be checked to ensure that complex poles are present, for if the quadratic can be factored to produce real poles, then the method of partial fractions should be used. In this example the discriminant of the quadratic formula, $B^2 - 4AC$, is negative (36-100), so we know that complex conjugate poles are present. We wish to express $F(s)$ in the form of pair 18 from the table. This can be accomplished by <u>completing the square</u> in s. Recall that we add and subtract one-half the square of the <u>coefficient of s to the</u> quadratic:

$$F(s) = \frac{1}{s^2 + 6s + 25} = \frac{1}{s^2 + 6s + (3)^2 + 25 - (3)^2} = \frac{1}{(s^2 + 6s + 9) + 16}$$

$$= \frac{1}{(s + 3)^2 + 4^2}$$

With reference to pair (18), we see that a = 3 and b = 4, and therefore

$$f(t) = \tfrac{1}{4} e^{-3t} \sin 4t$$

This function is representative of a type of response that is frequently encountered in practical circuits. It is called a <u>damped sine wave</u>, or <u>ringing</u> response, and can only exist if complex poles are present in the transform of the circuit function. The response can be sketched versus time by sketching the sine wave portion in such a way that the peak values decay exponentially with time-constant determined by the exponential term. That is, the envelope of the sine wave is the exponential decay. Figure 4 is a sketch of the function we have just found.

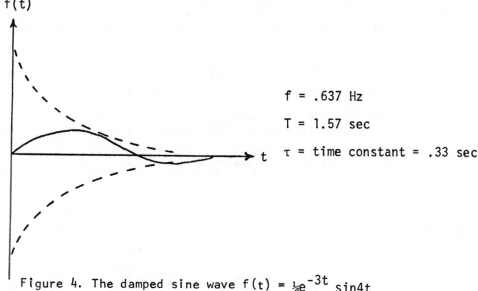

f = .637 Hz

T = 1.57 sec

τ = time constant = .33 sec

Figure 4. The damped sine wave $f(t) = \tfrac{1}{4} e^{-3t} \sin 4t$

The previous example could also have been solved using pair 20. The denominator in this case must be expressed in the form $s^2 + 2\zeta\omega_n s + \omega_n^2$, that is, we must identify the values of ζ and ω_n that are appropriate for our problem. In our example, we have

$$s^2 + 6s + 25 = s^2 + 2\zeta\omega_n s + \omega_n^2$$

from which it is apparent that

$$\omega_n^2 = 25, \text{ i.e., } \omega_n = 5$$

and $\qquad 2\zeta\omega_n = 6$

or, $\qquad 2\zeta(5) = 6$

$$\zeta = .6$$

Therefore, substituting into pair (20), we obtain

$$f(t) = \frac{1}{\omega_n\sqrt{1-\zeta^2}} \, e^{-\zeta\omega_n t} \sin(\omega_n\sqrt{1-\zeta^2}\, t)$$

$$= \frac{1}{5\sqrt{1-.36}} \, e^{-(.6)5t}\sin(5\sqrt{1-.36}\, t)$$

$$= \frac{1}{4}e^{-3t}\sin 4t$$

as before.

Finally, there is a method that can always be used when complex poles are present, regardless of what other terms are present in the numerator or denominator of the transform. This method does not rely upon the table of transform pairs. If there are any real poles present, their contribution to the inverse transform is found using the method of partial fractions exactly as before. This is best explained by way of an example. Suppose

$$F(s) = \frac{s + 1}{(s + 2)(s^2 + 2s + 26)}$$

This transform has one real pole at $s = -2$ and a pair of complex poles due to the quadratic. We first find the contribution of the real pole by doing a partial fraction expansion:

$$F(s) = \frac{s + 1}{(s + 2)(s^2 + 2s + 26)} = \frac{A}{s + 2} + X$$

Here, X denotes other terms which we recognize are required for the expansion but which we do not need to evaluate. At this step we need only evaluate coefficients A, B, ..., that correspond to real poles. Proceeding as before,

$$A = \cancel{(s + 2)} \left. \frac{(s + 1)}{\cancel{(s + 2)}(s^2 + 2s + 26)} \right|_{s = -2}$$

$$= \frac{(-2 + 1)}{(-2)^2 + (2)(-2) + 26)} = \frac{-1}{26}$$

Hence we know the contribution of the pole at s = -2 to the inverse will be $-1/26\ e^{-2t}$. This contribution will be added to the contribution of the complex poles due to the quadratic, which we now proceed to find.

Let K(s) denote what remains of F(s) after the quadratic term has been removed. In our example,

$$K(s) = \frac{s + 1}{s + 2}$$

Let $-\alpha$ = the real part of the complex poles due to the quadratic and ω = the imaginary part. Thus the complex conjugate poles are s = $-\alpha \pm j\omega$. In our example, by use of the quadratic formula, we find

$$s = \frac{-2 \pm\sqrt{4-104}}{2} = -1 \pm j5$$

so for our case, α = 1 and ω = 5. The next step is to find the magnitude M and angle θ.

$$M \underline{/\theta} = K(s)\Big|_{s = -\alpha + j\omega}$$

In our example,

$$M \underline{/\theta} = \frac{s + 1}{s + 2}\Big|_{s = -1 + j5} = \frac{-1 + j5 + 1}{-1 + j5 + 2}$$

$$= \frac{j5}{1 + j5} = \frac{5 \underline{/90^0}}{\sqrt{26} \quad \underline{/78.69^0}} = 0.98 \quad \underline{/11.31^0}$$

Thus, M = 0.98 and θ = 11.31°. Next, the portion of the inverse transform due to the quadratic is found by substituting the previously determined values of α, ω, M, and θ into the expression

$$f_1(t) = \frac{M}{\omega} e^{-\alpha t}\sin(\omega t + \theta)$$

In our case,

$$f_1(t) = \frac{0.98}{5} e^{-t}\sin(5t + 11.31^0)$$

$$= .196e^{-t}\sin(5t + 11.31^0)$$

Finally, the inverse transform is the sum of the contributions of the real poles and the contribution $f_1(t)$ just determined. So

$$f(t) = -\frac{1}{26} e^{-2t} + .196e^{-t} \sin(5t + 11.31^0)$$

In summary, the procedure is as follows :

1. Determine the portion of the inverse transform due to any real poles present, using the method of partial fractions.

2. Let $K(s)$ = what remains of $F(s)$ after the quadratic is removed.

3. Use the quadratic formula to determine the values of the real and imaginary parts of the complex poles, $s = -\alpha \pm j\omega$. (Note that α itself will always be a positive number.)

4. Find M and θ by evaluating

$$M \underline{/\theta} = K(s)\bigg|_{s = -\alpha + j\omega}$$

5. Find the portion of the inverse due to the quadratic by substituting values into

$$f_i(t) = \frac{M}{\omega}e^{-\alpha t}\sin(\omega t + \theta)$$

6. The total inverse is the sum of the portions found in steps (1) and (5).

EXERCISES

24. Find the inverse transform of each of the following:

(a) $F(s) = \dfrac{1}{s^2 + 6s + 34}$

(b) $V(s) = \dfrac{1}{s^2 + 4s + 10}$

(c) $I(s) = \dfrac{s + 5}{s^2 + 10s + 100}$

(d) $V(s) = \dfrac{1}{s^2 + 1.6s + 64}$

(e) $V(s) = \dfrac{s + 4}{s(s^2 + 2s + 10)}$

(f) $I(s) = \dfrac{s^2}{(s + 1)(s^2 + 4s + 20)}$

25. Sketch the inverses in (e) and (f) of problem 24 versus time.

ANSWERS TO EXERCISES

1. $v = 100\cos100t$ V

2. $i = .2\cos(10^6 t - 30^\circ)$ A

3. $v = 0$ $\left(\dfrac{di}{dt} = 0\right)$

4. $v = 16\sin10^5 t$ V

6. $\dfrac{dv}{dt} = \omega\cos\omega t;\quad \dfrac{d^2v}{dt^2} = -\omega^2\sin\omega t$

$\dfrac{d^2v}{dt^2} + \omega^2 v = -\omega^2\sin\omega t + \omega^2\sin\omega t = 0$

8. $\mathscr{L}(t) = \displaystyle\int_0^\infty te^{-st}\,t$

Let $U = t;\ dU = dt$

Let $dV = e^{-st}dt;\quad V = \dfrac{-e^{-st}}{s}$

$UV\Big|_0^\infty - \displaystyle\int_0^\infty V\,dU = \dfrac{-te^{-st}}{s}\Big|_0^\infty - \dfrac{e^{-st}}{s^2}\Big|_0^\infty$

$= 0 - \left(0 - \dfrac{1}{s^2}\right) = \dfrac{1}{s^2}$

9. (a) $10^3 - \dfrac{1}{2s}$

(b) $\dfrac{.25}{s(s + .5)} + \dfrac{1}{4s^2}$

(c) $\dfrac{50}{s^2} - \dfrac{4}{s} + \dfrac{1}{s + 4}$

(d) $\dfrac{100}{s(s + 5)}$

(e) $1 + \dfrac{1}{s} - \dfrac{1}{s^2}$

10. $v(t) = 12tu(t)$

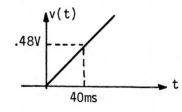

11. $100\delta(t);\quad .5u(t)$

13. (a) $\dfrac{3600}{(s + 7)^5}$

(b) $\dfrac{.04s}{s^2 + 5625}$

(c) $\dfrac{5}{(s + .5)}$

(d) $\dfrac{100}{(s + .05)^2 + 10^4}$

(e) $\dfrac{600}{s(s^2 + 1)}$

(f) $f(t) = 25\sin10^3t - 43.3\cos10^3t$

$F(s) = \dfrac{25 \times 10^3}{s^2 + 10^6} - \dfrac{43.3s}{s^2 + 10^6}$

(g) $f(t) = .0177\cos2t - .0177\sin2t$

$F(s) = \dfrac{.0177s}{s^2 + 4} - \dfrac{.035}{s^2 + 4}$

14. (a) $8 \times 10^4 e^{-4t})$

(b) $8.33(1-e^{-.4t})$

(c) $.01\sin100t$

(d) $1/3 (5e^{-5t} - 2e^{-2t})$

(e) $2.53 \times 10^{-3}\{999.9e^{-.1t} - 990e^{-10t}\}$

(f) $5 \times 10^4 t^2 e^{-5t}$

(g) $2e^{-4t}\sin5t$

15. $2/s$

16. $\dfrac{10s^2}{s + 5} - 10s + 50$

$= \dfrac{10s^2 -10s(s + 5) + 50(s + 5)}{s + 5} = \dfrac{2500}{s + 5} = \mathscr{L} f''(t)$

17. $\dfrac{8}{s(s + .5)}$

$\displaystyle\int_0^t 8e^{-t/2}dt = 16 - 16e^{-t/2}$

$$\mathscr{L}(16 - 16e^{-t/2}) = \frac{16}{s} - \frac{16}{s + .5} = \frac{8}{s(s + .5)}$$

18. $\mathscr{L}\{f'(t)\} = \frac{s}{s^2} - 0 = \frac{1}{s} = \mathscr{L}u(t)$

19. $\mathscr{L}\{f'(t)\} = \frac{\omega s}{s^2 + \omega^2} - 0 = \mathscr{L}(\omega\cos\omega t)$

20. $\mathscr{L}\left\{\int_0^t f(t)dt\right\} = \frac{1}{s}/s = \frac{1}{s^2} = \mathscr{L}(t)$

21. (a) $\dfrac{5 \times 10^7}{s}$

    (b) $.04s$

22. (a) $i(t) = 5e^{-20t}$

    (b) $v(t) = 5(1 - e^{-.2t})$

    (c) $i(t) = .2 + .8e^{-.5t}$

    (d) $v(t) = 10^4(1 - \frac{10}{9} e^{-t} + \frac{1}{9} e^{-10t})$

    (e) $i(t) = .75(1 - e^{-4t} - 4te^{-4t})$

    (f) $v(t) = \frac{-8}{65} e^{-8t} + \frac{1}{\sqrt{65}} \cos(t - 7.13°)$

23. (a) $f(t) = 0.8u(t) + .2e^{-5t}$

    (b) $i(t) = -\frac{1}{3} u(t) + \frac{1}{5} e^{-t} + \frac{17}{15} e^{-6t}$

    (c) $v(t) = \frac{4}{3} e^{-8t} - \frac{1}{3} e^{-2t}$

    (d) $f(t) = \frac{1}{25}u(t) + \frac{24}{25} e^{-5t} - \frac{16}{5} te^{-5t}$

    (e) $i(t) = \frac{5}{27} u(t) - \frac{1}{9} t - \frac{5}{27} e^{-3t} - \frac{4}{9} te^{-3t}$

24. (a) $f(t) = 0.2e^{-3t}\sin 5t$

    (b) $v(t) = \frac{1}{\sqrt{6}}e^{-2t} \sin\sqrt{6}\, t$

(c) $i(t) = e^{-5t}\cos 10t$

(d) $v(t) = 0.126e^{-.8t}\sin 7.96t$

(e) $v(t) = 0.4 + 0.447e^{-t}\sin(3t - 63.43°)$

(f) $i(t) = .0588e^{-t} + 1.21e^{-2t}\sin(4t + 129.1°)$

3 A Summary of BASIC Syntax

Most of the computer programs we will be using for digital simulation in this book are written in the BASIC computer language. Also, programming exercises require the use of BASIC. For these reasons, we summarize here the syntax of BASIC and illustrate some of the ways it can be used to perform computations typical of those we will encounter. BASIC was chosen for this book because it is an easy language to learn, is interactive, is very undemanding (i.e., very forgiving), and is probably the most widely available computer language today. Virtually every microcomputer marketed as a "personal computer" is programmable in BASIC, as are all large, time-shared computer systems. Despite its name (Beginner's All-purpose Symbolic Instruction Code), we should not regard it as a strictly elementary language with limited capabilities. In the author's view, it is the best all-around computer language available for scientific, technological, and engineering applications. APL is a cryptic language requiring a special keyboard and a long learning process, and FORTRAN and PASCAL have demanding syntaxes, especially in FORTRAN's input/output operations and PASCAL's so-called block structure. BASIC, like no other language, can be so readily learned and applied.

There are numerous "versions" of BASIC, some of which have extended capabilities and/or employ unusual or non-standard symbols. In our summary of BASIC, and in the programs we use in the book, we will restrict ourselves to the most common syntax and a basic BASIC that can be used with a majority of computers. We will mention from time to time some common variations encountered in the syntax of different versions.

Every BASIC statement must be preceded by a <u>statement number</u> that tells its order in the program. Any sequence of integers is permitted, but most programmers prefer to use 10, 20, 30, ..., a sequence that makes it easy to insert new statements between existing ones if necessary.

A <u>variable name</u> can be a single letter or a single letter followed by a single integer. (Many versions permit longer names.) <u>Value assignment</u> is accomplished using the keyword LET. For example,

        10 LET X = A

        20 LET A1 = 25.3

The quantity whose value is to be changed or assigned must always appear on the left of the equal sign. It would not be correct, for example, to write LET 5 = X. Most versions permit the omission of the keyword LET, so, for example, the statement 10 X = 4 would assign the value 4 to the variable X.

Numeric <u>constants</u> can be expressed with or without a decimal point, with or without a plus or minus sign, and with or without a positive or negative integer exponent, designated by the prefix E. Following are examples of constants correctly expressed in BASIC:

726

3.01

-5E7

42E-3

The symbols +, -, *, /, and ** are used to express addition, subtraction, multiplication, division, and exponentiation, respectively, though there is some variation among versions for the symbol used for exponentiation. Negative numbers cannot be raised to non-integer powers. Omission of the * symbol does NOT imply multiplication, as it does in ordinary algebra. For example, 7B does not mean 7*B.

In the <u>hierarchy</u> of operations, that is, the order in which expressions containing more than one arithmetic symbol are processed, exponentiation has the highest priority, multiplication and division are next with equal priority, and addition and subtraction are last, also with equal priority. Operations with equal priority are processed from left to right. Following are some examples:

$$3 + 8/2*2 = 3 + 4*2 = 3 + 8 = 11$$

$$3 + 8/2**2 = 3 + 8/4 = 3 + 2 = 5$$

$$4 - 12/2 + 4 = 4 - 6 + 4 = -2 + 4 = 2$$

$$6/2 - 2*3 = 3 - 2*3 = 3 - 6 = -3$$

<u>Parentheses</u> can be used to override the hierarchy of priorities. In expressions containing multiple sets of parentheses, expressions in the innermost sets are evaluated first, and the total number of left parentheses must always equal the total number of right parentheses, Following are some examples:

$$3 + 8/(2*2) = 3 + 8/4 = 3 + 2 = 5$$

$$(15/(3+ 2))*2 = (15/5)*2 = 3*2 = 6$$

$$(2**(9**.5))**2 = (2**3)**2 = 8**2 = 64$$

Value assignment can also be accomplished using the INPUT statement. This statement causes the computer to stop, print the ? prompt symbol, and wait for the user to enter a numeric value. For example, the program statement

INPUT Z2

can be used to assign the variable Z2 any value that the programmer wishes, simply by typing in that value when the question mark is displayed. Multiple value assignments may be made using a single INPUT statement simply by listing all the variable names, separated by commas, following the INPUT keyword. For example, if the statement

INPUT X, Y, Z

is executed, then the user can type in 1, 2, 3 after the ? prompt appears, resulting in the assignment of values 1, 2, and 3 to variables X, Y, and Z, respectively.

Following is an example of a BASIC program that uses the statements we have discussed thus far. Note that the last statement is END, a requirement in some versions of BASIC but optional in many.

```
10 INPUT A1, A2

20 LET X = A1/A2**2

30 LET Y = X

40 LET X = X + 1

50 LET Z = X/Y + 2

60 END
```

After the computer executes the INPUT statement at 10, suppose the user enters 8, 2. A1 and A2 are thus assigned the values 8 and 2, respectively. Statement number 20 assigns X the value 8/2**2 = 8/4 = 2. Statement 30 sets Y equal to X, namely 2, and statement 40 sets X equal to X + 1, namely 2 + 1, or 3. Statement 50 sets Z equal to 3/2 + 2 = 1.5 + 2 = 3.5.

The PRINT statement is used to display output values. The value of any variable whose name follows the keyword PRINT will be displayed when this instruction is executed. Multiple output values may be displayed by writing variable names, separated by commas, after the keyword PRINT. In the previous programming example, if we had included the statement

```
PRINT X, Y, Z
```

at the end, then the computer would have displayed:

```
3     2     3.5
```

An expression can also appear in a PRINT statement. For example, the combination

```
10 LET N = 4

20 PRINT 8 + N**.5
```

will cause the number 10 to be printed.

A _string_ is a set of characters that may include letters, numbers, or symbols, all of which are enclosed by a set of quotation marks. The computer does not interpret a string in any special way, like it does a keyword. It simply stores and reproduces the characters in exactly the same way they are written. A common application of strings is in the use of a PRINT statement to display a message. For example, if a BASIC program computes the value of a variable V to be, say, 12, then the statement

```
PRINT  "THE VALUE OF V IS" V
```

will cause the computer to display the following:

```
THE VALUE OF V IS 12
```

A string _variable_ may be assigned a string by use of the LET or INPUT statements. A string variable name consists of a single letter followed by a $ sign. For example, the statement

```
LET A$ = "YES"
```

assigns the string "YES" to the string variable A$.

EXERCISES

1. Determine which of the following are valid BASIC statements. State the errors in those that are incorrectly written.

   (a) 10 LET A2 = 4E4

   (b) 25 LET X = -3E.5

   (c) 15.5 PRINT X

   (d) 100 LET 3.14 = P

   (e) 40 INPUT 33

   (f) 120 PRINT X$, Y$, Z$

   (g) 300 LET P$ = "25"

   (h) 5 LET A$ = DAWN

   (i) 1 LET X = 12/E10

   (j) 50 LET W = 3Y

   (k) LET X = (-3)**.25

2. If A = 4, B = 12, C = 1, and D = 8, find the value of each of the following BASIC expressions:

   (a) A/C + 1

   (b) A**.5 + B-D/A

   (c) B-B/(A + D)

   (d) ((B-D)**.5 + C)**3/3

   (e) A*B-C/1E-2*D

   (f) 2**(A-10/(D + A/2))

3. Write each of the following algebraic expressions in BASIC:

   (a) $\sqrt{X^2 + Y^2}$

   (b) $\dfrac{5 \times 10^{-4}}{12A(W + Z)}$

   (c) $10 \left[(X-4)^2 + \dfrac{Z^3}{27} \right]^{1/4}$

(d) $\quad 2\left[90 - T\left(\dfrac{180}{\pi}\right)\right] - T1 - T2$

(e) $\quad \left(\dfrac{1}{\dfrac{1}{R_1} + \dfrac{1}{R_2} + \dfrac{1}{R_3}}\right)I_1 + \left(\dfrac{R_1 R_2}{R_1 + R_2}\right)I_2$

(f) $\quad \dfrac{\left[A - (6B)^{1/3}\right]4}{W(V-7)^2}$

When a BASIC program is executed, the statements are processed in the order specified by the statement numbers, unless a branch (or jump) type statement is encountered. The unconditional branch statement has the format

> GOTO sn

where sn is a programmer-supplied statement number. Execution of this statement results in the statement at sn being executed next. For example, in the program

> 10 LET X = 1
>
> 20 PRINT X
>
> 30 GOTO 10
>
> 40 END

the computer branches back to statement number 10 every time it reaches statement number 30 and thus never executes the END statement at 40. This program contains an infinite loop, which generally should be avoided.

A conditional branch statement causes the computer to branch to a specified statement number only if a certain condition is satisfied. If the condition is not satisfied, then the next statement in sequence is executed. The format for this statement is

> IF condition THEN sn

where the condition is one of those to be described below, and sn is the statement number to which the computer branches if the condition is satisfied. Conditions are expressed by use of conditional operators, as shown in the list below:

Condition	Symbol Used
less than	<
greater than	>
equal to	=
greater than or equal to	>=
less than or equal to	<=

not equal to   < >

Variable names, expressions, and constants can be used in conjunction with one of the symbols in the list to form a condition. Following are examples:

50 IF A < B THEN 100

80 IF X + 7 >= W**2 THEN 150

If at the time statement 50 is executed, the value of A is less than the value of B, then statement 100 is executed next. If at the time statement 80 is executed, the value of X + 7 is greater than or equal to the value of W^2, then statement 150 is executed next.

Following is an example of a BASIC program that uses a conditional branch statement to compute and print the sum of N consecutive integers, where N is entered by a user.

10 PRINT "ENTER A POSITIVE INTEGER"

20 INPUT N

30 LET S = 0

40 LET S = S + N

50 LET N = N - 1

60 IF N > 0 THEN 40

70 PRINT "THE SUM IS" S

80 END

To illustrate the operation of the program, suppose the user enters 3 when prompted by the INPUT statement. After the sum S is initialized to 0 by statement number 30, it is set equal to 0 + 3 = 3 at statement 40. N is then decremented to 2 at statement 50. Since 2 is greater than zero, the condition in statement number 60 is satisfied and a branch back to 40 is executed. Here S is assigned the new value S + N = 3 + 2 = 5. N is decremented again at 50, and again the condition at 60 is satisfied (N = 1 > 0). After one more "pass" through the loop, S becomes 6 and N becomes zero, so the condition at 60 is no longer satisfied. Hence statement 70 is executed next, resulting in the display

THE SUM IS 6

The preceding example illustrates a programming <u>loop</u>: the repeated execution of a set of statements. In BASIC, a programming loop can be set up automatically using the FOR TO and NEXT statements. The format is

FOR v = n_1 TO n_2

-
-
-

NEXT v

where v is a variable name and n_1 and n_2 are two integers, v is called the running (or counter, or index) variable. The loop consists of the statements between the FOR TO and NEXT statements. These statements are executed, first for v = n_1, next for v = n_2 + 1, and so on, up to and including v = n_2. In other words, v is automatically incremented each time the loop is executed, until v has value n_2. The loop must <u>always</u> be terminated by a NEXT statement. As an example, the following FOR TO, NEXT loop <u>prints</u> a table of the first ten integers, their squares, and their square roots.

```
10 PRINT "NUMBER", "SQUARE", "SQ. ROOT"

20 FOR I = 1 TO 10

30 LET S = I**2

40 LET R = I**.5

50 PRINT I, S, R

60 NEXT I

70 END
```

It is not permissible for any of the statements in the loop to alter the value of the running variable. For example, it would be incorrect to write statement 30 in the preceding program as

```
30 LET I = I**2
```

Either or both of the integers n_1 and n_2 in the FOR TO statement can be replaced by an integer-valued variable or expression. As an example, the program we wrote earlier for finding the sum of N consecutive integers could be written using a FOR TO, NEXT loop as follows:

```
10 PRINT "ENTER A POSITIVE INTEGER"

20 INPUT N

30 LET S = 0

40 FOR J = 1 TO N

50 LET S = S + J

60 NEXT J

70 PRINT S

80 END
```

In many programming applications it is desirable to be able to set up a FOR TO, NEXT loop in which the running variable v is incremented by a value other than one. We might, for example, want to execute a set of statements first for K = 2, next for K = 4, then for K = 6, and so on, up to, say, K = 12. This type of loop can be easily established by using the optional keyword STEP at the end of the FOR TO statement. The desired increment is written after the word STEP. For example, the following sequence

```
FOR F = 0 TO 36 STEP 3
-
-
-
NEXT F
```

sets up a loop that is executed first for F = 0, then for F = 3, then for F = 6, and so forth, up to F = 36. The increment that is specified after the word STEP may be an integer-valued variable or expression.

EXERCISES

4. Write BASIC statements that cause the following program branches to occur: (Note that more than one statement may be required in some cases.)

    (a) Branch to 100 if X is negative.

    (b) Branch to 100 if A3 is non-zero.

    (c) Branch to 50 if T is less than 1 and to 75 if T equals 1.

    (d) Branch to 30 if W1 is greater than or equal to 10^3; otherwise branch to 160.

5. Write the results displayed by the PRINT statement in each of the following:

    (a) 10 LET M = 5

         20 LET M = 2*M - 1

         30 IF M < 20 THEN 20

         40 PRINT M

         50 END

    (b) 10 LET D1 = 1

         20 LET D3 = (D1 + 1)**2

         30 IF D3 < = 25 THEN 20

         40 PRINT D3

         50 END

    (c) 10 LET S = 0

         20 FOR F = 1 TO 4

         30 LET S = S + 1/F

         40 NEXT F

         50 PRINT S

         60 END

    (d) 10 LET X = 2

         20 LET Y = 3**X

         30 LET S = 0

```
40 FOR J = 2*X TO Y + 1 STEP 2

50 LET S = S + J

60 NEXT J

70 PRINT S

80 END
```

6. Write a BASIC program that uses a FOR TO, NEXT loop to compute and print a table of values of $1 + 1 + 1^2 + 1^3$, $1 + 2 + 2^2 + 2^3$, $1 + 3 + 3^2 + 3^3$, and so forth, up to $1 + N + N^2 + N^3$, where the user enters the value of the integer N.

An array is a set of data values, each of which is identified by an integer-valued index. The value of the index is written in parentheses immediately following the array name (which is usually a single letter). For example, A(2) is entry number 2 in array A, X(5) is entry number 5 in array X, and so forth. The index can also be a variable name; for example, if the variable I has value 7, then A(I) refers to entry 7 in array A. An array is like a list, or a one-dimensional vector, and the index corresponds to a subscript in ordinary algebra. Most versions of BASIC are capable of handling 2-or-more-dimensional arrays (matrices) but we will not have occasion to use these and so will not discuss them. In many versions of BASIC, the "first" item in an array has index value 0 rather than 1, but the programmer can always use arrays and reference their contents under the assumption that 1 is the first index value.

The word dimension is used in two contexts in connection with arrays. By one use of this term we mean the number of index values required to identify an entry, that is, the number of subscripts that would have to be specified. Thus, for example, a two-dimensional array can be regarded as a matrix having rows and columns, and each entry is identified by its row and column number. In algebra we would write a_{ij}, and in BASIC, A(I, J). As we have already indicated, we will not be using arrays of dimension other than one (when we use the word dimension in this context). "Dimension" is also used to mean the maximum index value in an array which is 1-dimensional in the previous sense. For example, if the array A contained the 21 data values A(0), A(1), ..., A(20), then we would say it has dimension 20, in this new sense. Henceforth, our use of the word dimension will refer to this latter meaning, i.e., to the "size" of the array.

Most versions of BASIC permit a programmer to use one or more arrays with dimensions up to 10 (capable of storing 11 entries, if the first index value is 0), without having to specify the actual dimension. If a larger array is required, the programmer must use the DIM statement to specify its dimension. The format of this statement is

DIM a(n)

where a is an array name (a single letter, though some versions permit longer names), and n is the required dimension. More than one array can be dimensioned on a single line, as shown in the following example:

DIM A(20), X(15)

This statement specifies a dimension of 20 for array A and a dimension of 15 for array X. In some versions of BASIC, every array must be dimensioned, regardless of size. Also, in some versions of BASIC the dimension value in a DIM statement can be the name of an integer-valued variable.

As an example, following is a BASIC program that creates an array containing the cumulative sums of integers, that is, $S(1) = 1$, $S(2) = 1 + 2 = 3$, $S(3) = 1 + 2 + 3 = 6$, ...,

$S(N) = 1 + 2 + \ldots + N$, where N is a user-provided integer less than or equal to 100.

```
10 INPUT N
20 DIM S(100)
30 LET S(1) = 1
40 FOR I = 2 TO N
50 LET S(I) = S(I-1) + I
60 PRINT "S"("I") = "S(I)
70 NEXT I
80 END
```

This program sets the dimension of array S to 100 so it can contain values of S(I) up to S(100), depending on the value entered for N. In terms of memory conservation, a more efficient approach would be to write DIM S(N), if the version of BASIC being used permits this variation.

A BASIC function can be defined using a statement whose format is

```
DEF FNy(x) = expr
```

where y is any letter, x is any argument, and expr is an expression that defines the function in terms of the argument. For example,

```
DEF FNA(W) = 4*W**2-50
```

defines a function A of W to be $4W^2-50$. Once a function has been defined in this way, future references to the function need only specify a value of the argument. For example, FNA(10) would be evaluated as $4(10)^2-50 = 350$. The function name, with a value given for the argument, can be used in any subsequent expression or value assignment, such as,

```
LET M = 3*FNA(10) + 60
```

In this example, M would be assigned the value (3)(350) + 40 = 1090.

BASIC also has a certain number of "built-in" functions, called library functions, or intrinsic functions, that can be used without having been previously defined. Included in most libraries are the trigonometric, logarithmic, exponential, and absolute value functions. For example, the exponential function is designated by EXP(x), where x is a user-supplied argument value. This function returns the value e^x, where e is the natural logarithm base. As an example, consider the following program:

```
10 DEF FNE(T) = EXP(T) + EXP(-T)
20 FOR N = 1 TO 5
30 PRINT N, FNE(N)
40 NEXT N
50 END
```

This program defines FNE(T) to be the sum of the library functions EXP(T) and EXP(-T) and then prints the values of N and FNE(N) for N = 1 to N = 5.

Table 3.1 shows a list of the most common BASIC library functions and explains how each is defined.

Function	Finds the value of the
ABS(X)	absolute value of X, $|X|$
ATN(X)	arctangent of X, in radians
COS(X)	cosine of X, when X is in radians
COT(X)	cotangent of X, when X is in radians
EXP(X)	e^X, where e is the natural log base
LOG(X)	logarithm to the base e of X
SGN(X)	sign of X(1 if +, -1 if -, 0 if X = 0)
SIN(X)	sine of X, when X is in radians
SQR(X)	square root of X, provided $X \geqslant 0$
TAN(X)	tangent of X, when X is in radians

Table 3.1

Functions can be nested, in the sense that one function can appear in the argument of another function. For example, the statement

LET A = SIN(EXP(-.5))

assigns A the value $\sin(e^{-.5})$. Note that the arguments of the trigonometric functions have the units radians, and that the inverse trigonometric functions return values in radians. Thus, the value of A in the preceding example would be computed as sin(.606 rad) = 0.57.

A subroutine is a set of statements that have statement numbers outside the range of those in the main part of a program. A common situation in which a subroutine is useful occurs when the same computation must be performed several times during the course of a program, each computation using a different set of data values. For example, a programming application might require finding the maximum number in each of several sets of numbers. A subroutine could be written to find the maximum of any given set of numbers. Then the main program would generate the first set of numbers, go to the subroutine to find its maximum, return from the subroutine to generate a second set, go back to the subroutine to find the maximum of this set, and so forth.

The BASIC statement that causes the computer to go to a subroutine is

GOSUB sn

where sn is the statement number of the first statement in the subroutine. The last statement in the subroutine is always:

RETURN

By using the GOSUB statement in a main program and the RETURN statement at the end of the subroutine, the computer will automatically return from the subroutine to the next statement following the GOSUB. In this way, the same subroutine can be entered from any number of places in the main program and the computer will always return from the subroutine to the correct location in the main program. This automatic transfer could not be programmed using only GOTO statements.

Unlike subroutines written in FORTRAN and other languages, a BASIC subroutine is not isolated from the main program in the sense that data and variable values in one are unknown in the other. The results of any computations performed in the main program are fully accessible to the subroutine and vice-versa. Thus, there is no need for formally "passing" arguments or subroutine results back and forth between the two. The passing is automatic.

Following is an example of a program that uses a subroutine to compute the value of

$$\sqrt{X^2 + Y^2}$$

for two different sets of values of X and Y.

```
10 INPUT A, B
20 LET X = A + 1
30 LET Y = B - 1
40 GOSUB 200
50 PRINT "Z1 = "Z
60 LET X = A + 2
70 LET Y = B - 2
80 GOSUB 200
90 PRINT "Z2 = "Z
100 STOP
   -
   -
   -
200 LET Z = (X**2 + Y**2)**.5
210 RETURN
220 END
```

In this example, the initial values of X and Y are computed in lines 20 and 30 from user-supplied values of A and B. The subroutine is then used to compute Z =

$$\sqrt{X^2 + Y^2},$$

that is,

$$\sqrt{(A + 1)^2 + (B-1)^2}.$$

Upon returning from the subroutine, the main program prints this first value of Z, which is labeled Z1. Then the values of X and Y are modified in lines 60 and 70 and the subroutine is again used to compute Z =

$$\sqrt{X^2 + Y^2}$$

which this time is equivalent to

$$\sqrt{(A + 2)^2 + (B - 2)^2}$$

Upon returning to the main program, the new value of Z is printed with label Z2.

Note the STOP statement at line 100. This statement causes the computer to cease processing instructions at that point. Without it, the computer would enter the subroutine without having been instructed to do so by a GOSUB statement, and an error message would be generated. A STOP statement should always be written between the end of the main program and the beginning of a subroutine.

EXERCISES

7. Write a BASIC program that creates an array Y of dimension 20 such that Y(20) = 1, Y(19) = 2, ... , Y(1) = 20.

8. Given the following BASIC program:

```
10 DIM A(5), B(5), C(5)

20 LET B(1) = 0

30 FOR J = 2 TO 5

40 LET A(J) = J**2

50 LET B(J) = A(J) + B(J-1)

60 LET C(J) = A(J) + B(J)

70 PRINT 4*C(J)

80 NEXT J

90 END
```

Write the results of the PRINT statement as they would be displayed when this program is run.

9. Write a BASIC program that employs a user-defined function to compute and print values of

$$1/\sqrt{(W-50)^2}$$

for 11 equal-spaced values of W between W = 20 and W = 200 (inclusive).

10. Given the following BASIC program:

```
10 DIM V(5)

20 DEF FNJ(X) = 2*X**2

30 DEF FNK(Y) = 2**Y
```

```
40 FOR I = 1 TO 5

50 LET V(I) = FNJ(I) + FNK(I)

60 PRINT V(I)

70 NEXT I

80 END
```

Write the results of the PRINT statement as they would be displayed when this program is run.

11. Write a BASIC program that prints a table containing 19 equal-spaced angles from 0 to 180 degrees and the sines and cosines of those angles.

12. Given the following BASIC program:

```
10 LET R = 2

20 GOSUB 500

30 PRINT S

40 LET R = 3

50 GOSUB 500

60 PRINT S

70 STOP
  -
  -
  -
500 LET S = EXP(-R*ABS(2-R))

510 RETURN

520 END
```

Write the results of the PRINT statements.

ANSWERS TO EXERCISES

1. (a) Valid.

    (b) Invalid; E must be followed by an integer.

    (c) Invalid; statement number must be an integer.

    (d) Invalid; variable must be on the left of the = sign.

    (e) Invalid; cannot input a constant.

    (f) Valid.

    (g) Valid.

(h) Invalid; string must be enclosed in quotation marks. (Valid in some versions.)

(i) Invalid; E must be preceded by a constant. (Most versions will interpret E10 as zero.)

(j) Invalid; multiplication must be represented with *.

(k) Invalid; negative number raised to non-integer power.

2.   (a) 5

     (b) 12

     (c) 11

     (d) 9

     (e) -752

     (f) 8

3.   (a) (X**2Y**2)**.5

     (b) 5E-4/(12*A*(W + Z))

     (c) 10*((X-4)**2 + Z**3/27)**.25

     (d) 2*(90-T*180/3.1416)-T1-T2

     (e) (1/(1/R1 + 1/R2 + 1/R3))*I1+((R1*R2)/(R1 + R2))*I2

     (f) (A-(6*B)**(1/3))*4/(W*(V-7)**2)

4.   (a) IF X < 0 THEN 100

     (b) IF A3 < > 0 THEN 100

     (c) IF T < 1 THEN 50

         IF T = 1 THEN 75

     (d) IF W1 > = 1E3 THEN 30

         GOTO 160

5.   (a) 33

     (b) 676

     (c) 2.08333

     (d) 28

6.   10 PRINT "ENTER A POSITIVE INTEGER"

     20 INPUT N

     30 PRINT "I", "SUM OF POWERS"

```
40 FOR I = 1 TO N
50 PRINT I, 1 + I + I**2 + I **3
60 NEXT I
70 END
```

7.
```
10 DIM Y(20)
20 FOR I = 1 TO 20
30 LET Y(I) = 21-I
40 NEXT I
50 END
```

8. 32

    88

    180

    316

9.
```
10 DEF FNA(W) = 1/(((W-50)**2)**.5)
20 PRINT "W", "F(W)"
30 FOR W = 20 TO 200 STEP 18
40 PRINT W, FNA(W)
50 NEXT W
60 END
```

10. 4

     12

     26

     48

     82

11.
```
10 PRINT "ANGLE", "SINE", "COSINE"
20 FOR I = 0 TO 180 STEP 20
30 LET A = I*3.1416/180
40 PRINT I, SIN(A), COS(A)
50 NEXT I
60 END
```

12. 1

     4.97871E-2

4 Computing Frequency Response

OBJECTIVES

1. To learn how to write a BASIC program for computing the gain magnitude and angle, versus frequency, of a transfer function.

2. To develop an appreciation for the power that a computer has to produce rapid, accurate results in linear circuit computations and to learn how this potential can be used to improve understanding of network behavior.

3. To investigate and verify intuitive understanding of the frequency characteristics of several widely used circuits.

DISCUSSION

The accurate determination of the frequency response of a network often requires a considerable amount of lengthy and tedious calculation, particularly if the transfer function of the network is somewhat complex. The wide accessibility of computers today, large and small, and the widespread use of the BASIC computer language, provide a means for relieving investigators from repetitious calculations, in addition to providing more accurate results. The ability to use a computer for this purpose is therefore a valuable, time-saving skill that can be used to improve and refine our understanding of the behaviour of linear systems.

The first step in setting up a BASIC program for investigation of frequency response is to express the gain magnitude and phase angle of the transfer function in forms which are compatible with the computational abilities of BASIC. We must therefore express these functions in terms of operations such as multiplication, division, exponentiation, and inverse trigonometric functions. This is a relatively easy task when the transfer function is expressed as a quotient of product terms involving $s = j\omega$. It is only necessary to write the mathematical operations required to convert each factor to polar form and then to express the overall magnitude and angle of the transfer function using the rules of polar arithmetic. Suppose, for example, that

$$G(s) = \frac{2-4s}{3s(5s + 6)}$$

Then

$$G(j\omega) = \frac{2-j4\omega}{j3\omega(j5\omega + 6)}$$

Now

$$|2-j4\omega| = \sqrt{4 + (4\omega)^2}$$

$$|j3\omega| = 3\omega$$

and

$$|j5\omega + 6| = \sqrt{(5\omega)^2 + 36}$$

so,
$$|G| = \frac{|2-j4\omega|}{|j3\omega|\ |j5\omega + 6|}$$

$$= \frac{\sqrt{4 + (4\omega)^2}}{3\omega\sqrt{(5\omega)^2 + 36}}$$

This last expression of $|G|$ is in a form which readily lends itself to computation using BASIC. Similarly,

$$\underline{/(2-j4\omega)} = \arctan(-4\omega/2) = -\arctan(2\omega)$$

$$\underline{/j\omega3} = 90^0 = \pi/2 \text{ radians}$$

$$\underline{/(j5\omega + 6)} = \arctan(5\omega/6)$$

Therefore,
$$\underline{/G} = \underline{/(2-j4\omega)} - \underline{/j\omega3} - \underline{/(j5\omega + 6)}$$

$$= -\arctan(2\omega) - \pi/2 - \arctan(5\omega/6)$$

Again, this is a form that can be easily computed in BASIC using the ATN function (and remembering that most versions of BASIC return an angle in radians).

To determine the behavior of $|G|$ and $\underline{/G}$ as frequency varies, we will of course have to make some provision for having the program evaluate these functions at different values of ω (or f). This is best accomplished through use of a FOR-TO, NEXT loop. This loop can be written so that it will repeat the same set of computations while values of frequency are automatically incremented, until some final value of frequency is reached. For example, the loop

```
10  FOR F = 0 TO 1000 STEP 100

20  PRINT (6 + F**2) **.5

30  NEXT F
```

would cause the computer to calculate and print values of

$$\sqrt{6 + F^2}$$

for F = 0, 100, 200, . . . , up to F = 1000. F is automatically incremented in steps of size 100 so that a total of 11 values are printed. Recall that all statements written between the FOR-TO statement and the NEXT statement will be repeated in such a loop.

To illustrate how BASIC can be used to generate frequency response data, we will write a program to compute the gain magnitude and phase of the transfer function of the network shown in Figure 4.1.

The impedance Z of the parallel L-R combination is

$$Z(s) = \frac{(400)(.5s)}{400 + .5s} = \frac{200s}{400 + .5s}$$

By the voltage divider rule,

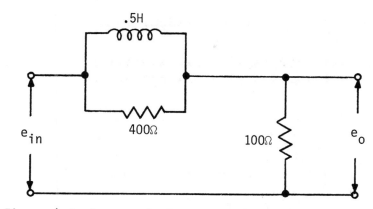

Figure 4.1 A network whose transfer function is analyzed using BASIC. The program in Figure 4.2 computes gain magnitude and angle versus frequency.

$$E_0(s) = \frac{100}{100 + Z} E_{in}(s)$$

and therefore

$$G(s) = \frac{E_0(s)}{E_{in}(s)} = \frac{100}{100 + \dfrac{200s}{400 + .5s}} = \frac{50s + 4 \times 10^4}{250s + 4 \times 10^4}$$

$$G(j\omega) = \frac{4 \times 10^4 + j\omega 50}{4 \times 10^4 + j\omega 250}$$

Then

$$|G| = \sqrt{\frac{16 \times 10^8 + (50\omega)^2}{16 \times 10^8 + (250\omega)^2}}$$

and

$$\underline{/G} = \arctan\left(\frac{50\omega}{4 \times 10^4}\right) - \arctan\left(\frac{250\,\omega}{4 \times 10^4}\right)$$

$$= \arctan(12.5 \times 10^{-4}\omega) - \arctan(62.5 \times 10^{-4}\omega)$$

Figure 4.2 shows a listing of the program along with output data obtained from a program run. Note that the program is written to provide output in Hz and degrees. The statement on line 20 converts frequency in Hz to radians/sec ($\omega = 2\pi f$) as required for the computations, and the angle computation in line 50 converts radians to degrees using the scale factor 57.296. A Bode plot based upon this output is shown in Figure 4.3.

From the output data and the Bode plot, we see that the gain magnitude starts at unity and approaches .2 as frequency increases. These results agree with our intuitive understanding of the network in Figure 4.1. Since the inductor is a short circuit at DC, all the input will appear across the output at zero frequency, and at high frequencies the large impedance of the inductor makes the circuit behave like a resistive voltage divider with gain 100/500 = .2. Note that the phase angle begins at zero degrees, decreases to around -41 degrees in the vicinity of 60 Hz, and then gradually increases back towards zero degrees. Again, at very high frequencies, the parallel inductive reactance contributes little, and the circuit becomes predominantly resistive.

```
10 PRINT "FREQUENCY,HZ","MAGNITUDE","ANGLE,DEG"
20 FOR F=0 TO 250 STEP 10
30 LET W=6.28319*F
40 LET M=((16E8+(50*W)**2)/(16E8+(250*W)**2))**.5
50 LET A=57.296*(ATN(12.5E-4*W)-ATN(62.5E-4*W))
60 PRINT F,M,A
70 NEXT F
80 END
```

Figure 4.2(a)   A BASIC program that computes gain magnitude
and angle of the network transfer function shown in Figure 4.1.

FREQUENCY,HZ	MAGNITUDE	ANGLE,DEG
0	1	0
10	.93366788	−16.9491856
20	.79608207	−29.2190978
30	.664849103	−36.4164957
40	.562906857	−40.0779303
50	.487566677	−41.5707184
60	.431888565	−41.7715148
70	.390123522	−41.2085828
80	.358217199	−40.201453
90	.333402612	−38.9467991
100	.313784527	−37.5674994
110	.298044856	−36.1408865
120	.285249829	−34.7155001
130	.274725582	−33.3213477
140	.265977251	−31.9763696
150	.258635561	−30.6906055
160	.252420894	−29.4689254
170	.24711869	−28.3128404
180	.242562314	−27.221713
190	.238620902	−26.1935679
200	.235190645	−25.2256367
210	.232188419	−24.3147214
220	.229547089	−23.4574352
230	.227211999	−22.65036
240	.225138314	−21.8901477
250	.223289013	−21.1735812

Figure 4.2(b)   Output data obtained from a run of
the program in Figure 4.2(a). Frequency range is
0-250 Hz.

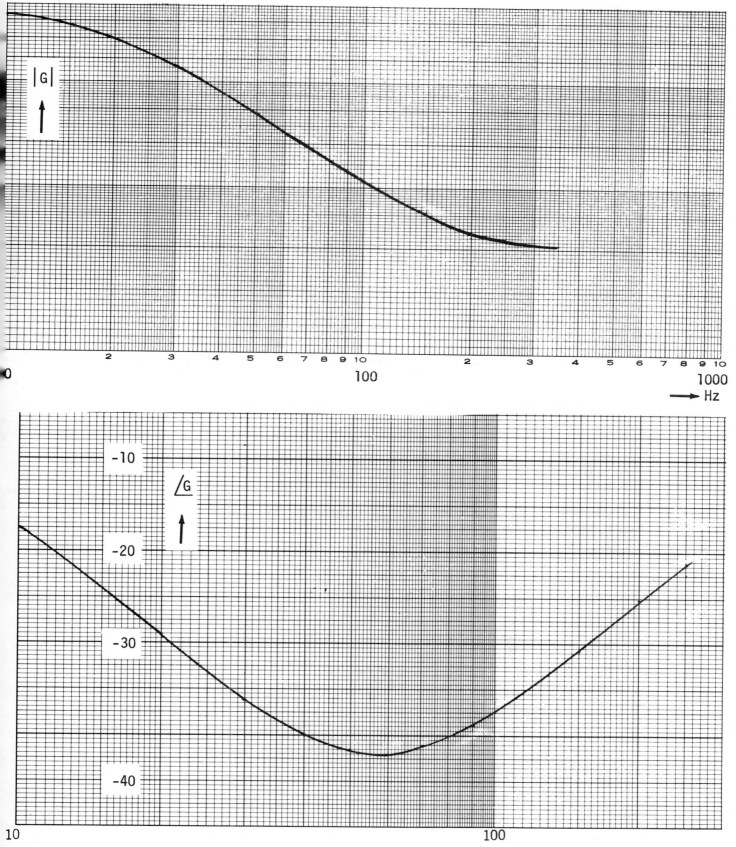

Figure 4.3   Bode plot based on the data in Figure 4.2(b).

54

EXERCISES

1. Modify the program shown in Figure 4.2 so that it prints frequency in radians/sec, angle in radians, and outputs data at 50 equally spaced values of ω between 0 and 3000 rad/sec. Run your program to check its operation.

2. Write a BASIC program that can be used to generate frequency response data for the network shown in Figure 4.4.

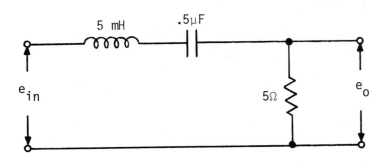

Figure 4.4

3. Run your program for f = 2 kHz to 4 kHz in steps of 50 Hz and record the results. (Get a hard copy if possible.) Modify the program and run it again for f = 3050 Hz to f = 3250 Hz in steps of 10 Hz. Record these results also.

4. Rewrite your program so that the user may input values of R while the program is running. (Use the BASIC INPUT statement.) Then run the program several times for f = 3 kHz to 3.4 kHz in steps of 20 Hz, using the following values of R: 2 Ω, 10 Ω, and 50 Ω.

5. Write a BASIC program that can be used to generate frequency response data for the "lead" network shown in Figure 4.5.

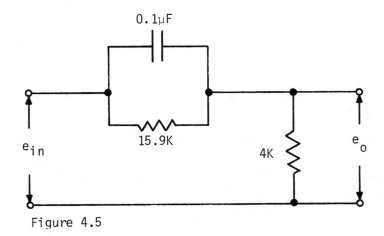

Figure 4.5

Run your program and record gain magnitude and angle at frequencies from 10 Hz to 1 KHz in steps of 20 Hz.

6. The transfer function of the circuit shown in Figure 4.6 is $G = Z_2 Z_4 / Z_1 Z_3$.

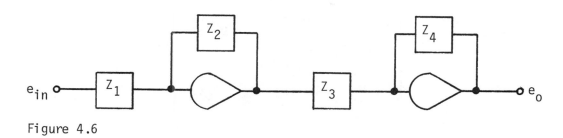

Figure 4.6

Write a BASIC program that can be used to generate frequency response data when Z_1 is a 100 K resistor, Z_2 is a 0.1 μF capacitor in parallel with a 10 K resistor, Z_3 is a 500 K resistor, and Z_4 is a 1.0 μF capacitor. Run your program using a frequency range that is adequate for construction of a Bode plot that shows all significant trends in the response. (Hint: there is a break frequency due to the parallel R-C combination in Z_2.) Record enough data to construct the Bode plot.

QUESTIONS (Note: Submit well-documented copies of all programs written for this experiment.)

1. Check the program you wrote in step 2 of the Procedure by hand calculating $|G|$ and $\underline{/G}$ at one of the frequencies used in the program. Show your calculations.

2. Construct a Bode plot showing $|G|$ and $\underline{/G}$ versus frequency using the data obtained in step 3 of the Procedure. It is not necessary to plot every point computed by your program.

3. Construct Bode plots using the data obtained in step 4 of the Procedure. Plot the response curves for all values of R on the same sheet of graph paper so they can be easily compared. Describe the effect that circuit resistance has on the frequency response, as observed in your plots.

4. Repeat questions 1 and 2 for the data obtained in step 5 of the Procedure. Referring to your results, explain why the network of Figure 4.5 is called a "lead network." Based upon your data, what do you believe are the values that $|G|$ and $\underline{/G}$ approach as f approaches 0 and as f approaches infinity? Are these trends in your data supported by your intuitive understanding of the network? Explain.

5. Construct a Bode plot using the data obtained in step 6 of the Procedure. Where does your data indicate that a break frequency occurs in the response? Based upon your data, what do you believe are the values of $|G|$ and $\underline{/G}$ as f approaches infinity? What would the frequency response of the circuit in Figure 4.6 look like if Z_1 and Z_2 were interchanged and at the same time Z_3 and Z_4 were interchanged?

5 Iterative Computations

1. To learn how certain kinds of computational problems can be solved by performing iterations until a specified accuracy criterion is satisfied.

2. To learn how to write a BASIC program that permits the user to initiate iterations through interactive control.

3. To gain experience in the use of iterative computations by finding the frequency at which a transfer function has a phase angle of -180^0.

4. To learn how iterations can be performed automatically in a BASIC program.

DISCUSSION

In many practical problems it is necessary to perform a certain set of computations over and over again. Each time the computations are performed in this type of problem, we obtain a result that is closer to the solution we are seeking. Furthermore, we use that result in the next repetition of the computations in such a way that the next result is even closer to the solution. This process is called iterative computation, and we say that we have performed an iteration each time the computations are repeated. In practice, the iterations are continued until the result obtained meets some predetermined criterion, for example, until the difference between the result of an iteration and the true solution is equal or less than some acceptable value. Thus, each time an iteration is completed, we must test the results to see if they meet the criterion.

To illustrate iterative computations, suppose we wished to find $\sqrt{5}$ using a calculator that had no square root function. Our procedure is to choose a number and square it. If the result is less than 5, then we choose a larger number; otherwise we choose a smaller number. We might start by choosing 2; since $2^2 = 4$ and 4 is less than 5, we try 3 for our next iteration. In this case $3^2 = 9$ is too large, so we try a number between 2 and 3, say 2.5. Since $2.5^2 = 6.25$ is still too large, we iterate again with a number between 2 and 2.5. If we want our solution to produce a square that is within .01 of 5, then we would continue this process until an iteration produced the result 2.236. In this example, the test of the result of an iteration is to square the number and see if it is within the range 4.99 to 5.01.

Many problems in linear systems analysis can be solved using iterative techniques. Digital computers are particularly well suited for this type of analysis because of the high speed at which they can perform iterations, and because they can be programmed to do automatic iterations. Automatic iterative computation occurs when the computer is programmed to perform the test of each iteration's results and automatically initiate the next iteration with whatever new values are required to improve the results.

We will begin our study of iterative computations with an example in which the programmer examines the results of each iteration, modifies the computational parameters as dictated by these results, and then initiates another iteration. BASIC is an ideal language for this kind of computational process since it was designed for just such interactive communication between programmer and computer. By using the INPUT statement, the programmer can cause the computer to pause during its computations and wait for new data to be entered.

A common problem in linear systems analysis is to find the frequency which the phase angle of a transfer function has a particular value, such as -180^0. Suppose for example that we wished to determine the frequency at which the phase is -180^0 when the transfer function has the general form:

$$G(s) = \frac{K}{s(s + a)(s + b)} \tag{1}$$

Where K is any positive constant. Note that

$$\underline{/G} = -90^0 - \arctan(\omega/a) - \arctan(\omega/b) \tag{2}$$

Figure 5.1 shows a flowchart for a program that computes and prints the angle of G at equally spaced frequencies over a user-selected range of frequencies. The computed angles are examined by the user after each iteration, and the user is given the opportunity either to terminate the computations or to initiate another interation using a new set of frequencies.

By narrowing the frequency range in each iteration, it is possible to "home in" on the frequency where the phase is as close as desired to -180^0. In the flowchart, f_1 is the lowest frequency at which the computation of equation (2) is performed, f_2 is the highest frequency, and N is the total number of frequency intervals between f_1 and f_2. Note that none of f_1, f_2, or N can be zero.

Figure 5.2 shows a BASIC program that implements the flowchart of figure 5.1. Note in this program that it is necessary to convert frequency values in Hz to radians/sec, since the BASIC function ATN must have its argument expressed in radians. Hence the statement in 120 defines the value of Π, and that value is used in the computation at 140.

Figure 5.3 shows the results of three runs (iterations) of the program of Figure 5.2, using the values a = 10 and b = 100. Inspection of the first run reveals that the required frequency must be somewhere between 4.8 Hz and 6.7 Hz, where the phase angles are seen to be -178.439^0 and -189.467^0, respectively. Therefore, in the next iteration we compute 10 new values between the frequency extremes f_1 = 4.8 Hz and f_2 = 6.7 Hz. The results now show that the required frequency is between 4.99 Hz and 5.18 Hz. These frequencies are used for f_1 and f_2 in the next run. In this last run we settle for a phase angle of -179.968^0 at the frequency 5.028 Hz.

Testing the result of an iteration to determine if some accuracy criterion has been met and modifying the computational parameters in a way that will improve the results of the next iteration are tasks that were performed by the user in the previous example. When a program is written in such a way that these tasks are left to the computer, then we say that we have automatic iterative computations. To illustrate this process, we will solve the same problem that was solved in the previous example by writing a program that requires no intervention by the user, other than the initial entering of data. The flowchart for this program is shown in Figure 5.4.

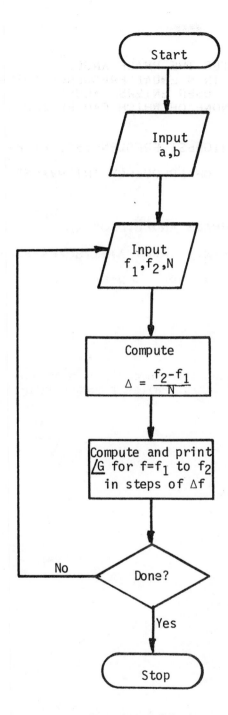

Figure 5.1. A flowchart for iterative computation of the frequency at which the phase angle of $G(s) = K/s(s + a)(s + B)$ equals -180^0. The program is shown in Figure 5.2

```
10 REM    THIS PROGRAM COMPUTES THE PHASE ANGLE
20 REM    OF G=K/S(S+A)(S+B) IN N EQUAL FREQUENCY INTERVALS
30 REM    BETWEEN F1 AND F2.  USER ENTERS VALUES
40 REM    FOR F1,F2, AND N, NONE OF WHICH CAN BE ZERO.
50 PRINT "ENTER A,B"
60 INPUT A,B
70 PRINT "ENTER LOWEST AND HIGHEST FREQUENCIES, F1,F2, IN HZ"
80 INPUT F1,F2
90 PRINT "ENTER TOTAL NUMBER OF FREQUENCY INTERVALS"
100 INPUT N
110 LET D=(F2-F1)/N
120 LET P=3.1415927
130 PRINT "FREQUENCY,HZ",,"PHASE ANGLE,DEG"
140 FOR F=F1 TO F2 STEP D
150    PRINT F,,-90-(180/P)*ATN((2*P*F)/A)-(180/P)*ATN((2*P*F)/B)
160 NEXT F
170 PRINT "CHANGE FREQUENCIES? TYPE Y OR N"
180 INPUT A$
190 IF A$="Y" THEN 70
200 END
>
```

Figure 5.2   A BASIC program for iterative computation of the frequency at which the phase angle of $G(s)=K/s(s+a)(s+b)$ equals -180°.

```
ENTER A,B
 10              100
ENTER LOWEST AND HIGHEST FREQUENCIES, F1,F2, IN HZ
 1               20
ENTER TOTAL NUMBER OF FREQUENCY INTERVALS
 10
FREQUENCY,HZ                    PHASE ANGLE,DEG
 1                              -125.737
 2.90000                       -161.568
 4.80000                       -178.439
 6.70000                       -189.467
 8.60000                       -197.900
 10.5000                       -204.795
 12.4000                       -210.609
 14.3000                       -215.589
 16.2000                       -219.897
 18.1000                       -223.649
 20.0000                       -226.938
CHANGE FREQUENCIES? TYPE Y OR N
Y
ENTER LOWEST AND HIGHEST FREQUENCIES, F1,F2, IN HZ
 4.80000        6.70000
ENTER TOTAL NUMBER OF FREQUENCY INTERVALS
 10
FREQUENCY,HZ                    PHASE ANGLE,DEG
 4.80000                       -178.439
 4.99000                       -179.718
 5.18000                       -180.949
 5.37000                       -182.136
 5.56000                       -183.283
 5.75000                       -184.392
 5.94000                       -185.467
 6.13000                       -186.510
 6.32000                       -187.523
 6.51000                       -188.508
 6.70000                       -189.467
CHANGE FREQUENCIES? TYPE Y OR N
Y
ENTER LOWEST AND HIGHEST FREQUENCIES, F1,F2, IN HZ
 4.99000         5.18000
ENTER TOTAL NUMBER OF FREQUENCY INTERVALS
 10
FREQUENCY,HZ                    PHASE ANGLE,DEG
 4.99000                       -179.718
 5.00900                       -179.843
 5.02800                       -179.968
 5.04700                       -180.092
 5.06600                       -180.216
 5.08500                       -180.339
 5.10400                       -180.462
 5.12300                       -180.584
 5.14200                       -180.706
 5.16100                       -180.828
 5.18000                       -180.949
CHANGE FREQUENCIES? TYPE Y OR N
N
!
```

Figure 5.3. The results of three iterations of the program in Figure 5.2;
a=10, b=100.

62

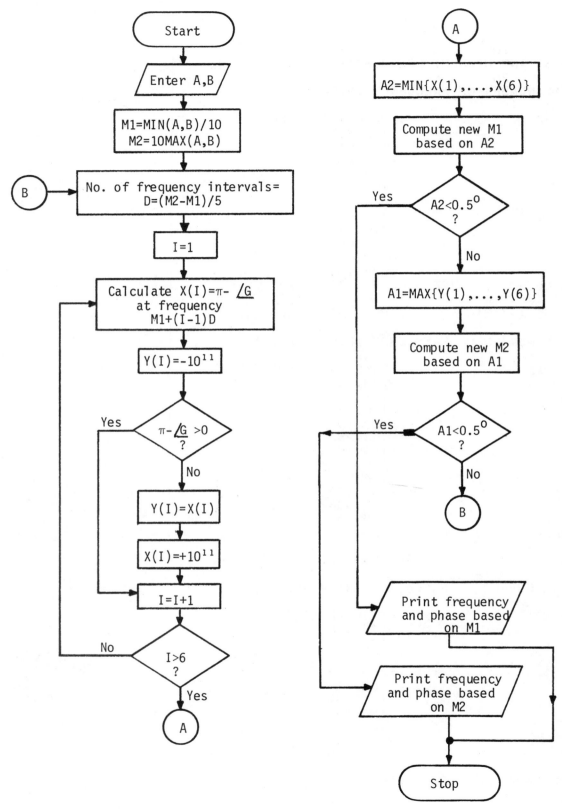

Figure 5.4. A flowchart for automatic iterative computation of the frequency at which $G(s)=K/s(s+a)(s+b)$ equals -180°. The program is shown in Figure 5.5.

The general strategy represented by the flowchart of Figure 5.4 is to bracket the frequency at which the phase is -180° by finding, in each iteration, frequencies at which the phase is greater than -180° and frequencies at which it is less than -180°. In each iteration the differences between 180°. In each iteration the differences between 180° (actually π radians) and the computed angles are determined, thus producing both positive and negative values. (Since $\underline{/G} = -\pi/2 - \arctan(\omega/a) - \arctan(\omega/b)$, we find the difference between 180° and $\underline{/G}$ by computing $\pi - \underline{/G} = \pi/2 - \arctan(\omega/a) - \arctan(\omega/b)$ for each value of ω.) The maximum of the negative values (that is, the one closest to zero) and the minimum of the positive values are then calculated and the frequencies corresponding to these two values then form the frequency boundaries for the next iteration. To illustrate, suppose that an iteration produced the following results:

Frequency: 100 200 300 400 500 600

180 - $\underline{/G}$: + 12   + 5   -2   -8   -12   -20

Since -2 is the maximum of the negative values and + 5 is the minimum of the positive values, the next iteration will compute 6 new values corresponding to frequencies in the range from M1 = 200 to M2 = 300.

This process continues until the computed difference 180 - $\underline{/G}$ is less than 0.5°. Note that the first iteration computes values in the range from one decade below the minimum of A and B to one decade above the maximum of A and B. This range will ensure that the frequencies used on the first iteration will produce phase angles both less than and greater than -180 degrees.

Figure 5.5 shows the actual program. In this program the array X is used to store positive values of $\pi - \underline{/G}$ and the array Y is used to store negative values. If a value is positive, then a very large negative value (-10^{11}) is stored in the corresponding position of the Y array, so that it has no hope of being selected as the maximum of the negative values. Similarly, if a value of $\pi - \underline{/G}$ is negative, then a very large positive value ($+ 10^{11}$) is stored in its place in the $\overline{X}$ array.

The accuracy test is performed in lines 270 and 350, where the minimum positive value of $\pi - \underline{/G}$ is compared to $(0.5°)(\pi/180)$ radians, and the maximum negative value of $\pi - \underline{/G}$ is compared to this same quantity. Note that all computations are performed in radians or radians/sec.

```
10 REM THIS PROGRAM FINDS THE FREQUENCY AT WHICH
20 REM THE ANGLE OF K/S(S+A)(S+B) IS -180 DEGREES
30 REM PLUS OR MINUS 0.5 DEGREES. USER ENTERS A AND B.
40 PRINT "G=K/S(S+A)(S+B). ENTER A AND B."
50 INPUT A,B
60 DIM X(6),Y(6)
61 REM      M1=LOWEST FREQ (RAD/SEC) AT WHICH INITIAL ANGLE
62 REM       COMPUTATIONS WILL BE MADE; M2=HIGHEST FREQ (RAD/SEC)
63 REM       AT WHICH INITIAL ANGLE COMPUTATIONS WILL BE MADE
70 LET M1=(MIN(A,B))/10
80 LET M2=10*MAX(A,B)
81 REM       DEFINE THE CONSTANT PI
90 LET P=3.1415926
91 REM       D=FREQ INTERVAL BETWEEN COMPUTATIONS
100 LET D=(M2-M1)/5
101 REM     LOOP TO CONSTRUCT ARRAY X OF POSITIVE VALUES OF
102 REM     PI/2-(COMPUTED ANGLE) AND ARRAY Y OF NEGATIVE
103 REM     VALUES OF PI/2-(COMPUTED ANGLE)
110 FOR I=1 TO 6
111 REM     X(I)=PI/2-(COMPUTED ANGLE)
120   LET X(I)=P/2-ATN((M1+(I-1)*D)/A)-ATN((M1+(I-1)*D)/B)
121 REM     INITIALIZE Y(I) TO VERY LARGE NEGATIVE VALUE
130   LET Y(I)=-10E10
131 REM     IF X(I) IS POSITIVE, GO TO NEXT I; NOTE THAT Y(I) REMAINS NE
GATIVE
140   IF X(I)>=0 THEN 170
141 REM     X(I) IS NEGATIVE; SET Y(I) EQUAL TO THIS NEGATIVE VALUE
142 REM     AND SET X(I) TO A VERY LARGE POSITIVE VALUE
150   LET Y(I)=X(I)
160   LET X(I)=10E10
170 NEXT I
171 REM     INITIALIZE A1 AND A2 IN PREPARATION FOR FINDING
172 REM     MIN X(I) AND MAX Y(I)
180 LET A1=Y(1)
190 LET A2=X(1)
191 REM  LOOP THAT FINDS MIN X(I) VALUE AND SETS A2 EQUAL TO THIS MIN;
192 REM     AT END OF LOOP, K IS THE POSITION (INDEX) OF MIN VALUE IN AR
RAY X
200 LET K=1
210 FOR J=2 TO 6
220   IF A2 < X(J) THEN 250
230   LET A2=X(J)
240   LET K=J
250 NEXT J
251 REM     OBTAIN FREQUENCY VALUE CORRESPONDING TO MIN X(I)
252 REM     AND SET THAT FREQUENCY EQUAL TO M1
260 LET M1=M1+(K-1)*D
261 REM     IF A2 SATISFIES ACCURACY CRITERION (.5 DEGREES), GO PRINT RE
SULT
270 IF A2 < (2.77778E-3)*P THEN 370
271 REM     OTHERWISE, FIND MAX Y(I) VALUE AND SET A1 EQUAL TO THIS MAX
272 REM     AT END OF LOOP, K IS THE POSITION (INDEX) OF MAX VALUE IN AR
```

Figure 5.5 (Continued on next page)

```
RAY Y
 280 LET K=1
 290 FOR J=2 TO 6
 300    IF A1 > Y(J) THEN 330
 310    LET A1=Y(J)
 320    LET K=J
 330 NEXT J
 331 REM     OBTAIN FREQUENCY VALUE CORRESPONDING TO MAX Y(I)
 332 REM     AND SET THAT FREQUENCY EQUAL TO M2
 340 LET M2=M2-(6-K)*D
 341 REM     IF A1 SATISFIES ACCURACY CRITERION (.5 DEGREES),GO PRINT RES
ULT
 350 IF ABS(A1) < (2.77778E-3)*P THEN 390
 351 REM     OTHERWISE, GO BACK AND COMPUTE NEW FREQUENCY INTERVALS
 352 REM     BASED ON NEW VALUES OF M1 AND M2 AND DO ANOTHER ITERATION
 360 GOTO 100
 370 PRINT "AT";M1;"RAD/SEC, THE ANGLE IS";-90-(ATN(M1/A)+ATN(M1/B))*(18
0/P)
 380 GOTO 400
 390 PRINT "AT";M2;"RAD/SEC, THE ANGLE IS";-90-(ATN(M2/A)+ATN(M2/B))*(18
0/P)
 400 END
>
```

Figure 5.5. A BASIC program for automatic iterative computation of the frequency at which the angle of $G(s)=K/s(s+b)(s+b)$ equals $-180°$; $\pm 0.5°$.

Figure 5.5 (continued)

We should note that the MIN and MAX functions used in statement numbers 70 and 80 are not available in some versions of BASIC. However, it is easy to write a set of statements that are equivalent to both, as for example:

```
70 IF A > B THEN 80

71 LET M1 = A/10

72 LET M2 = 10*B

73 GOTO 90

80 LET M1 = B/10

81 LET M2 = 10*A
```

The operations performed by the program may be better understood by studying the following sequence of important quantities that are computed during the 4 iterations required to find the frequency at which the angle of $G = K/s(s + 1)(s + 10)$ is $-180° \pm .5°$. (Values have been rounded for clarity.)

$$A = 1, B = 10$$

$$M1 = 1/10 = .100 \quad (\text{line } 70)$$

$$M2 = 10 \times 10 = 100 \quad \text{(line 80)}$$

The first completion (all 6 executions) of the loop in lines 110 through 170 produces the following X and Y arrays (values of $\pi/2$ - arctan ω/a - arctan ω/b):

$$X = \begin{bmatrix} 1.461 \\ + 10^{11} \\ + 10^{11} \\ + 10^{11} \\ + 10^{11} \\ + 10^{11} \end{bmatrix} \qquad Y = \begin{bmatrix} -10^{11} \\ -1.10 \\ -1.30 \\ -1.39 \\ -1.43 \\ -1.46 \end{bmatrix}$$

Note that whenever $X(I)$ has a positive value, a large negative value (-10^{11}) has been inserted in the corresponding position of the Y array, and that whenever $Y(I)$ has a negative value, a large positive value has been inserted in the corresponding position of the X array.

In lines 180 and 190, A1 and A2 are set equal (initialized) to the first entries in Y (-10^{11}) and X ($+ 1.46$), in preparation for finding the minimum X value and maximum Y value. The loop in lines 200 through 250 finds the minimum X value, A2 = + 1.46, at its conclusion. Also K = 1 at its conclusion, indicating that the minimum X value, i.e., the minimum positive difference, is in position 1 of the X array.

Using K = 1, the statement at line 260 finds the frequency (.1 rad/sec) corresponding to the minimum X value and sets M1 equal to .1. (In this case, M1 retains its old value of .1.)

In line 270, the accuracy criterion (.5 degrees) is checked to see if the minimum X value, A2, satisfies it. In this case it does not, so the program enters the loop in lines 280 through 330 to find the maximum Y value. At the conclusion of the loop, the maximum Y value is set equal to A1 (-1.10) and K = 2, indicating that -1.10 is in position 2 of the Y array.

In line 340 the frequency corresponding to A1 (20.08) is determined and M2 is set equal to this frequency. In line 350, the accuracy criterion is checked against A1, the maximum negative difference, and, in the present example, fails. Consequently another iteration begins at line 100, where the new values of M1 and M2 are used to compute the new frequency interval D between subsequent calculations.

The next iteration, between ω = M1 = .1 rad/sec and ω = M2 = 20.08 rad/sec yields the following:

$$X = \begin{bmatrix} + 1.46 \\ + 10^{11} \\ + 10^{11} \\ + 10^{11} \\ + 10^{11} \\ + 10^{11} \end{bmatrix} \qquad Y = \begin{bmatrix} -10^{11} \\ -.149 \\ -.550 \\ -.797 \\ -.950 \\ -1.06 \end{bmatrix}$$

```
A2  =   1.46, K = 1, M1 = .100
A1  =   -.149, K = 2, M2 = 4.096
```

Subsequent iterations produce the following:

$$X = \begin{bmatrix} +\ 1.46 \\ +\ .748 \\ +\ .363 \\ +\ .136 \\ +\ 10^{11} \\ +\ 10^{11} \end{bmatrix} \qquad Y = \begin{bmatrix} -10^{11} \\ -10^{11} \\ -10^{11} \\ -10^{11} \\ -.024 \\ -.150 \end{bmatrix}$$

```
A2 = .136, K = 4, M1 = 2.497
A1 = -.024, K = 5, M2 = 3.29
```

$$X = \begin{bmatrix} +\ .136 \\ +\ .100 \\ +\ .067 \\ +\ .035 \\ +\ .005 \\ +\ 10^{11} \end{bmatrix} \qquad Y = \begin{bmatrix} -10^{11} \\ -10^{11} \\ -10^{11} \\ -10^{11} \\ -10^{11} \\ -.024 \end{bmatrix}$$

```
A2 = .005, K = 5, M1 = 3.13696
```

In this last iteration, A2 satisfies the accuracy criterion, so A1 is not computed; instead, the iterations are terminated with the output statement at line 370:

AT 3.13696 RAD/SEC THE ANGLE IS -179.735 DEGREES.

Figure 5.6 shows the results of several runs of the program in Figure 5.5, using various combinations of values for a and b. Note that all final angles are with $\pm$ .5° of -180°.

```
G=K/S(S+A)(S+B). ENTER A AND B.
A=   1   B=   10
AT   3.13696  RAD/SEC, THE ANGLE IS   -179.735
G=K/S(S+A)(S+B). ENTER A AND B.
A=   20   B=   100
AT   45.1136  RAD/SEC, THE ANGLE IS   -180.373
G=K/S(S+A)(S+B). ENTER A AND B.
A=   5   B=   1000
AT   67.6966  RAD/SEC, THE ANGLE IS   -179.649
G=K/S(S+A)(S+B). ENTER A AND B.
A=   .500000   B=   2
AT   1.00760  RAD/SEC, THE ANGLE IS   -180.347

!
```

Figure 5.6 The results of 4 different runs of the program shown in Figure 5.5

EXERCISES

1. Write a BASIC program that can be used to determine the frequency, in Hz, at which the phase angle of

    $$G = \frac{K}{(s + a)\ (s + b)\ (s + c)}$$

    is -180°. K is any positive constant. Write your program in such a way that the user enters values for a, b, and c and the frequencies at which computations are performed, and then controls the iterations by entering new frequency ranges in response to the results produced.

2. Run your program to determine the frequency at which the phase angle of

    $$G = \frac{K}{(s + 2)\ (s + 10)\ (s + 25)}$$

    is $-180^\circ \pm 0.1^\circ$. Record or submit a hard copy of the results of all iterations.

3. Repeat step 2 for a = 5, b = 20, and c = 200.

4. Modify the automatic iterative computation program given in Figure 5.5 of the Discussion so it can be used to determine the frequency, in Hz, at which

    $$G = \frac{K}{(s + a)\ (s + b)\ (s + c)}$$

    is $-180^\circ \pm 0.1^\circ$. Run your program for a = 2, b = 10, and c = 25 and record the result.

5. Run the modified program for a = 5, b = 20, and c = 200 and record the result.

6 Computing DC Transients in RL and RC Networks

OBJECTIVES

1. To learn how to use two general equations to predict the DC transient current or voltage in any RL or RC network.

2. To learn how to determine initial and steady-state currents and voltages in RL and RC networks.

3. To learn how to write a BASIC computer program that produces equations for transient current and voltage and computes instantaneous values of each.

4. To learn through observation of computer generated data and plots the effects of time-constants and initial conditions on transient behavior.

DISCUSSION

When a DC voltage is switched into a network containing both resistive and reactive components, we know that a transient current will flow, until such time as equilibrium (steady-state) conditions are reached. The transient(s) cause transient voltages to be developed across the components of the network. In this experiment, we will restrict our attention to networks that contain only resistance and inductance, or only resistance and capacitance.

In the circuit shown in Figure 6.1, a DC source is switched into an RL network at t = 0. We assume no initial current in the inductor.

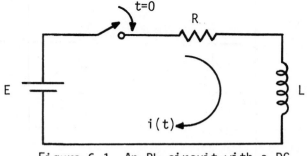

Figure 6.1. An RL circuit with a DC source switched in at t=0.

Transforming the circuit for analysis by Laplace transform methods, we obtain Figure 6.2.

By Kirchhoff's voltage law,

$$\frac{E}{s} = I(s)R + I(s)Ls$$

69

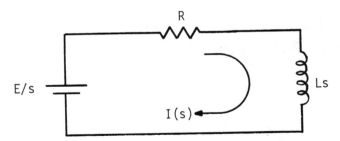

Figure 6.2. The transform of the circuit in Figure 6.1.

$$I(s) = \frac{E}{s(R + Ls)} = \frac{E/L}{s(s + R/L)} \tag{1}$$

Inverting,

$$i(t) = \frac{E}{R}\{1 - e^{-(R/L)t}\} = \frac{E}{R}\{1 - e^{-t/\tau}\} \tag{2}$$

where τ = L/R = the circuit time-constant. Note that the initial current in the circuit, I(t) evaluated at t = 0, is i(0) = E/R(1-1) = 0, while the steady-value, $\lim_{t\to\infty} i(t)$, is i(∞) = E/R. The voltage across the inductor L is found from

$$V(s) = I(s)Ls = \frac{E}{s + R/L} \tag{3}$$

$$v(t) = Ee^{-t/\tau} \tag{4}$$

The initial voltage is v(0) = E, and the steady-state voltage is v(∞) = 0.

Figure 6.3(a) shows an RC circuit containing a capacitor with an initial voltage V_0. The switch is closed at t = 0, and the transformed equivalent circuit is shown in Figure 6.3(b).

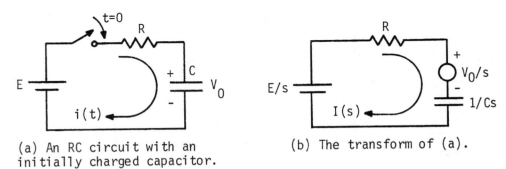

(a) An RC circuit with an
initially charged capacitor.

(b) The transform of (a).

Figure 6.3

$$I(s) = \frac{E-V_o}{s(R + 1/Cs)} = \frac{(E-V_o)/R}{s + 1/RC} \tag{5}$$

and

$$I(t) = \frac{(E-V_o)}{R} e^{-t/RC} \tag{6}$$

where the time constant $\tau = RC$. The initial current is $i(0) = (E-V_o)/R$ and the steady-state current is $i(\infty) = 0$. The voltage across the capacitor is

$$V(s) = I(s)(1/Cs) + V_o/s$$

$$= \frac{(E-V_o)}{RCs(s + 1/RC)} + V_o/s \tag{7}$$

$$v(t) = (E-V_o)(1 - e^{-t/RC}) + V_o$$

$$= E - (E-V_o)E^{-t/RC} \tag{8}$$

In this case, $v(0) - V_o$ and $v(\infty) = E$.

We note in the above examples a similarity in the forms of the equations for the currents and voltages in RC and RL networks. Every voltage and every current in every RL and every RC circuit will fit one of the following two forms:

$$A_1 e^{-t/\tau} \tag{9}$$

$$A_1 + A_2 e^{-t/\tau} \tag{10}$$

where A_1 and A_2 are constants whose values depend on circuit components and initial conditions. For example, equation (2) fits equation (10) with $A_1 = E/R$ and $A_2 = -E/R$, equation (4) fits equation (9) with $A_1 = E$, and equation (8) fits equation (10) with $A_1 = E$ and $A_2 = -(E-V_o)$. We can capitalize on these similarities in form to construct a BASIC program that calculates $v(t)$ or $i(t)$ in any RL or RC network.

The voltage or current in an RL or RC network may be found using the following general form[1], which is expressed in terms of initial and steady-state values of current voltage, and which will always reduce to one of the two forms of equations (9) and (10):

$$y(t) = y(\infty) + [y(0) - y(\infty)] e^{-t/\tau} \tag{11}$$

where y represents either a voltage across or a current through some component in the circuit, $y(0)$ is the initial value of that quantity (the value at $t = 0$), $y(\infty)$ is the steady-state value of that quantity, and τ is the time-constant.

To use equation (11), it is necessary to know how to find initial and steady-state values in a network. These values can be easily determined without completely solving the network, simply by reducing the network with its equivalent circuits at $t = 0$ and $t = \infty$. The rules for finding these equivalent circuits are summarized below.

(i) At t = 0

    Replace all inductors with open-circuits,
Replace all capacitors with short-circuits.

(ii) At t = ∞

    Replace all inductors with short-circuits.
Replace all capacitors with open-circuits.

In both cases (i) and (ii), insert a voltage source V_0 in series with (the short or open representing) a capacitor that has an initial voltage v_0, and insert a current source I_0 in parallel with (the short or open representing) an inductor with an initial current I_0.

    To illustrate these rules, we will determine $i(0)$, $i(\infty)$, $v_R(0)$, and $v_R(\infty)$ in the circuit shown in Figure 6.4(a). The equivalent circuits at t = 0 and t = ∞ are shown in Figures 6.4(b) and 6.4(c), respectively.

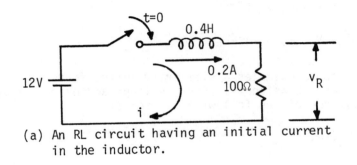

(a) An RL circuit having an initial current in the inductor.

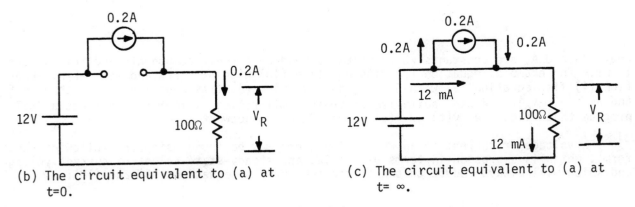

(b) The circuit equivalent to (a) at t=0.

(c) The circuit equivalent to (a) at t= ∞.

Figure 6.4

Note in Figure 6.4(b) that the .4 H inductor is replaced by an open circuit in parallel with a .2A current source,while in Figure 6.4(c) the inductor has been replaced by a short-circuit in parallel with a..2A current source. It is easy now to see that

$$i(0) = .2A, \quad V_R(0) = (.2A)(100\ \Omega) = 20\ V.$$

1. See: Stanley, Transform Circuit Analysis for Engineering and Technology, Prentice-Hall (1968), p. 112.

$$i(\infty) = 12 \text{ V}/100 \ \Omega = 120 \text{ mA, and } v_R (\infty) = (120 \text{ mA})(100 \ \Omega) = 12 \text{ V.}$$

In the equivalent circuit for t = ∞, the shorted current source may be omitted for clarity, since it contributes nothing to the rest of the circuit. Similarly, in the equivalent circuit at t = ∞ for an RC network containing a capacitor with initial voltage v_0, the open circuited voltage source V_0 may be omitted. Using the initial and steady-state values determined above in equation (11), we find

$$i(t) = i(\infty) + \{i(0) - i(\infty)\} \ e^{-t/\tau}$$

$$= \ 120 \text{ mA} + \{200 \text{ mA} - 120 \text{ mA}\} \ e^{-t/.004}$$

$$= \ 120 + 80e^{-t/.004} \text{mA}$$

and

$$v_R(t) = v_R (\infty) + \{v_R (0) - v_R(\infty)\} \ e^{-t/\tau}$$

$$= 12 + \{20 - 12\} \ e^{-t/.004}$$

$$= 12 + 8e^{-t/.004} \text{ V}$$

The general series RL circuit is shown in Figure 6.5. Note that the initial current I_0 may be either positive (as shown) or negative (opposite to that shown).

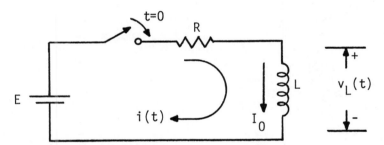

Figure 6.5. A general series RL circuit. I_0 may be positive or negative.

Using the rules discussed earlier, we find that

$$i(0) = I_0, \ i(\infty) \ = E/R \qquad\qquad\qquad\qquad\qquad (12)$$

$$v_L(0) = E - I_0R, \ v_L(\infty) = 0 \qquad\qquad\qquad\qquad\qquad (13)$$

$$v_R(0) = I_0R, \ v_R(\infty) = E \qquad\qquad\qquad\qquad\qquad (14)$$

The general series RC circuit is shown in Figure 6.6. Again, the initial voltage V_0 across the capacitor is assumed positive with the polarity shown, and would be expressed as a negative quantity if the polarity were reversed.

The initial and steady-state values of the circuit parameters are

$$i(0) = (E-V_0)/R \qquad i(\infty) = 0 \qquad\qquad\qquad\qquad\qquad (15)$$

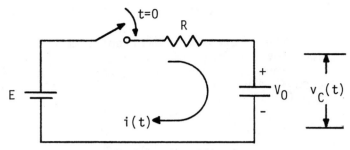

Figure 6.6. A general series RC circuit. V_0 may be positive or negative.

$$v_C(0) = V_0 \qquad v_C(\infty) = E \tag{16}$$

$$v_R(0) = E + V_0 \qquad v_R(\infty) = 0 \tag{17}$$

Figure 6.7 shows a flowchart for a BASIC program that can be used to solve equation (11) for the voltage across and current through the reactive element of either an RC or RL circuit. The program prints the solutions $v(t)$ and $i(t)$ in equation form and prints a table of instantaneous values of $v(t)$ and $i(t)$ for 21 instants of time ranging from $t = 0$ to $t = 5$ time constants $(t = 5\tau)$.

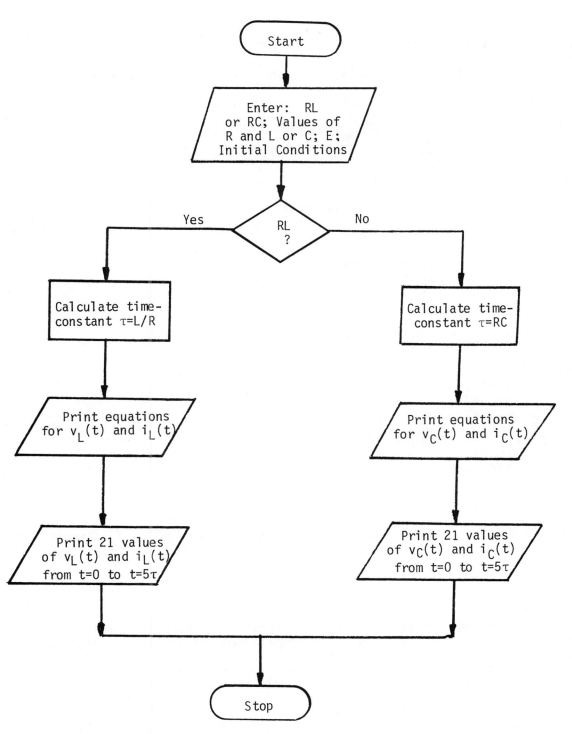

Figure 6.7. A flowchart for computing v(t) and i(t) in an RL or RC circuit. The BASIC program is shown in Figure 6.8.

```
100 PRINT "ENTER RL OR RC"
110 INPUT A$
120 PRINT "ENTER RESISTANCE VALUE IN OHMS"
130 INPUT R
140 PRINT "ENTER INDUCTANCE IN HENRIES OR CAPACITANCE IN FARADS"
150 INPUT X
160 PRINT "ENTER INITIAL CURRENT IN AMPS OR INITIAL VOLTAGE IN VOLTS"
170 INPUT F
180 PRINT "ENTER APPLIED SOURCE VOLTAGE IN VOLTS"
190 INPUT E
200 DIM T(21),V(21),I(21)
210 IF A$="RL" THEN 320
220 LET C=R*X
230 PRINT "V(T)="E"+("F-E")(EXP(-T/"C")"
240 PRINT "I(T)="((E-F)/R)"EXP(-T/"C")"
250 PRINT
260 FOR K=1 TO 21
270    LET T(K)=.25*C*(K-1)
280    LET V(K)=E+(F-E)*EXP(-T(K)/C)
290     LET I(K)=((E-F)/R)*EXP(-T(K)/C)
300 NEXT K
310 GOTO 410
320 LET C=X/R
330 PRINT "V(T)="E-F*R"EXP(-T/"C")"
340 PRINT "I(T)="E/R"+("F-E/R")EXP(-T/"C")"
350 PRINT
360 FOR K=1 TO 21
370 LET T(K)=.25*C*(K-1)
380 LET V(K)=(E-F*R)*EXP(-T(K)/C)
390    LET I(K)=E/R+(F-E/R)*EXP(-T(K)/C)
400 NEXT K
410 PRINT "TIME,SEC","VOLTAGE,VOLTS   CURRENT,AMPS"
420 FOR K=1 TO 21
430    PRINT T(K),V(K),I(K)
440 NEXT K
450 END
>
```

Figure 6.8. A BASIC program that computes v(t) and i(t) in an RL or RC circuit.

Figure 6.8(a) shows the results of a program run for an RC circuit using values R=4K, C=200μF, V_o= -5 volts, and E=10V. Figures 6.9(b) and 6.9(c) show plots of $v_c(t)$ and i(t) versus time, based on the results of the program run. Note that the capacitor voltage is -5V at t=0, as we would expect, since V_o = -5. The voltage then rises towards its final value of +10V with a time constant of (4×10^3) (2×10^{-4}) = 0.8 sec. The equation for $v_C(t)$ is seen from the printout to be $v_C(t) = 10 - 15e^{-t/.8}$, while the current is $i(t) = .00375e^{-t/.8}$. The computed initial value of current is 3.75 mA, which agrees with the calculation

$$i(0) = \frac{V - V_o}{R} = \frac{15}{4K} = 3.75 \times 10^{-3} \text{ A.}$$

```
ENTER RL OR RC
ENTER RESISTANCE VALUE IN OHMS
 4000
ENTER INDUCTANCE IN HENRIES OR CAPACITANCE IN FARADS
 2.00000E-04
ENTER INITIAL CURRENT IN AMPS OR INITIAL VOLTAGE IN VOLTS
-5
ENTER APPLIED SOURCE VOLTAGE IN VOLTS
 10
V(T)= 10+(-15)(EXP(-T/ .800000)
I(T)= 3.75000E-03EXP(-T/ .800000)
TIME,SEC          VOLTAGE,VOLTS      CURRENT,AMPS
 0                -5                 3.75000E-03
 .200000          -1.68201          2.92050E-03
 .400000          .902040           2.27449E-03
 .600000          2.91450           1.77137E-03
 .800000          4.48181           1.37955E-03
1.00000           5.70243           1.07439E-03
1.20000           6.65305           8.36738E-04
1.40000           7.39339           6.51652E-04
1.60000           7.96997           5.07507E-04
1.80000           8.41901           3.95247E-04
2.00000           8.76873           3.07819E-04
2.20000           9.04108           2.39729E-04
2.40000           9.25319           1.86702E-04
2.60000           9.41839           1.45403E-04
2.80000           9.54704           1.13240E-04
3.00000           9.64723           8.81915E-05
3.20000           9.72527           6.86836E-05
3.40000           9.78604           5.34909E-05
3.60000           9.83337           4.16587E-05
3.80000           9.87022           3.24439E-05
4.00000           9.89893           2.52673E-05

!
```

Figure 6.9(a). Results of a run of the program in Figure 6.8.
R=4K, C=200μF, V_0=-5V, E=10V.

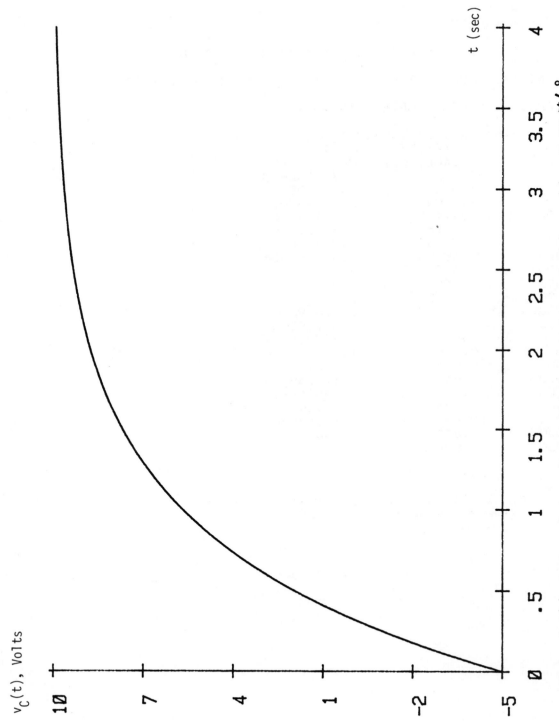

Figure 6.9(b). A plot of the voltage $v_C(t)$ found in Figure 6.9(a). $v_C(t) = 10-15e^{-t/.8}$ V.

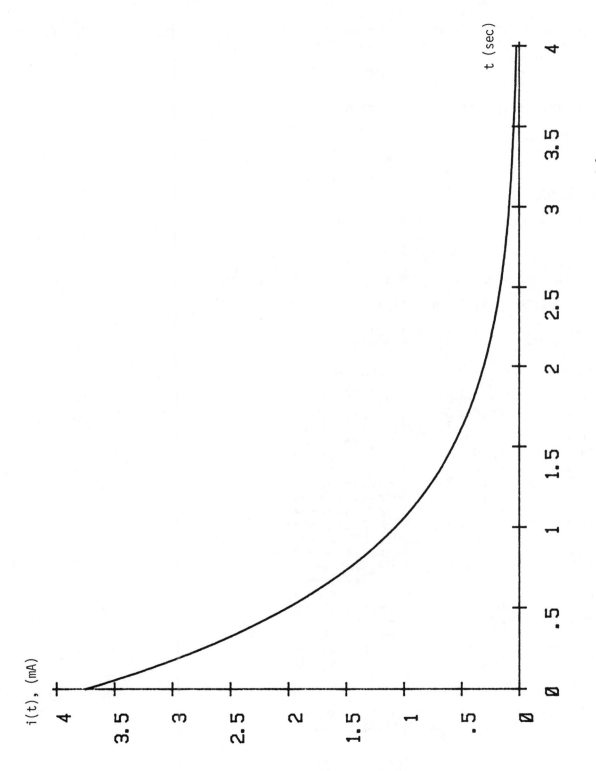

Figure 6.9(c). A plot of the current i(t) found in Figure 6.9(a). $i(t) = 3.75e^{-t/.8}$ mA.

Figure 6.10 (a) shows the results of another program run for the same RC circuit, this time for an initial capacitor voltage $V_0 = +20$ V. We see that $v_C(t)$ in this case <u>decays</u> from its initial value of 20 V to its final value of 10 V with the same 0.8 sec time constant. A plot of $v_C(t)$ based on the computed data is shown in Figure 6.10 (b). Figure 6.10 (c) is a plot of $i(t)$. We note that the current now has initial value -2.5 mA =

$$\frac{10-20}{4K}$$

and rises towards its final value of zero.

```
ENTER  RL OR RC
RC
ENTER  RESISTANCE VALUE IN OHMS
 4000
ENTER  INDUCTANCE IN HENRIES OR CAPACITANCE IN FARADS
 2.00000E-04
ENTER  INITIAL CURRENT IN AMPS OR INITIAL VOLTAGE IN VOLTS
 20
ENTER  APPLIED SOURCE VOLTAGE IN VOLTS
 10
V(T)= 10+( 10)(EXP(-T/ .800000)
I(T)=-2.50000E-03EXP(-T/ .800000)
```

TIME,SEC	VOLTAGE,VOLTS	CURRENT,AMPS
0	20	-2.50000E-03
.200000	17.7880	-1.94700E-03
.400000	16.0653	-1.51633E-03
.600000	14.7237	-1.18092E-03
.800000	13.6788	-9.19699E-04
1.00000	12.8650	-7.16262E-04
1.20000	12.2313	-5.57825E-04
1.40000	11.7377	-4.34435E-04
1.60000	11.3534	-3.38338E-04
1.80000	11.0540	-2.63498E-04
2.00000	10.8208	-2.05212E-04
2.20000	10.6393	-1.59820E-04
2.40000	10.4979	-1.24468E-04
2.60000	10.3877	-9.69355E-05
2.80000	10.3020	-7.54935E-05
3.00000	10.2352	-5.87944E-05
3.20000	10.1832	-4.57891E-05
3.40000	10.1426	-3.56606E-05
3.60000	10.1111	-2.77725E-05
3.80000	10.0865	-2.16292E-05
4.00000	10.0674	-1.68449E-05
!		

Figure 6.10(a). Results of a run of the program in Figure 6.8. R=4K, C=200µF, V_0=20V, E=10V.

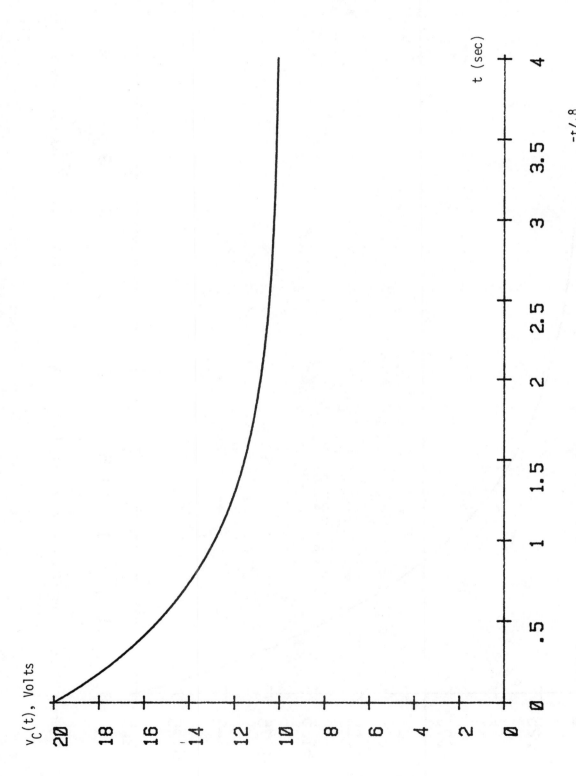

Figure 6.10(b). A plot of the voltage $v_C(t)$ found in Figure 6.10(a). $v_C(t) = 10 + 10e^{-t/.8}$ V. Compare with Figure 6.9(b).

82

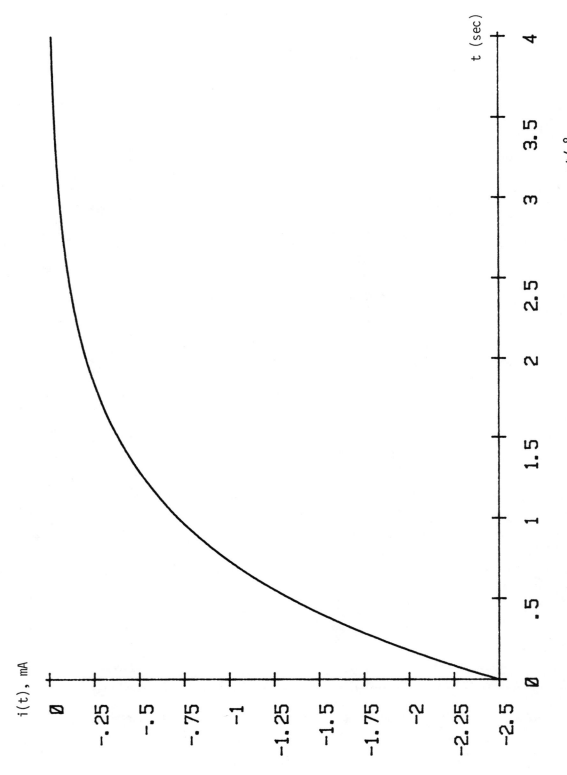

Figure 6.10(c). A plot of the current i(t) found in Figure 6.10(a). $i(t) = -2.5e^{-t/.8}$ mA. Compare with Figure 6.9(c).

Figure 6.11 (a) shows the results of a program for an RL circuit in which R = 1.5 K, L = 30 mH, I_0 = 7.5 mA, and E = 30 V. We see that $v_L(t) = 18.75e^{-t/2 \times 10^{-5}}$ V and i(t) = $.02 - .0125e^{-t/2 \times 10^{-5}}$ A. The data are plotted in Figures 6.11 (b) and 6.11 (c), respectively. The current has initial value 7.5 mA, as expected, and rises towards its final value of .02 A = 30 V/1.5 K. The voltage has initial value 18.75 V (30-.0075 x 1.5 K) and decays toward zero.

```
ENTER RL OR RC
RL
ENTER RESISTANCE VALUE IN OHMS
 1500
ENTER INDUCTANCE IN HENRIES OR CAPACITANCE IN FARADS
 3.00000E-02
ENTER INITIAL CURRENT IN AMPS OR INITIAL VOLTAGE IN VOLTS
 7.50000E-03
ENTER APPLIED SOURCE VOLTAGE IN VOLTS
 30
V(T)= 18.7500EXP(-T/ 2.00000E-05)
I(T)= 2.00000E-02+(-1.25000E-02)EXP(-T/ 2.00000E-05)
TIME,SEC        VOLTAGE,VOLTS    CURRENT,AMPS
 0               18.7500          7.50000E-03
 5.00000E-06     14.6025          1.02650E-02
 1.00000E-05     11.3724          1.24184E-02
 1.50000E-05     8.85687          1.40954E-02
 2.00000E-05     6.89774          1.54015E-02
 2.50000E-05     5.37196          1.64187E-02
 3.00000E-05     4.18369          1.72109E-02
 3.50000E-05     3.25826          1.78278E-02
 4.00000E-05     2.53754          1.83083E-02
 4.50000E-05     1.97624          1.86825E-02
 5.00000E-05     1.53909          1.89739E-02
 5.50000E-05     1.19865          1.92009E-02
 6.00000E-05     .933508          1.93777E-02
 6.50000E-05     .727016          1.95153E-02
 7.00000E-05     .566201          1.96225E-02
 7.50000E-05     .440958          1.97060E-02
 8.00000E-05     .343418          1.97711E-02
 8.50000E-05     .267454          1.98217E-02
 9.00000E-05     .208294          1.98611E-02
 9.50000E-05     .162219          1.98919E-02
 1.00000E-04     .126337          1.99158E-02

!
```

Figure 6.11(a). Results of a run of the program in Figure 6.8.
R=1.5K, L=30mH, I_0=7.5mA, E=30V.

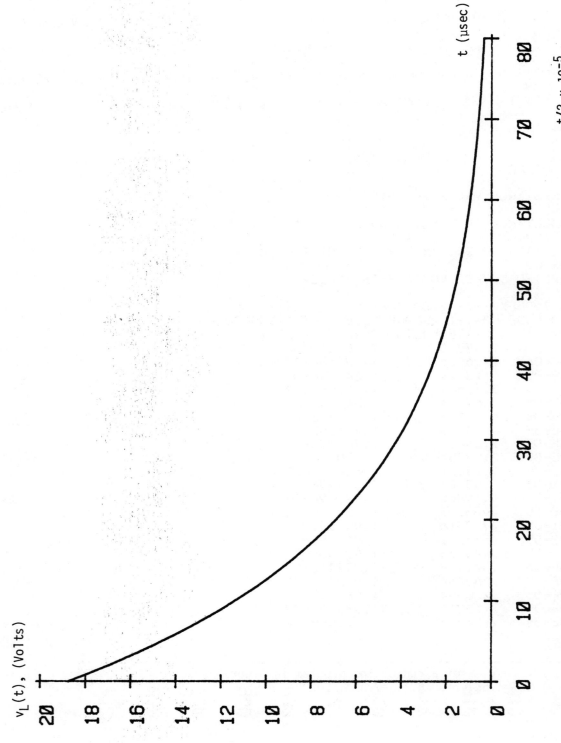

Figure 6.11(b). A plot of the voltage $v_L(t)$ found in Figure 6.11(a). $v_L(t) = 18.75e^{-t/2} \times 10^{-5}$ V.

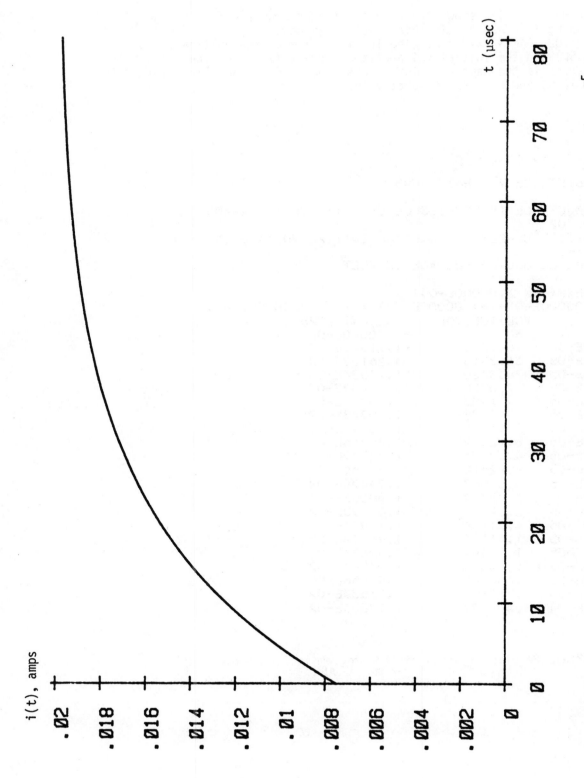

Figure 6.11(c). A plot of the current i(t) found in Figure 6.11(a). $i(t) = .02 - .0125e^{-t/2} \times 10^{-5}$ A.

Finally, Figure 6.12(a) shows the results of a program run for the same RL circuit, using I_0 = -20mA. In this case we see that $v(t) = 60e^{-t/2 \times 10^{-5}}$V and $i(t) = .02 - .04e^{-t/2 \times 10^{-5}}$ A. The initial value of the voltage is 60V (30+.02x1.5K) and the initial value of the current is -.02A. The final value of the current is the same as before, .02A = 30V/1.5K. These are plotted in Figures 6.12(b) and 6.12(c), respectively.

```
ENTER RL OR RC
RL
ENTER RESISTANCE VALUE IN OHMS
 1500
ENTER INDUCTANCE IN HENRIES OR CAPACITANCE IN FARADS
 3.00000E-02
ENTER INITIAL CURRENT IN AMPS OR INITIAL VOLTAGE IN VOLTS
-2.00000E-02
ENTER APPLIED SOURCE VOLTAGE IN VOLTS
 30
V(T)= 60EXP(-T/ 2.00000E-05)
I(T)= 2.00000E-02+(-4.00000E-02)EXP(-T/ 2.00000E-05)
TIME,SEC        VOLTAGE,VOLTS   CURRENT,AMPS
 0              60              -2.00000E-02
 5.00000E-06    46.7280         -1.11520E-02
 1.00000E-05    36.3918         -4.26123E-03
 1.50000E-05    28.3420          1.10534E-03
 2.00000E-05    22.0728          5.28482E-03
 2.50000E-05    17.1903          8.53981E-03
 3.00000E-05    13.3878          1.10748E-02
 3.50000E-05    10.4264          1.30490E-02
 4.00000E-05    8.12012          1.45866E-02
 4.50000E-05    6.32395          1.57840E-02
 5.00000E-05    4.92510          1.67166E-02
 5.50000E-05    3.83567          1.74429E-02
 6.00000E-05    2.98722          1.80085E-02
 6.50000E-05    2.32645          1.84490E-02
 7.00000E-05    1.81184          1.87921E-02
 7.50000E-05    1.41106          1.90593E-02
 8.00000E-05    1.09894          1.92674E-02
 8.50000E-05    .855854          1.94294E-02
 9.00000E-05    .666540          1.95556E-02
 9.50000E-05    .519102          1.96539E-02
 1.00000E-04    .404277          1.97305E-02

!
```

Figure 6.12(a). Results of a run of the program in Figure 6.8. R=1.5K, L=30mH, I_0=-20mA, E=30V.

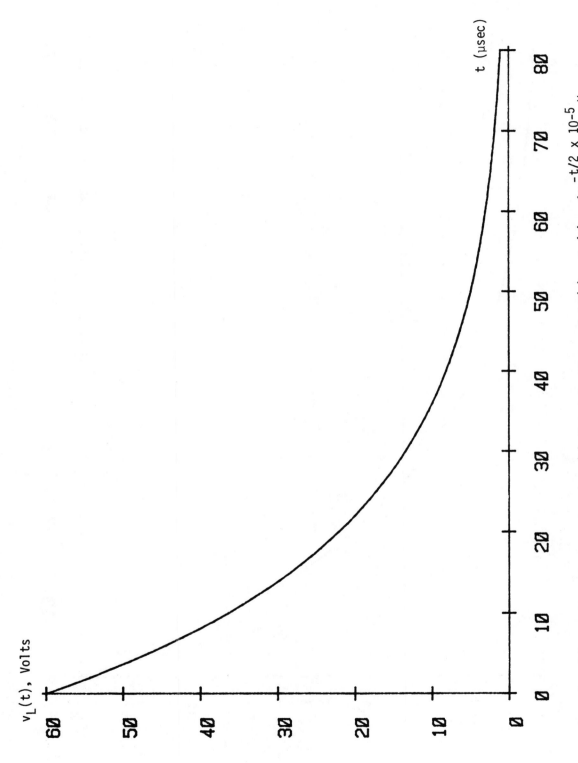

Figure 6.12(b). A plot of the voltage $v_L(t)$ found in Figure 6.12(a). $v_L(t) = 60e^{-t/2} \times 10^{-5}$ V. Compare with Figure 6.11(b).

88

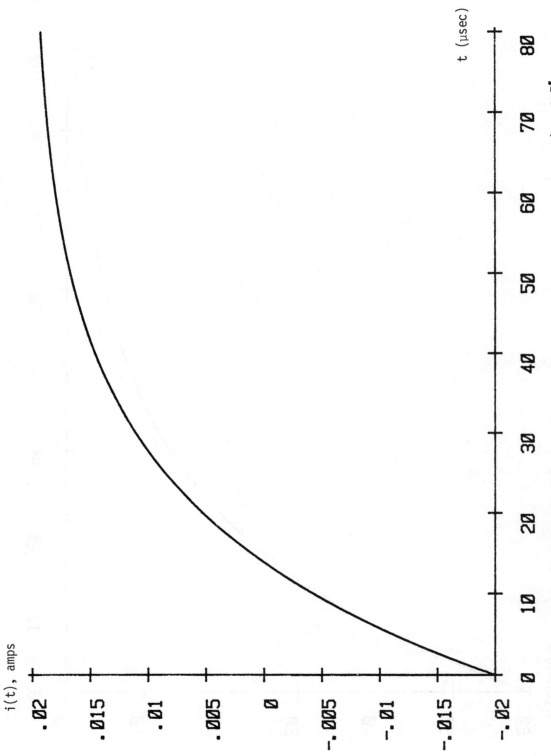

Figure 6.12(c). A plot of the current $i(t)$ found in Figure 6.12(a). $i(t) = .02 - .04e^{-t/2} \times 10^{-5}$ A. Compare with Figure 6.11(c).

The program shown in Figure 6.8 is written for series RL or RC circuits. To use the program for a different circuit configuration, it is necessary to reduce the configuration to a series equivalent, i.e., to a Thevenin equivalent circuit. Suppose, for example, that we want to use the program to find $v_C(t)$ and $i_C(t)$ in the circuit shown in Figure 6.13 (a). Figure 6.13 (b) shows the Thevenin equivalent circuit with respect to the terminals A-B.

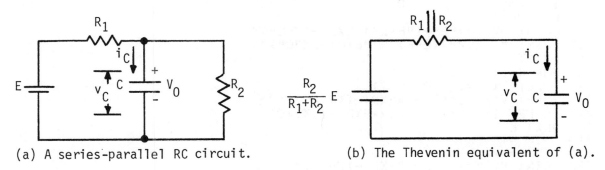

(a) A series-parallel RC circuit.   (b) The Thevenin equivalent of (a).

Figure 6.13

When using the program to analyze the circuit of Figure 6.13 (a), we would therefore type the value of $R_1 \| R_2$ when prompted to enter a resistance value, and the value of

$$\left(\frac{R_2}{R_1 + R_2} \right) E$$

when prompted to enter the applied source voltage.

Alternatively, if a particular (non-series) circuit configuration is to be analyzed repeatedly using different parameter values, we can easily modify the program so that it will compute the Thevenin equivalent values necessary for subsequent computations. In the program listing of Figure 6.14, the original program has been modified to find $v_C(t)$ and $i_C(t)$ for the general circuit shown in Figure 6.13(a). The user now enters values for R1, R2, and E1 (= E in Figure 6.9) and the program computes R = (R1 x R2)/(R1 + R2) and E = E1(R2/(R1 + R2)) for use in subsequent computations.

EXERCISES

1. Use the program of Figure 6.8 to determine the voltage across and current through the capacitor in Figure 6.15 after the switch is closed at t = 0. What are the theoretical initial and final values of the capacitor current and voltage? Show your computations. Use the data computed by the program to sketch v(t) and i(t) versus time.

2. Repeat Exercise 1 when the initial capacitor voltage is + 12 V (with the same polarity as the 4 V shown in Figure 6.15) and the applied voltage is -12 V (with the opposite polarity of the 4V source shown in Figure 6.15).

3. Use the program of Figure 6.8 to find the voltage across and current through the inductor in the circuit of Figure 6.16 after the switch is closed at t = 0.

```
100 PRINT "ENTER R1 AND R2 IN OHMS"
110 INPUT R1,R2
120 PRINT "ENTER CAPACITANCE IN FARADS"
130 INPUT X
140 PRINT "ENTER APPLIED SOURCE VOLTAGE IN VOLTS"
150 INPUT E1
160 LET R=(R1*R2)/(R1+R2)
170 LET E=E1*(R2/(R1+R2))
180 LET F=0
200 DIM T(21),V(21),I(21)
210 IF A$="RL" THEN 320
220 LET C=R*X
230 PRINT "V(T)="E"+("F-E")(EXP(-T/"C")"
240 PRINT "I(T)="((E-F)/R)"EXP(-T/"C")"
250 PRINT
260 FOR K=1 TO 21
270    LET T(K)=.25*C*(K-1)
280    LET V(K)=E+(F-E)*EXP(-T(K)/C)
290     LET I(K)=((E-F)/R)*EXP(-T(K)/C)
300 NEXT K
310 GOTO 410
320 LET C=X/R
330 PRINT "V(T)="E-F*R"EXP(-T/"C")"
340 PRINT "I(T)="E/R"+("F-E/R")EXP(-T/"C")"
350 PRINT
360 FOR K=1 TO 21
370 LET T(K)=.25*C*(K-1)
380 LET V(K)=(E-F*R)*EXP(-T(K)/C)
390    LET I(K)=E/R+(F-E/R)*EXP(-T(K)/C)
400 NEXT K
410 PRINT "TIME,SEC","VOLTAGE,VOLTS  CURRENT,AMPS"
420 FOR K=1 TO 21
430    PRINT T(K),V(K),I(K)
440 NEXT K
450 END
```

!

Figure 6.14. A BASIC program that computes $v_c(t)$ and $i(t)$ for
the circuit shown in Figure 6.13.

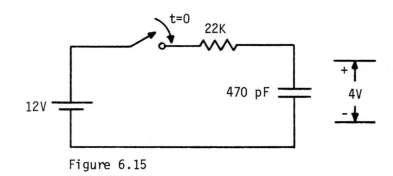

Figure 6.15

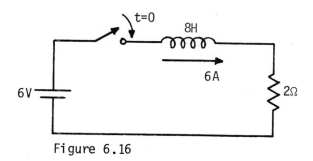

Figure 6.16

What are the theoretical initial and final values of the inductor current and voltage? Use the data computed by the program to sketch v(t) and i(t) versus time.

4. Repeat Exercise 3 when the initial current is zero.

5. Modify the program of Figure 6.8 so it can be used to find the voltage across the re-sistor, in addition to the current and voltage across the capacitor or inductor. Also, have the program compute and print the <u>sum</u> of the voltages across R and C (or, across R and L) at each time point. Then run your program for the circuits of Exercises 1 and 3. How are the computed sums related? Explain why they have the values they do.

6. Modify the program of Figure 6.8 so it can be used to find the voltage across and cur-rent through the inductor in a circuit of the general form of Figure 6.17 after the switch is closed at t = 0. User enters values of E, I_0, R_1, R_2, R_3, and L. Print 21 values of v and i from t = 0 to t = 5 time constants.

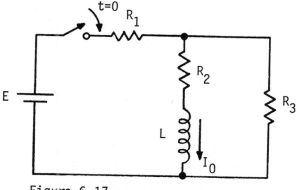

Figure 6.17

Run your program for the case E = 60 V, R_1 = 3 K, R_2 = 1 K, R_3 = 6 K, L = .6 H, and I_0 = 20 mA. What are the theoretical initial and final values of the current and voltage, and how do these compare with computed values?

1. Calculate the circuit period and use these values to determine current and voltage. Use the data compiled by the program to calculate and plot the current.

2. Repeat step 2 with the initial conditions as shown.

3. Run the program in Figure 8-8 so it can proceed to...

7 Computing AC Transients in RL and RC Networks

OBJECTIVES

1. To gain experience writing BASIC programs to solve AC network equations, based on the results of analysis using Laplace transform methods.

2. To verify through analysis and computer generated data the existence of a transient in the response of RL and RC networks to an AC excitation.

3. To learn how to select time intervals for computing instantaneous values of voltage and current based on the frequency of the AC excitation and the circuit time constant.

DISCUSSION

When an AC voltage is switched into an RL or an RC network, there is a transient component in the current that flows, just as there is when a DC source is applied. If the AC voltage is sinusoidal, e = Asin(ωt + θ), then the transient component of the resulting current oscillates at the same frequency ω. We can identify the transient by performing a transform analysis of the circuit. See Figure 7.1.

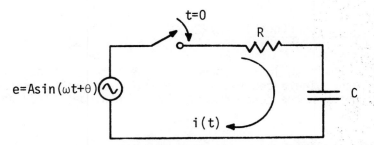

Figure 7.1. An RC circuit having an AC source switched in at t=0.

Since e = Asin(ωt + θ) equals A(sinθcosωt + cosθsinωt), the transform of e may be expressed as

$$E(s) = \frac{(As)\sin\theta}{s^2 + \omega^2} + \frac{(A\omega)\cos\theta}{s^2 + \omega^2}$$

$$= \frac{(As)\sin\theta + (A\omega)\cos\theta}{s^2 + \omega^2} \tag{1}$$

93

Then,

$$I(s) = \frac{E(s)}{R + \frac{1}{Cs}} = \frac{(As)\sin\theta + (A\omega)\cos\theta}{(\frac{Rcs + 1}{Cs})(s^2 + \omega^2)}$$

$$= \frac{(A/R)(s^2\sin\theta + s\omega\cos\theta)}{(s + 1/RC)(s^2 + \omega^2)} \tag{2}$$

To invert equation (2) we first use the partial fraction technique to find the component of the inverse due to the pole at s = -1/RC.

$$I(s) = \frac{C_1}{s + 1/RC} + \frac{C_2}{s + j\omega} + \frac{C_3}{s - j\omega} \tag{3}$$

$$C_1 = \frac{(A/R)(s^2\sin\theta + s\omega\cos\theta)}{s^2 + \omega^2}\bigg|_{s = -1/RC}$$

With some algebraic manipulation, we find

$$C_1 = \frac{(A/R)(\sin\theta - \omega RC\cos\theta)}{1 + (\omega RC)^2}$$

We therefore know that one term in the equation for i(t), call it $i_1(t)$, will be the inverse of the first fraction in equation (3), that is, the inverse of

$$\frac{(A/R)(\sin\theta - \omega RC\cos\theta)}{\{1 + (\omega RC)^2\}(s + 1/RC)}$$

So, $$i_1(t) = \frac{(A/R)(\sin\theta - \omega RC\cos\theta)}{1 + (\omega RC)^2} e^{-t/RC} \tag{4}$$

Equation (4) accounts for the transient component of the total current. The steady-state component can be determined using a general technique[1] for inverting transforms having a quadratic with complex roots in the denominator. This technique yields an inverse of the form

$$i_2(t) = \frac{M}{\omega}e^{-\alpha t} \sin(\omega t + \Psi) \tag{5}$$

where $\alpha \pm j\omega$ are the complex roots of the quadratic

and   M and Ψ are determined by evaluating

$$M \underline{/\Psi} = K(s)\bigg|_{s = -\alpha + j\omega}$$

where K(s) is that portion of the transform remaining after the quadratic is removed.

    In the present example, the quadratic is $s^2 + \omega^2$ and its complex roots are $s = \pm j\omega$. Note that $\alpha = 0$. Removing the quadratic from equation (2), we obtain

-----
1. See Bogart, Laplace Transforms: Theory and Experiments (Wiley), 1983.

$$K(s) = \frac{(A/R)(s^2 \sin\theta + s\omega\cos\theta)}{(s + 1/RC)}$$

and therefore

$$M \underline{/\Psi} = \frac{(A/R)(s^2 \sin\theta + s\omega\cos\theta)}{(s + 1/RC)} \bigg|_{s = j\omega}$$

$$= (A/R) \frac{(-\omega^2 \sin\theta + j\omega^2 \cos\theta)}{j\omega + 1/RC} \tag{6}$$

The magnitude of M of (6) is

$$M = \frac{A}{R} \sqrt{\frac{\omega^4 \sin^2\theta + \omega^4 \cos^2\theta}{\omega^2 + (1/RC)^2}}$$

$$= \frac{A\omega^2 C}{\sqrt{1 + (\omega RC)^2}} \tag{7}$$

and the angle Ψ of (6) is

$$\Psi = \Theta + \arctan(1/\omega RC) \tag{8}$$

Using (7) and (8) in (5), we obtain

$$i_2(t) = \frac{A\omega C}{1 + (\omega RC)^2} \sin(\omega t + \Psi) \tag{9}$$

where $\Psi = \theta + \arctan(1/\omega RC)$

The total current i(t) is the sum of $i_1(t)$, the component due to the pole at s = -1/RC, and $i_2(t)$, the component due to the complex poles s = $\pm$ jω. Thus, from equations (4) and (9),

$$i(t) = \frac{(A/R)(\sin\theta - \omega RC\cos\theta)}{1 + (\omega RC)^2} e^{-t/RC} \tag{10}$$

$$+ \frac{A\omega C}{\sqrt{1 + (\omega RC)^2}} \sin(\omega t + \Psi)$$

where $\Psi = \theta + \arctan(1/\omega RC)$

To obtain an expression for the voltage $v_R(t)$ across the resistor R in Figure 4.1, we simply multiply equation (10) by R: $v_R(t) = i(t) R$.

For the special case where $\theta = 90^0$, i.e. e(t) = Asin(ωt + 90^0) = Acos(ωt), the voltage $v_R(t)$ becomes

$$v_R(t) = \frac{-A\omega C}{1 + (\omega RC)^2} \; e^{-t/RC} \; + \; \frac{A\omega C}{\sqrt{1 + (\omega RC)^2}} \; \sin(\omega t + \Psi) \qquad (11)$$

where $\qquad \Psi = 90^0 + \arctan(1/\omega RC)$

Figure 7.2 shows a typical example of the voltage waveform predicted by equation (11). The contribution of the negative-valued exponential in (11) is clearly apparent in the figure. Note how the peaks of the sinusoidal oscillation gradually rise toward their steady-state value as the exponential in (11) (the transient component) gradually decays to zero with increasing time.

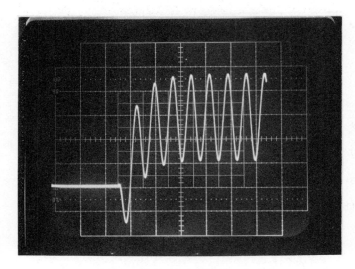

Figure 7.2 The voltage $v_R(t)$ across the resistor in Figure 7.1. See equation (11).

Consider now the series RL circuit shown in Figure 7.3.

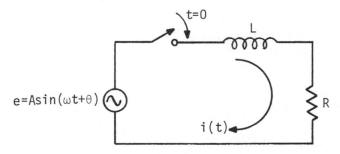

Figure 7.3. An RL circuit having an AC source switched in at t=0.

After the switch is thrown at t = 0, we have

$$I(s) = \frac{E(s)}{Ls + R} = \frac{(As)\sin\theta + (A\omega)\cos\theta}{(Ls + R)(s^2 + \omega^2)}$$

$$= \frac{(A/L)\{(s)\sin\theta + \omega\cos\theta\}}{(s^2 + \omega^2)(s + R/L)} = \frac{C_1}{(s + R/L)} + \frac{C_2}{s + j\omega} + \frac{C_3}{s - j\omega}$$

$$C_1 = \frac{(A/L)\{(s)(\sin\theta) + \omega\cos\theta\}}{s^2 + \omega^2}\Bigg|_{s = -R/L}$$

$$= \frac{A/L\{(-R/L)\sin\theta + \omega\cos\theta\}}{\omega^2 + (R/L)^2}$$

$$i_1(t) = \frac{(A/L)\{(-R/L)\sin\theta + \omega\cos\theta\}}{\omega^2 + (R/L)^2} e^{-t/(L/R)} \tag{12}$$

$$M\,\underline{/\Psi} = \frac{(A/L)\{(s)(\sin\theta) + \omega\cos\theta\}}{(s + R/L)}\Bigg|_{s = j\omega}$$

$$= \frac{(A/L)(j\omega\sin\theta + \omega\cos\theta)}{j\omega + R/L}$$

$$M = \frac{A\omega}{\sqrt{R^2 + (\omega L)^2}} \qquad \Psi = \theta - \arctan(\omega L/R)$$

From (5),

$$i_2(t) = \frac{A}{\sqrt{R^2 + (\omega L)^2}} \sin(\omega t + \Psi) \tag{13}$$

where $\qquad \Psi = \theta - \arctan(\omega L/R)$

Combining (12) and (13),

$$i(t) = i_1(t) + i_2(t)$$

$$= (A/L)\frac{\{(-R/L)\sin\theta + \omega\cos\theta\}}{\omega^2 + (R/L)^2} e^{-t/(L/R)}$$

$$+ \frac{A}{\sqrt{R^2 + (\omega L)^2}} \sin(\omega t + \Psi) \tag{14}$$

where $\qquad \Psi = \theta - \arctan(\omega L/R)$

Figure 7.4 is a listing of a BASIC program that finds the equations for the current through and voltage across the resistor in an RL or an RC circuit when a sinusoidal excitation is applied at t = 0. It also computes and prints out values of current and voltage at 21 time points up to 5 time-constants. The logic of the program is quite straightforward

```
10 REM   THIS PROGRAM FINDS THE EQUATIONS FOR THE CURRENT THROUGH
20 REM   AND VOLTAGE ACROSS THE RESISTOR IN AN RL OR AN RC CIRCUIT
30 REM   WHEN A SINUSOIDAL EXCITATION IS APPLIED AT T=0.
40 REM   IT ALSO COMPUTES AND PRINTS OUT VALUES OF CURRENT AND
50 REM   VOLTAGE AT 21 TIME POINTS UP TO 5 TIME-CONSTANTS.
100 PRINT "ENTER RL OR RC"
110 INPUT A$
120 PRINT "ENTER RESISTANCE IN OHMS"
130 INPUT R
140 PRINT "ENTER INDUCTANCE IN H OR CAPACITANCE IN F"
150 INPUT X
160 PRINT "ENTER PEAK VALUE A IN VOLTS, FREQ W IN RAD/SEC"
165 PRINT "AND PHASE ANGLE D IN DEGREES"
170 PRINT "A=": "W=": "D=":
180 INPUT A,W,D
190 LET P=3.1415927
200 LET Z=D*P/180
210 DIM T(21),V(21),I(21)
220 IF A$="RL" THEN 370
230 LET S=Z+ATN(1/(W*R*X))
250 LET N=SIN(Z)-W*R*X*COS(Z)
260 LET D1=1+(W*R*X)**2
270 LET D2=D1**.5
280 PRINT "I(T)="(A/R)*N/D1"EXP(-T/"R*X")+"A*W*X/D2"SIN("W"T+("S*180/P")
)"
290 PRINT "V(T)="A*N/D1"EXP(-T/"R*X")+"A*W*X*R/D2"SIN("W"T+("S*180/P"))"
300 PRINT
310 FOR K=1 TO 21
320    LET T(K)=.25*R*X*(K-1)
330    LET I(K)=(A/R)*(N/D1)*EXP(-T(K)/(R*X))+(A*W*X/D2)*SIN(W*T(K)+S)
340    LET V(K)=R*I(K)
350 NEXT K
360 GOTO 490
370 LET S=Z-ATN(W*X/R)
380 LET N=(-R/X)*SIN(Z)+W*COS(Z)
390 LET D1=W**2+(R/X)**2
400 LET D2=D1**.5
410 PRINT "I(T)="(A/X)*(N/D1)"EXP(-T/"X/R")+"A/(D2*X)"SIN("W"T+("S*180/P
"))"
420 PRINT "V(T)="(A*R/X)*(N/D1)"EXP(-T/"X/R")+"(A*R)/(D2*X)"SIN("W"T+("S
*180/P"))"
430 PRINT
440 FOR K=1 TO 21
450    LET T(K)=.25*(X/R)*(K-1)
460 LET I(K)=(A/X)*(N/D1)*EXP(-T(K)/(X/R))+(A/(D2*X))*SIN(W*T(K)+S)
470 LET V(K)=R*I(K)
480 NEXT K
490 PRINT"TIME,SEC","CURRENT,AMPS  VOLTAGE,VOLTS"
500 FOR K=1 TO 21
510    PRINT T(K),I(K),V(K)
520 NEXT K
530 END
```

Figure 7.4. A BASIC program that computes v(t) and i(t) in an RL or RC circuit with an ac excitation.

and very similar to that shown in the flowchart for computing DC transients (Chapter 6). The only significant difference is that the equations printed in lines 280, 290, 410, and 420, and the computations performed in lines 330, 340, 460, and 470 are based on equations 10 and 14 of the Discussion (the time-domain solutions for an AC excitation), rather than on solutions based on DC excitation. Also, this program computes voltage and current relations in the resistor rather than in the reactive element, and zero initial conditions are assumed for each circuit.

Figure 7.5 shows the results of one computer run of the program in Figure 7.4. The program was used to compute the current through and voltage across a 500 K resistor in a circuit containing a 4 μF capacitor, when the excitation e = 10sin(t + 30^0) V is applied. We see that the (rounded) solutions are

$$i = -4.93e^{-t/2} + 17.89\sin(t + 56.56^0)\ \mu A$$

$$v = -2.46e^{-t/2} + 8.94\sin(t + 56.56^0)\ V$$

Note the oscillatory nature of the values printed out in the table. The time-constant of the transient is two seconds and the period of the sinusoidal oscillation is τ = 6.28 seconds. Thus in the five time-constant period of time shown, the sinewave undergoes somewhat less than two complete cycles of oscillation. These cycles are apparent from an examination of the data.

For large values of t, the transient represented by the exponential term will have decayed to zero, and we can confirm the remaining (steady-state) solution using conventional AC circuit analysis. By the voltage divider rule,

$$v_R = \left(\frac{R}{R - jX_C}\right)E\underline{/\theta} = \frac{.5 \times 10^6}{.5 \times 10^6 - j/(4 \times 10^{-6})}\ 10\ \underline{/30^0}$$

$$= (.894\ \underline{/26.56^0})(10\underline{/30^0}) = 8.94\ \underline{/56.56^0}$$

$$= 8.94\sin(t + 56.56^0)\ V$$

This result agrees well with the computer generated solution for the steady-state component of v(t).

Figure 7.6 shows the results of running the program for an RL circuit in which R = 10 ohms, L = 10 H, and e = 10sin(100t + 45^0) V. The solutions are

$$i(t) = 7e^{-t} + 10\sin(100t - 44.43^0)\ mA$$

and $$v(t) = .07e^{-t} + 0.1\sin(100t - 44.43^0)\ V$$

In this case the time constant of the transient is one second, while the period of the oscillation is .0628 seconds. Consequently, each value of voltage and current printed in the table occurs .25/.0628 $\approx$ 4 complete cycles later than the preceding value. Therefore, the rather slow oscillation that the data values seem to infer cannot be interpreted as the frequency at which the values are truly changing. There is just too large a time interval between calculated values to see the true frequency of oscillation.

```
ENTER RL OR RC
RC
ENTER RESISTANCE IN OHMS
 500000
ENTER INDUCTANCE IN H OR CAPACITANCE IN F
 4.00000E-06
ENTER PEAK VALUE A IN VOLTS, FREQ W IN RAD/SEC AND PHASE ANGLE D IN DEG.
A=   W=   D=
 10          1              30


I(T)=-4.92820E-06EXP(-T/ 2)+ 1.78885E-05SIN( 1T+( 56.5651))

V(T)=-2.46410EXP(-T/ 2)+ 8.94427SIN( 1T+( 56.5651))

TIME,SEC        CURRENT,AMPS VOLTAGE,VOLTS
 0               1.00000E-05   5.00000
 .500000         1.39881E-05   6.99403
 1               1.33705E-05   6.68526
 1.50000         8.55978E-06   4.27989
 2               9.37096E-07    .468548
 2.50000        -7.47280E-06  -3.73640
 3              -1.44875E-05  -7.24375
 3.50000        -1.82935E-05  -9.14674
 4              -1.78840E-05  -8.94202
 4.50000        -1.33012E-05  -6.65058
 5              -5.62151E-06  -2.81076
 5.50000         3.31002E-06   1.65501
 6               1.13342E-05   5.66711
 6.50000         1.65079E-05   8.25396
 7               1.75811E-05   8.79056
 7.50000         1.43041E-05   7.15203
 8               7.48920E-06   3.74460
 8.50000        -1.18704E-06   -.593520
 9              -9.59428E-06  -4.79714
 9.50000        -1.56693E-05  -7.83467
 10             -1.79211E-05  -8.96056

 !
```

Figure 7.5. The results of a run of the program in Figure 7.4
            R=500K, C=4μF, e=10sin(t+30°) V.

```
ENTER RL OR RC
?RL
ENTER RESISTANCE IN OHMS
?10
ENTER INDUCTANCE IN H OR CAPACITANCE IN F
?10
ENTER PEAK VALUE A IN VOLTS, FREQ W IN RAD/SEC
AND PHASE ANGLE D IN DEGREES
A=  W=  D=  ?10,100,45
I(T)= 6.99966E-03EXP(-T/ 1)+ 9.99950E-03SIN( 100T+(-44.4271))
V(T)= 6.99966E-02EXP(-T/ 1)+ 9.99950E-02SIN( 100T+(-44.4271))
```

TIME,SEC	CURRENT,AMPS	VOLTAGE,VOLTS
0	4.33681E-18	4.33681E-17
.250000	-2.43187E-03	-2.43187E-02
.500000	-4.38256E-03	-4.38256E-02
.750000	-5.91471E-03	-5.91471E-02
1	-7.07690E-03	-7.07690E-02
1.25000	-7.90748E-03	-7.90748E-02
1.50000	-8.43766E-03	-8.43766E-02
1.75000	-8.69378E-03	-8.69378E-02
2	-8.69912E-03	-8.69912E-02
2.25000	-8.47522E-03	-8.47522E-02
2.50000	-8.04287E-03	-8.04287E-02
2.75000	-7.42281E-03	-7.42281E-02
3	-6.63616E-03	-6.63616E-02
3.25000	-5.70473E-03	-5.70473E-02
3.50000	-4.65109E-03	-4.65109E-02
3.75000	-3.49863E-03	-3.49863E-02
4	-2.27137E-03	-2.27137E-02
4.25000	-9.93841E-04	-9.93841E-03
4.50000	3.09206E-04	3.09206E-03
4.75000	1.61307E-03	1.61307E-02
5	2.89342E-03	2.89342E-02

```
    530 HALT
>
```

Figure 7.6. The results of a run of the program in Figure 7.4.
R=10Ω, L=10H, e=10sin(100t+45°) V.

EXERCISES

1. Rewrite the program given in the Discussion section so it computes the equation for and prints instantaneous values of the voltage across the <u>reactive</u> element in the circuit (L or C) instead of the current in the circuit. In addition to printing values of the voltage across R (v_R) and the voltafe across the reactive element (v_X) in your table, include two new columns containing (1) the instantaneous values of the AC input, and (2) of the sum of the instananeous values of v_R and v_X.

2. Run your program for an RC circuit using R = 150 K, C + .05μF, and e = 120 sin(377t-60°) V. What network law do your results confirm? Submit copies of your program and results.

3. Repeat step 2 for an RL circuit using R = 220Ω, L = 100 mH, and e = 10 sin(10^4t + 60°)V.

4. Rewrite the program given in the Discussion section so that instead of computing instantaneous values for 21 time points ranging up to 5 time constants, it prints instantaneous values during the first 5 cycles of the oscillation. Print 5 values for each cycle of the oscillation so that every 5 values are one period (T) of time apart.

5. Run your program using the same values for R,L, and e that were used for the example whose results are shown in Figure 7.6 of the Discussion. Compare your results with those of Figure 7.6. Submit copies of your program and results.

6. Using Laplace transforms, find i(t) in the RC and RL networks of Figures 7.1 and 7.3 when initial conditions are present (initial voltage across the capacitor and initial current in the inductor). Then write a BASIC program that prints the equation for i(t) and 21 instantaneous values of i(t) up to 5 time-constants.

7. Run your program using the values given in step 2 above and an initial capacitor voltage of 40 volts.

8. Run your program using the values given in step 3 above and an initial inductor current of -50 mA.

8 Computing Inverse Transforms

OBJECTIVES

1. To learn how to write a program that can be used to find the inverse of a transform when the transform is of a specific type but has general parameters.

2. To learn how to develop inverse transform equations with generalized parameters so the equations can be evaluated by computer for specific user-supplied parameter values.

3. To use the computer to investigate the effects of parameter changes on the nature of an inverse transform, specifically in regard to its classification as over, under, or critically damped.

4. To use the computer to investigate the effect of pole locations on the peak overshoot of an inverse transform and on the time required for the inverse to reach its steady-state value.

DISCUSSION

In the last two chapters we used Laplace transforms to find general expressions for voltage and current in a specific type of circuit. The time-domain functions we obtained and solved on the computer were therefore written in terms of the circuit parameters: R, L, C, and so forth. For example, in Chapter 6 we used Laplace transforms to solve for the current in a series RC network and found

$$i(t) = \frac{(E-V_0)}{R} e^{-t/RC}$$

We then wrote a computer program to solve this equation based on user-supplied values for R, C, E, and V_0.

In this experiment we will take a different approach. We will write programs that can be used to find the time-domain functions (inverse transforms) that correspond to Laplace transforms of certain general types. For example, we will write a BASIC program that finds the inverse transform of

$$F(s) = \frac{K(s + a)}{s(s + b)(s + c)} \tag{1}$$

In this case, the user will be required to enter values for K, a, b, and c instead of specific circuit parameters. The advantage to this approach is that the transform in (1)

103

may arise from a number of different problems or circuit types and so the computer program will be applicable to a wider range of situations. The disadvantage is that the user may be required to calculate values for K, a, b, and c in terms of the specific problem parameters before using the program.

We can find the inverse transform of (1) in terms of K, a, b, and c by using the partial fractions technique:

$$\frac{K(s + a)}{s(s + b)(s + c)} = \frac{A_1}{s} + \frac{A_2}{s + b} + \frac{A_3}{s + c} \tag{2}$$

The coefficients A_1, A_2, and A_3 are found as follows:

$$A_1 = \frac{K(s + a)}{(s + b)(s + c)} \bigg|_{s = 0} = \frac{Ka}{bc} \tag{3}$$

$$A_2 = \frac{K(s + a)}{s(s + c)} \bigg|_{s = -b} = \frac{K(-b + a)}{-b(-b + c)} \tag{4}$$

$$A_3 = \frac{K(s + a)}{s(s + b)} \bigg|_{s = -c} = \frac{K(-c + a)}{-c(-c + b)} \tag{5}$$

We know that the inverse transform corresponding to (2) is of the form

$$f(t) = A_1 + A_2 e^{-bt} + A_3 e^{-ct} \tag{6}$$

Thus, we can write our BASIC program to compute the values of A_1, A_2, and A_3 in accordance with equations (3), (4), and (5) and use these values in equation (6) to compute values of f(t). Our program will print the time-domain solution f(t) in the form of (6) and compute values of f(t) at user-selected time points. To permit the user to experiment with different ranges of the time interval over which the solution values are computed, we include in the program a provision for looping back, at the user's option, to alter the range of time and the number of time intervals at which solution values are found. Figure 8.1 shows a flowchart for the program.

Figure 8.2 is a listing of the BASIC program which implements the flowchart of Figure 8.1. Note that we require positive (and non-zero) values for K, a, b, and c and do not permit the case b = c. Otherwise, the inverse transforms will not fit the form of equation (6). (Some of these special cases will be exercises.) Note also the use of the "define function" (DEF FN) capability of BASIC in line 160 of the program, which we use to compute values of equation (6) in a FOR TO, NEXT loop. If this capability is not available in the user's version of BASIC, the computation can be performed within the PRINT statement, as we have done in previous programs.

Figure 8.3 shows the results of a run of the program in Figure 8.2 for the case K = 200, a = 5, b = 1, and c = 100, that is, for

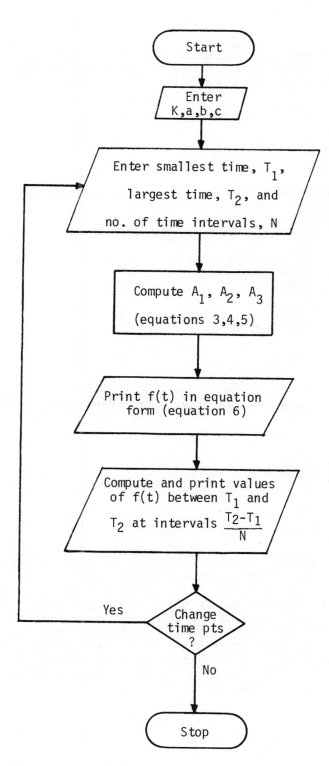

Figure 8.1. A flowchart for computing the
inverse transform of $F(s)=K(s+a)/s(s+b)(s+c)$.
The program is shown in Figure 8.2.

```
10 REM THIS PROGRAM FINDS THE INVERSE OF K(S+A)/S(S+B)(S+C).
20 REM K,A,B, AND C MUST BE POSITIVE. B CANNOT=C. THE INVERSE IS
30 REM COMPUTED AT N EQUAL TIME INTERVALS BETWEEN T1 AND T2.
40 PRINT
50 PRINT "G=K(S+A)/S(S+B)(S+C)"
60 PRINT "ENTER K,A,B,C"
70 INPUT K,A,B,C
80 PRINT "ENTER T1,T2,N"
90 INPUT T1,T2,N
100 LET A1=K*A/(B*C)
110 LET A2=(K*(-B+A))/((-B)*(-B+C))
120 LET A3=(K*(-C+A))/((-C)*(-C+B))
130 PRINT "THE INVERSE TRANSFORM IS:"
140 PRINT A1"+("A2")EXP("(-B)"T)+("A3")EXP("(-C)"T)"
150 PRINT
160 DEF FNI(T)=A1+A2*EXP(-B*T)+A3*EXP(-C*T)
170 PRINT "TIME,SEC","INVERSE"
180 FOR T=T1 TO T2 STEP (T2-T1)/N
190     PRINT T,FNI(T)
200 NEXT T
210 PRINT "CHANGE TIME POINTS? (Y OR N)."
220 INPUT A$
230 IF A$="Y" THEN 80
240 END
!
```

Figure 8.2 A BASIC program for computing the inverse transform of F(s)=K(s+a)/s(s+b)(s+c).

$$F(s) = \frac{200(s + 5)}{s(s + 1)(s + 100)}$$

The inverse transform is seen to be

$$f(t) = 10 - 8.08e^{-t} - 1.92e^{-100t} \tag{7}$$

We chose initially to have the program evaluate (7) at N = 10 time intervals between T_1 = 0 and T_2 = 1 seconds. The results of these computations are shown in the first table. We then noticed from equation (7) that the steady-state value of f(t) should be 10 (after sufficient time has elapsed for the exponentials in (7) to decay to zero). Since the last value computed in the first run was only 7.08, we elected to expand the time by setting T_2 = 4 seconds in the second run. We also increased N to 20 for better resolution. The results are shown in the second table of values, and it is clear now that f(t) is approaching 10 asymptotically. Note also that f(t) should be identically zero at t = 0, but in both tables the value shown at t = 0 is 2.22×10^{-16}. This non-zero value is due to round-off error but is for all practical purposes zero.

```
ENTER K,A,B,C
 200            5              1              100
ENTER T1,T2,N
 0             1              10
THE INVERSE TRANSFORM IS:
 10+(-8.08081)EXP(-1T)+(-1.91919)EXP(-100T)

TIME,SEC        INVERSE
 0              2.22045E-16
 .100000        2.68810
 .200000        3.38399
 .300000        4.01359
 .400000        4.58327
 .500000        5.09874
 .600000        5.56516
 .700000        5.98719
 .800000        6.36906
 .900000        6.71459
1.00000         7.02724
CHANGE TIME POINTS? (Y OR N).
Y
ENTER T1,T2,N
 0             4              20
THE INVERSE TRANSFORM IS:
 10+(-8.08081)EXP(-1T)+(-1.91919)EXP(-100T)

TIME,SEC        INVERSE
 0              2.22045E-16
 .200000        3.38399
 .400000        4.58327
 .600000        5.56516
 .800000        6.36906
1.00000         7.02724
1.20000         7.56611
1.40000         8.00730
1.60000         8.36851
1.80000         8.66425
2.00000         8.90638
2.20000         9.10462
2.40000         9.26693
2.60000         9.39981
2.80000         9.50861
3.00000         9.59768
3.20000         9.67061
3.40000         9.73032
3.60000         9.77920
3.80000         9.81923
4.00000         9.85199
CHANGE TIME POINTS? (Y OR N).
N
!
```

Figure 8.3 The results of a run of the program in Figure 8.2.
           F(s)=200(s+5)/s(s+1)(s+10).

Another commonly encountered transform type is

$$F(s) = \frac{C}{s(s^2 + as + K)} \tag{8}$$

where a, C, and K are constants. Depending on the magnitudes of a and K, the quadratic in the denominator of (8) may have real and unequal roots, real and equal roots, or complex conjugate roots. The poles of F(s) due to the quadratic are therefore in one of these same categories, since the roots of the denominator are by definition the poles of the transfer function. Using the quadratic formula to find the roots, we have

$$s = \frac{-a \pm \sqrt{a^2 - 4K}}{2} \tag{9}$$

We therefore see that the nature of the poles (real or complex, equal or unequal) depends on the quantity $a^2 - 4K$. The three cases, $a^2 > 4K$, $a^2 = 4K$, and $a^2 < 4K$, produce three distinct forms of inverse transforms and correspond to what are called the underdamped, critically damped, and underdamped cases, respectively.

We will derive the inverse transform of (8) for each of the three cases listed above, and then write a program that computes the correct inverse according to the case it determines is applicable.

1. The overdamped case ($a^2 > 4K$).

In this case we know that the quadratic in the denominator of (8) has two real and unequal factors p_1 and p_2 :

$$F(s) = \frac{C}{s(s + p_1)(s + p_2)} \tag{10}$$

We can therefore perform a partial fraction expansion of (10):

$$F(s) = \frac{A_1}{s} + \frac{A_2}{s + p_1} + \frac{A_3}{s + p_2}$$

From (9), we know that

$$P_1 = \frac{a}{2} + \frac{\sqrt{a^2 - 4K}}{s}$$

$$P_2 = \frac{a}{2} - \frac{\sqrt{a^2 - 4K}}{2}$$

(Note that the factors have signs that are opposite those of the roots or poles.) Evaluating the coefficients A_1, A_2, and A_3, we find:

$$A_1 = \left. \frac{C}{(s + p_1)(s + p_2)} \right|_{s = 0} = \frac{C}{p_1 p_2} \tag{11}$$

$$A_2 = \left. \frac{C}{s(s + p_2)} \right|_{s = p_1} = \frac{C}{-p_1(-p_1 + p_2)} \tag{12}$$

$$A_3 = \left. \frac{C}{s(s + p_1)} \right|_{s = -p_2} = \frac{C}{-p_2(-p_2 + p_1)} \tag{13}$$

The inverse transform is

$$A_1 + A_2 e^{-p_1 t} + A_3 e^{-p_2 t} \tag{14}$$

where A_1, A_2, and A_3 are computed from equations 11, 12, 13.

2. The critically damped case $(a^2 = 4K)$.

   In this case, the factors of the quadratic are real and, from (9), both equal to $a/2$:

$$F(s) = \frac{C}{s(s + a/2)^2}$$

Using the partial fraction technique applicable to repeated poles, we write

$$F(s) = \frac{A_1}{s} + \frac{A_2}{(s + a/2)} + \frac{A_3}{(s + a/2)^2}$$

where

$$A_1 = \left. \frac{C}{(s + a/2)^2} \right|_{s = 0} = 4C/a^2$$

$$A_2 = \left. \frac{d(C/S)}{ds} \right|_{s = -a/2} = \left. \frac{-C}{s^2} \right|_{s = -a/2} = \frac{-4C}{a^2}$$

$$A_3 = \left. \frac{C}{s} \right|_{s = -a/2} = \frac{-2C}{a}$$

The inverse transform is then

$$A_1 + A_2 e^{-(a/2)t} + A_3 t e^{-(a/2)t} \tag{15}$$

3. The underdamped case $(a^2 < 4K)$.

   In this case, the roots are complex conjugates of each other:

$$s = \frac{-a}{2} \pm \frac{j \sqrt{4K-a^2}}{2} \tag{16}$$

We will use the method described in Chapter 7 to find the inverse transform. Recall that the contribution of the quadratic to the inverse is

$$\frac{M}{\omega} e^{-\alpha t} \sin(\omega t + \theta) \tag{17}$$

where $\qquad M\underline{/\theta} = K(s)\Big|_{s = -\alpha + j\omega}$

and $K(s)$ is what remains of $F(s)$ when the quadratic is removed. From (16),

$$\alpha = a/2 \quad \text{and} \quad \omega = \frac{\sqrt{4K-a^2}}{2}$$

Therefore,

$$M\underline{/\theta} = \frac{C}{s}\Big|_{s = -\frac{a}{2} + j\frac{\sqrt{4K-a^2}}{2}}$$

$$= \frac{C}{-\frac{a}{2} + j\frac{\sqrt{4K-a^2}}{2}}$$

$$M = \frac{C}{\sqrt{(a^2/4) + (4K-a^2)/4}} = \frac{C}{\sqrt{K}}$$

$$\theta = -\arctan\frac{\sqrt{4K-a^2}}{-a}$$

$$= \arctan\left(\frac{\sqrt{4K-a^2}}{a}\right) - \pi$$

The contribution of the quadratic to the inverse is therefore (from equation 17):

$$\frac{\frac{C}{\sqrt{K}}}{\frac{\sqrt{4k-a^2}}{2}} e^{-(a/2)t} \sin\left(\frac{\sqrt{4K-a^2}}{2} t + \theta\right)$$

$$= \frac{2C}{\sqrt{K(4K-a^2)}} e^{-(a/2)t} \sin\left(\frac{\sqrt{4K-a^2}}{2} t + \theta\right) \qquad (18)$$

The steady-state term in the inverse (due to the s in the denominator of F(s), i.e., due to the pole at s = 0) is

$$A_1 = \left.\frac{C}{s^2 + as + K}\right|_{s=0} = C/K \qquad (19)$$

Thus, combining (18) and (19),

$$f(t) = \frac{C}{K} + \frac{2C}{\sqrt{K(4k-a^2)}} e^{-(a/2)t} \sin\left(\frac{\sqrt{4K-a^2}}{2} t + \theta\right) \qquad (20)$$

where $\quad \theta = \arctan\left(\frac{\sqrt{4K-a^2}}{a}\right) - \pi$

Figure 8.4 shows a flowchart for a BASIC program that determines which of the three cases above is applicable, displays the inverse f(t) in equation form, and prints out values of the inverse at user-selected time intervals.

Figure 8.5 shows the program listing the flowchart of Figure 8.4. In the program we again make use of the DEF FN statement, this time in three different places (lines 180, 340, and 460), corresponding to the three different types of inverse functions. Even though only one of these functions will be evaluated in any one computer run, we must assign them different names (FNI, FNJ, and FNK) to prevent the computer from generating an error message.

Figure 8.6 through 8.8 show the results of several computer runs of the program given in Figure 8.5. In all runs the values of a and C were fixed at 12 and 100, respectively, and the value of K was changed to investigate its effects on the inverse. In the first run shown (Figure 8.6), K was set to 20. The transform to be inverted in this case was therefore

$$\frac{C}{s(s^2 + as + K)} = \frac{100}{s(s^2 + 12s + 20)} = \frac{100}{s(s + 2)(s + 10)}$$

This is clearly the overdamped case, and the inverse is seen from the printout to be

$$f(t) = 5 + 1.25e^{-10t} - 6.25e^{-2t} \qquad (21)$$

Note how the values rise towards 5, the steady-state value of (21). Note also that the pole at s= -2 is the <u>dominant</u> pole, in the sense that the time constant (1/2 sec.) in (21) is much longer than the time constant of the other exponential (1/10 sec.), and is therefore much more significant in determining how long the transient portion takes to die out. For this reason, f(t) was evaluated at time points up to t = 2 seconds.

112

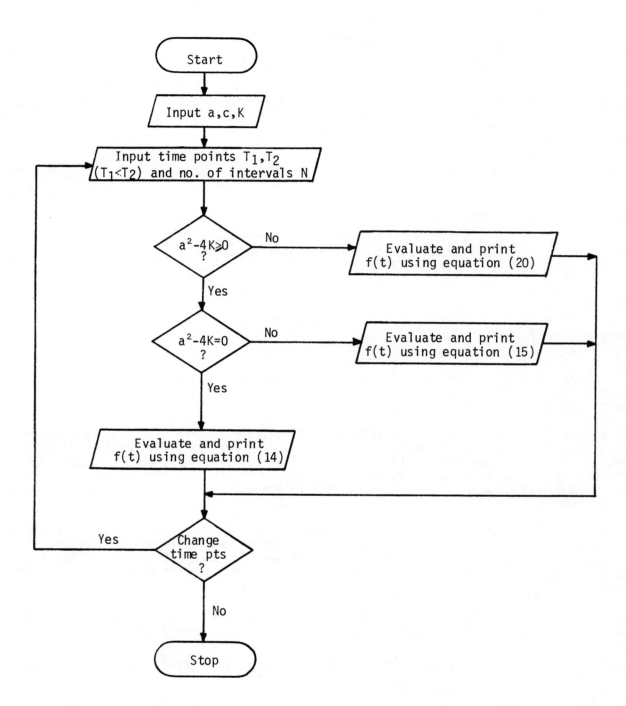

Figure 8.4. A flowchart for computing the inverse transform of $F(s)=C/s(s^2+as+K)$. The BASIC program is shown in Figure 8.5.

```
10 REM THIS PROGRAM FINDS THE INVERSE
20 REM TRANSFORM OF F(S)=C/S(S**2+AS+K).
30 REM A,C, AND K MUST BE > 0. COMPUTATIONS
40 REM ARE BETWEEN T1 AND T2 IN N INTERVALS.
50 PRINT "F(S)=C/S(S**2+AS+K)"
60 PRINT "ENTER C,A,K"
70 INPUT C,A,K
80 PRINT "ENTER LOWEST TIME T1, LARGEST TIME T2, AND NO. OF INTERVALS, N
."
90 INPUT T1,T2,N
100 LET D=A*A-4*K
110 IF D>=0 THEN 250
120 LET S=-D
130 LET W=(SQR(S))/2
140 LET Z=ATN((SQR(S))/A)-3.1416
150 LET M=C/SQR(K)
160 PRINT "THE INVERSE IS:"
170 PRINT C/K"+"2*C/(SQR(K*S))"EXP("(-A/2)"T)SIN("SQR(S)/2"T+("Z*57.29578"
))"
180 DEF FNI(T)=C/K+2*C/(SQR(K*S))*EXP((-A/2)*T)*SIN((SQR(S)/2)*T+Z)
190 PRINT
200 PRINT "TIME,SEC","INVERSE"
210 FOR T=T1 TO T2 STEP (T2-T1)/N
220     PRINT T,FNI(T)
230 NEXT T
240 GOTO 520
250 IF D=0 THEN 410
260 LET P=(SQR(D))/2
270 LET P1=(A/2)+P
280 LET P2=(A/2)-P
290 LET A1=C/(P1*P2)
300 LET A2=C/((-P1)*(-P1+P2))
310 LET A3=C/((-P2)*(-P2+P1))
320 PRINT "THE INVERSE IS:"
330 PRINT A1"+("A2")EXP("(-P1)")T+("A3")EXP("(-P2)")T"
340 DEF FNJ(T)=A1 +A2*EXP(-P1*T)+A3*EXP(-P2*T)
350 PRINT
360 PRINT "TIME,SEC","INVERSE"
370 FOR T=T1 TO T2 STEP (T2-T1)/N
380     PRINT T,FNJ(T)
390 NEXT T
400 GOTO 520
410 LET A1=4*C/(A**2)
420 LET A2=A1
430 LET A3=2*C/A
440 PRINT "THE INVERSE IS:"
450 PRINT A1"-"A2"EXP("(-A/2)"T)-"A3"T(EXP("(-A/2)"T))"
460 DEF FNK(T)=A1-A2*EXP(-A*T/2)-A3*T*EXP(-A*T/2)
470 PRINT
480 PRINT "TIME,SEC","INVERSE"
490 FOR T=T1 TO T2 STEP (T2-T1)/N
500     PRINT T,FNK(T)
510 NEXT T
520 PRINT "CHANGE T? (Y OR N)."
530 INPUT A$
540 IF A$="Y" THEN 80
550 END
```

!

Figure 8.5 A BASIC program for computing the inverse transform of $F(s)=C/s(s^2+as+K)$.

```
F(S)=C/S(S**2+AS+K)
ENTER C,A,K
 100           12              20
ENTER LOWEST TIME T1, LARGEST TIME T2, AND NO. OF INTERVALS, N.
 0            2              15
THE INVERSE IS:
 5+( 1.25000)EXP(-10)T+(-6.25000)EXP(-2)T

TIME,SEC         INVERSE
 0               0
 .133333         .542444
 .266667        1.42032
 .400000        2.21459
 .533333        2.85507
 .666667        3.35411
 .800000        3.73857
 .933333        4.03362
1.06667         4.25977
1.20000         4.43302
1.33333         4.56573
1.46667         4.66738
1.60000         4.74524
1.73333         4.80487
1.86667         4.85054
2.00000         4.88553
CHANGE T? (Y OR N).
N
!
```

Figure 8.6. The results of a run of the program in Figure 8.5 when
F(s)=100/s(s^2+12s+20). The inverse is overdamped.

In the second run (see Figure 8.7), K was set to 36. In this case

$$F(s) = \frac{100}{s + 12s + 36} = \frac{100}{(s + 6)^2}$$

This corresponds to the critically damped case, and the inverse is seen from the printout
to be

$$f(t) = 2.78 - 2.78e^{-6t} - 16.7te^{-6t} \tag{22}$$

Note how the values of f(t) rise towards their steady-state value (2.78) faster than those
of the previous case.

In the last run, shown in Figure 8.8, K was set to 52. In this case

$$F(s) = \frac{100}{s(s^2 + 12s + 52)}$$

and the poles are the complex conjugates s = -6 $\pm$ j4. This is the underdamped case and the
inverse is seen from the printout to be

$$f(t) = 1.92 + 3.47e^{-6t}\sin(4t - 146.3^0) \tag{23}$$

```
F(S)=C/S(S**2+AS+K)
ENTER C,A,K
 100          12              36
ENTER LOWEST TIME T1, LARGEST TIME T2, AND NO. OF INTERVALS, N.
 0            1.50000         15
THE INVERSE IS:
 2.77778- 2.77778EXP(-6T)- 16.6667T(EXP(-6T))

TIME,SEC         INVERSE
 0                0
 .100000         .338615
 .200000         .937146
 .300000        1.49212
 .400000        1.92100
 .500000        2.22459
 .600000        2.42864
 .700000        2.56118
 .800000        2.64519
 .900000        2.69748
1.00000         2.72958
1.10000         2.74906
1.20000         2.76077
1.30000         2.76776
1.40000         2.77191
1.50000         2.77435
CHANGE T? (Y OR N).
N
!
```

Figure 8.7. The results of a run of the program in Figure 8.5 when
          $F(s)=100/(s^2+12s+36)$. The inverse is critically damped.

Note how the values of f(t) rise towards 1.92, overshoot, and oscillate about 1.92. In
this type of problem, the peak overshoot is often of interest. We note in the first set
of values shown in Figure 8.8 that the maximum, 1.94026, occurs at t = 0.8 seconds. To
refine our determination of the peak overshoot, we initiate a second tun to compute values of (23) between t = 0.7 and t = 0.9 seconds. The results of this run are shown in
the second table of Figure 8.8, from which we conclude that the peak overshoot falls between t = 0.78 and t = 0.79 seconds, and is approximately 1.94034.

PROCEDURE

1. Use the program given in the Discussion section to find the inverse f(t) of

$$F(s) = \frac{100(s + 10)}{s(s + 5)(s + 20)}$$

    Determine values of f(t) up to approximately 90% of its steady-state value. What is
    the dominant pole of F(s)? How do the data values obtained from your computer run
    confirm this?

2. Investigate the effect of the location of the zero of the transform in step 1 on the
    nature of the inverse of that transform. (Since a = 10 in step 1, the zero is at s =
    -10; use the program to determine values of f(t) when a is less than 5 and when a is
    greater than 20.) Compare computed values of f(t) from the standpoint of time required

```
F(S)=C/S(S**2+AS+K)
ENTER C,A,K
 100            12             52
ENTER LOWEST TIME T1, LARGEST TIME T2, AND NO. OF INTERVALS, N.
 0              1              20
THE INVERSE IS:
 1.92308+ 3.46688EXP(-6T)SIN( 4T+(-146.310))

TIME,SEC         INVERSE
 0               2.11916E-05
 5.00000E-02     .102286
 .100000         .334498
 .150000         .615569
 .200000         .896272
 .250000         1.14963
 .300000         1.36347
 .350000         1.53495
 .400000         1.66659
 .450000         1.76365
 .500000         1.83233
 .550000         1.87880
 .600000         1.90358
 .650000         1.92633
 .700000         1.93576
 .750000         1.93970
 .800000         1.94026
 .850000         1.93891
 .900000         1.93663
 .950000         1.93407
 1.00000         1.93160
CHANGE T? (Y OR N).
Y
ENTER LOWEST TIME T1, LARGEST TIME T2, AND NO. OF INTERVALS, N.
 .700000        .900000         20
THE INVERSE IS:
 1.92308+ 3.46688EXP(-6T)SIN( 4T+(-146.310))

TIME,SEC         INVERSE
 .700000         1.93576
 .710000         1.93691
 .720000         1.93786
 .730000         1.93863
 .740000         1.93924
 .750000         1.93970
 .760000         1.94003
 .770000         1.94024
 .780000         1.94034
 .790000         1.94034
 .800000         1.94026
 .810000         1.94011
 .820000         1.93988
 .830000         1.93961
 .840000         1.93928
 .850000         1.93891
 .860000         1.93850
 .870000         1.93806
 .880000         1.93760
 .890000         1.93713
 .900000         1.93663
CHANGE T? (Y OR N).
N

!
```

Figure 8.8 The results of a run of the program in Figure 8.5 when $F(s) = 100/(s + 12s + 52)$. The inverse is underdamped.

to approach steady-state values.

3. Modify the program shown in Figure 8.2 of the Discussion so it can be used to find the inverse of the transform

$$F(s) = \frac{K(s + a)}{s(s + b)(s + c)}$$

for the case b = c (in addition to the case b ≠ c). Run your program to find the inverse of

(a) $F(s)$ $\dfrac{500(s + 40)}{s(s + 25)(s + 50)}$

(b) $F(s) = \dfrac{500(s + 40)}{s(s + 25)^2}$

Compare the values computed for f(t) in each case, from the standpoint of steady-state value and time required to reach steady-state. Check the results of your program by hand calculating the value of f(t) in each case at t = 0.

4. Using the program in Figure 8.5, determine the maximum value of the inverse of each of the following transforms:

(a) $F(s) = \dfrac{100}{s(s^2 + s + 100)}$

(b) $F(s) = \dfrac{100}{s(s^2 + 5s + 25)}$

5. Modify the program in Figure 8.5 so it can be used for the case a = 0, i. e., to find the inverse of

$$F(s) = \frac{C}{s(s^2 + K)}$$

in addition to the cases for which it was originally written. Use your program to find the inverse of

$$F(s) = \frac{50}{s(s^2 + 100)}$$

Based on data values obtained from your run, plot a graph of f(t) versus time.

6. Write a BASIC program that can be used to find the inverse transform of

$$F(s) = \frac{C(s + a)}{s(s^2 + bs + K)}$$

User enters values for a, b, C and K. Specify whatever restrictions you assume on the permissible values of the constants. Run your program and obtain values of f(t) at a sufficient number of time points to discern its general behavior for each of the following:

(a) $F(s) = \dfrac{10(s + 10)}{s(s^2 + 15s + 50)}$

(b) $F(s) = \dfrac{50(s + 100)}{s(s^2 + s + 10)}$

(c) $F(s) = \dfrac{50(s + 100)}{s(s^2 + 20s + 100)}$

Compare the results obtained from your run of (a) above with results obtained using the appropriate values of K, a, b, and C in a run of the program shown in Figure 8.2. (Notice that (a) above can be made to fit equation (1) in the Discussion.)

9 Computing Transients in RLC Networks

1. To learn how a program written to find the inverse of a transform of a specific type can be used to analyze the transient response of a variety of RLC networks.

2. To learn through observation of computer generated results how the characteristics of voltage and current transients depend on circuit parameters.

3. To learn the criteria for under, over, and critical damping in series and parallel RLC circuits and to confirm these criteria by observation of computer generated response data.

DISCUSSION

In this experiment, the computer method introduced in Experiment 5 will be used for the transient analysis of RLC networks. That is, we will write a program that inverts a transform of a specific type and use the program to solve a variety of RLC network types. We will see how network parameters (values of R, L, and C) determine whether the inverse transform represents a response that is over, under, or critically damped.

The transform we will invert is

$$F(s) = \frac{K(as^2 + bs + c)}{s(s^2 + ds + e)} \tag{1}$$

As we shall see, this transform can be made to fit current and voltage transforms for a wide variety of RLC circuits, by making a suitable choice of values for the coefficients a, b, c, d, and e (some of which may be zero). As in Experiment 5, to invert (1) we must consider three cases: real and unequal poles, real and equal poles, and complex conjugate poles. As before, the case that applies depends on the quadratic in the denominator of (1). specifically on the quantity d^2-4e.

1. $\underline{d^2-4e > 0}$

In this case,

$$F(s) = \frac{K(as^2 + bs + c)}{s(s + p_1)(s + p_2)}$$

where

$$p_1 = \frac{d + \sqrt{d^2 - 4e}}{2} \quad \text{and} \quad p_2 = \frac{d - \sqrt{d^2 - 4e}}{2}$$

Omitting the constant K for the moment (we will multiply K by the inverse we ultimately find), we write the partial fraction expansion:

$$F(s) = \frac{A_1}{s} + \frac{A_2}{s + p_1} + \frac{A_3}{s + p_2}$$

where

$$A_1 = \left. \frac{as^2 + bs + c}{(s + p_1)(s + p_2)} \right|_{s = 0} = c/(p_1 p_2)$$

$$A_2 = \left. \frac{as^2 + bs + c}{s(s + p_2)} \right|_{s = -p_1} = \frac{a p_1^2 - b p_1 + c}{-p_1(-p_1 + p_2)}$$

$$A_3 = \left. \frac{as^2 + bs + c}{s(s + p_1)} \right|_{s = -p_2} = \frac{a p_2^2 - b p_2 + c}{-p_2(-p_2 + p_1)}$$

Therefore,

$$f(t) = KA_1 + KA_2 e^{-p_1 t} + KA_3 e^{-p_2 t} \tag{2}$$

2. $\underline{d^2 - 4e = 0}$

   In this case, the factors of the quadratic are real and equal:

$$F(s) = \frac{K(as^2 + bs + c)}{s(s + p)^2}$$

where $p = d/2$

Omitting K again,

$$F(s) = \frac{A_1}{s} + \frac{A_2}{(s + d/2)^2} + \frac{A_3}{s + d/2}$$

where

$$A_1 = \left. \frac{as^2 + bs + c}{(s + d/2)^2} \right|_{s = 0} = 4c/d^2$$

$$A_2 = \left. \frac{as^2 + bs + c}{s} \right|_{s = -d/2} = \frac{-ad}{2} + b - \frac{2c}{d}$$

$$A_3 = \left. \frac{d}{ds}\left(\frac{as^2 + bs + c}{s}\right) \right|_{s = -d/2} = \left. a - \frac{c}{s^2} \right|_{s = -d/2} = a - \frac{4c}{d^2}$$

Then

$$f(t) = KA_1 + KA_2 te^{-(dt/2)} + KA_3 e^{-(dt/2)} \qquad (3)$$

3. $\underline{d^2 - 4e < 0}$

In this case, the poles are complex conjugates and

$$F(s) = \frac{K(as^2 + bs + c)}{s(s + \alpha + j\omega)(s + \alpha - j\omega)}$$

where

$$\alpha = d/2 \quad \text{and} \quad \omega = \frac{\sqrt{4e-d^2}}{2}$$

Letting $K(s) = \frac{as^2 + bs + c}{s}$,

We have

$$M\underline{/\theta} = K(s)\Big|_{s = -\alpha + j\omega} = \frac{as^2 + bs + c}{s}\Big|_{s = -\alpha + j\omega}$$

$$= \frac{a(-\alpha + j\omega)^2 + b(-\alpha + j\omega) + c}{-\alpha + j\omega}$$

$$= \frac{\{a(\alpha^2 - \omega^2) - \alpha b + c\} + j(\omega b - 2a\alpha\omega)}{-\alpha + j\omega}$$

Letting

$$A_2 = a(\alpha^2 - \omega^2) - \alpha b + c$$

$$A_3 = \omega b - 2a\alpha\omega$$

We have

$$M = \sqrt{\frac{A_2^2 + A_3^2}{\alpha^2 + \omega^2}}$$

and

$$\theta = \arctan(A_3/A_2) - \arctan(\omega/-\alpha)$$

The contribution of the pole at $s = 0$ is found from

$$\frac{as^2 + bs + c}{s^2 + ds + e}\Big|_{s = 0} = c/e$$

Therefore,

$$f(t) = Kc/e + \frac{KM}{\omega} e^{-\alpha t} \sin(\omega t + \theta) \qquad (4)$$

where

$$\theta = \arctan(A_3/A_2) - \arctan(\omega/-\alpha)$$

A BASIC program that computes the inverse of (1) based on the equations derived above is shown in Figure 9.1. The logic of this program is straightforward and has a flowchart very similar to that shown in Figure 8.4 of the previous chapter. The one major difference is the inclusion in this program of a <u>subroutine</u> for computing the phase angle θ in case 3 (equation 4). This subroutine is necessary because of the complexity of the arctan computation required and because of the fact that the BASIC ATN function does not recognize differences in arctan computations based on the algebraic signs of the numerator and denominator of its argument. For example, the ATN function will return the same angle for ATN (-2/ + 3) as it does for ATN(+ 2/-3), even though these angles are in different quadrants. Also, we must allow for cases where x is zero in ATN(y/x), a computation which would result in an error message if we do not anticipate it and generate the correct angles ($\pm \pi/2$) for those cases.

The subroutine logic is based on the following considerations:

Let $Z = \arctan(|y|/|x|)$, where x and y may be any real numbers, positive, negative, or zero. Then the actual value of θ, based on the true algebraic values of x and y, is computed in the subroutine as follows:

1. If $x > 0$ and $y > 0$, then the arctan computation above is correct, i.e., $\theta = Z$.

2. If $x > 0$ and $y < 0$, then $\theta = -Z$.

3. If $x < 0$ and $y > 0$, then $\theta = 180^0 - Z$.

4. If $x < 0$ and $y < 0$, then $\theta = Z - 180^0$.

5. If $x = 0$ and $y > 0$, then $\theta = + 90^0$.

6. If $x = 0$ and $y < 0$, then $\theta = -90^0$.

The flowchart used to implement this logic for the subroutine is shown in Figure 9.2

Consider now the series RLC circuit whose transform is shown in Figure 9.3. A DC voltage V is applied when the switch is closed at $t = 0$.

The current I(s) that flows in the circuit is

$$I(s) = \frac{V(s)}{Z(s)} = \frac{V/s}{Ls + R + 1/Cs} = \left(\frac{V}{\frac{LCs^2 + RCs + 1}{Cs}} \right) = \frac{V/L}{s^2 + \frac{R}{L}s + \frac{1}{LC}} \quad (5)$$

The quadratic in the denominator of (4) has roots

$$s = \frac{-R/L \pm \sqrt{(R/L)^2 - 4/LC}}{2}$$

Therfore, the response will be overdamped, critically damped, or underdamped depending on whether $(R/L)^2$ is greater than, equal to, or less than $4/LC$, respectively. For critical damping,

$$(R/L)^2 = 4/LC$$

```
10 REM THE INVERSE TRANSFORM OF K(AS**2+BS+C)/S(S**2+DS+E)
20 REM IS EVALUATED AT N TIME INTERVALS BETWEEN TIME T1 AND TIME T2
50 PRINT "F(S)=K(AS**2+BS+C)/S(S**2+DS+E)"
60 PRINT "ENTER K,A,B,C,D,E"
70 INPUT K,A,B,C,D,E
80 PRINT "ENTER T1,T2,N"
90 INPUT T1,T2,N
100 LET D1=D*D -4*E
110 IF D1<=0 THEN 260
120 LET D2=SQR(D1)
130 LET P1=(D+D2)/2
140 LET P2=(D-D2)/2
150 LET A1=C/(P1*P2)
160 LET A2=(A*(P1**2)-B*P1+C)/((-P1)*(-P1+P2))
170 LET A3=(A*(P2**2)-B*P2+C)/((-P2)*(-P2+P1))
180 PRINT "THE INVERSE IS:"
190 PRINT K*A1"+("K*A2")EXP("(-P1)")T+("K*A3")EXP("(-P2)")T"
200 PRINT
210 PRINT "TIME,SEC","INVERSE"
220 FOR T=T1 TO T2 STEP (T2-T1)/N
230 PRINT T,K*A1+K*A2*EXP(-P1*T)+K*A3*EXP(-P2*T)
240 NEXT T
250 GOTO 590
260 IF D1<0 THEN 380
270 LET A1=(4*C)/(D**2)
280 LET A2=-A*D/2+B-2*C/D
290 LET A3=A-(4*C)/(D**2)
300 PRINT "THE INVERSE IS:"
310 PRINT K*A1"+("K*A2"T)EXP(" (-D/2) "T)+("K*A3")EXP("(-D/2)"T)"
320 PRINT
330 PRINT "TIME,SEC","INVERSE"
340 FOR T=T1 TO T2 STEP (T2-T1)/N
350 PRINT T, K*A1+K*A2*T*EXP(-D*T/2)+K*A3*EXP(-D*T/2)
360 NEXT T
370 GOTO 590
380 LET A1=D/2
390 LET W=(SQR(4*E-D**2))/2
400 LET A2=A*(A1**2-W**2)-A1*B+C
410 LET A3=W*B-2*A*A1*W
420 LET M=(SQR(A2**2+A3**2))/SQR(A1**2+W**2)
430 LET X=A2
440 LET Y=A3
450 GOSUB 670
460 LET Z1=Z
470 LET X=-A1
480 LET Y=W
490 GOSUB 670
500 LET Z2=Z
510 LET S=Z1-Z2
520 PRINT "THE INVERSE IS:"
530 PRINT K*C/E"+("K*M/W")EXP("-A1"T)SIN("W"T+("S*57.29578"))"
540 PRINT
550 PRINT "TIME,SEC","INVERSE"
560 FOR T=T1 TO T2 STEP (T2-T1)/N
570 PRINT T, K*C/E+(K*M/W)*EXP(-A1*T)*SIN(W*T+S)
```

Figure 9.1 (continued on next page)

```
580 NEXT T
590 PRINT "CHANGE TIME? (Y OR N)."
600 INPUT A$
610 IF A$="Y" THEN 80
620 STOP
630 REM SUBROUTINE THAT COMPUTES ARCTAN(Y/X) USING THE BASIC
640 REM ATN FUNCTION AND CORRECTS FOR THE SIGN OF X AND Y.
670 IF X=0 GOTO 780
680 LET Z=ATN(ABS(Y)/ABS(X))
690 IF X>0 GOTO 750
700 IF Y<0 GOTO 730
710 LET Z=3.1416-Z
720 GOTO 820
730 LET Z=-(3.1416-Z)
740 GOTO 820
750 IF Y>0 GOTO 820
760 LET Z=-Z
770 GOTO 820
780 IF Y>0 GOTO 810
790 LET Z=-1.5708
800 GOTO 820
810 LET Z=1.5708
820 RETURN
830 END
!
```

Figure 9.1. A BASIC program that computes the inverse transform of $F(s)=\dfrac{K(as^2+bs+c)}{s(s^2+ds+e)}$.

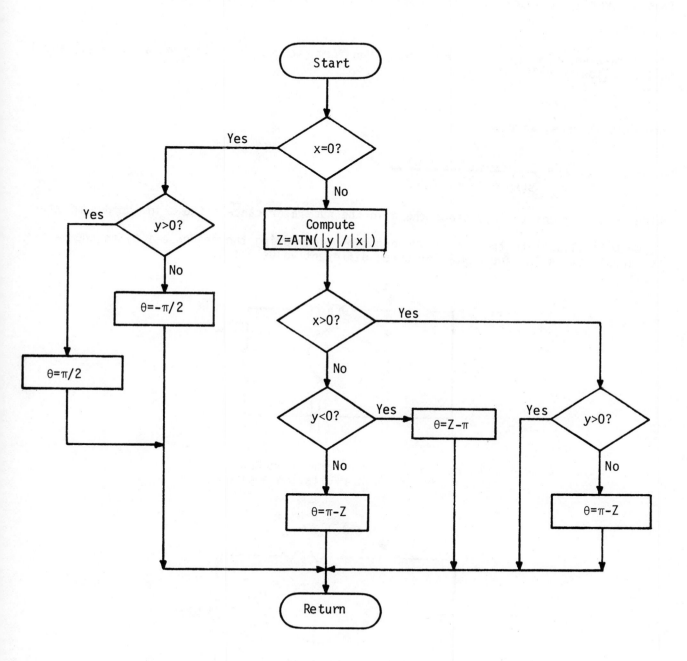

Figure 9.2. A flowchart for the subroutine that computes angle in Figure 9.1.

or, $\quad R = 2\sqrt{L/C}$

Thus an overdamped response occurs when $R > 2\sqrt{L/C}$, and an underdamped response occurs when $R < 2\sqrt{L/C}$.

To make equation (5) fit our general transform, we must set the constants in (1) equal to the following values:

$K = V/L$, $a = 0$, $b = 1$, $c = 0$, $d = R/L$, and $e = 1/LC$.

When this is done, we have

$$I(s) = \frac{V/L(0 + s + 0)}{s(s^2 + \frac{R}{L}s + 1/LC)}$$

which is equivalent to (5), since the s in the numerator cancels the s in the denominator.

We will illustrate the use of our program by computing the response $i(t)$ in the series RLC circuit shown in Figure 9.4 for three different values of R.

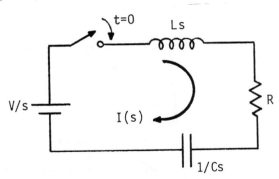

Figure 9.3 The transform of an RLC circuit having a DC excitation applied at t=0.

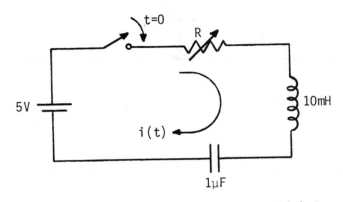

Figure 9.4. An RLC circuit in which $i(t)$ is computed for 3 different values of R.

1. R = 400 Ω.

With the values shown in Figure 9.4, we find

$$K = V/L = 5/10^{-2} = 500$$

$$d = R/L = 400/10^{-2} = 4 \times 10^4$$

$$e = 1/LC = \frac{1}{10^{-2} \times 10^{-6}} = 10^8$$

Figure 9.5 (a) shows the results of a computer run using these values (and b = 1, a = c = 0, as noted before). The response equation is seen to be

$$i(t) = -1.44 \times 10^{-2} e^{-3.73 \times 10^4 t} + 1.44 \times 10^{-2} e^{-2.68 \times 10^3 t} \text{ amps} \tag{6}$$

Values of i(t) are displayed at time points ranging from 0 to 0.2 ms in .01 ms increments. Note that some experimentation may be required to find a range of time values that reveals this transient portion of i(t). For example, the choices $t_1 = 0$, $t_2 = 1$, and n = 10 would yield a table of all zero values, since i(t) reaches its peak and decays back to zero in less than one millisecond. This rapid variation is due to the small magnitudes of the time-constants of the exponential terms:

$$1/37,320.5 = .0268 \text{ ms and}$$

$$1/2,679.49 = .373 \text{ ms.}$$

Figure 9.5 (b) shows a plot of i(t) versus t, based on the values computed and displayed in the table of Figure 9.5 (a). Note that i(t) reaches its maximum value of 10.92 mA at t = 80 μsec, that is, 80 μsec after the switch is closed.

The transient response obtained in this example and plotted in Figure 9.5 (b) is typical of the overdampled case. Note that

$$R = 400 \ \Omega > 2\sqrt{L/C} = 200 \ \Omega$$

so the criterion for overdamping is met. Regardless of the damping, it should be intuitively clear that the steady-state current in Figure 9.4 must be zero, since the capacitor must eventually charge to 5 V.

2. R = 200 Ω.

In this case,

$$d = R/L = 200/10^{-2} = 2 \times 10^4$$

while, as before, K = V/L = 500, a = 0, b = 1, c = 0, and e = 1/LC = 10^8. Figure 9.6 (a) shows the results of a computer run using these values. The printout shows that

$$i(t) = 0 + 500te^{-1000t} + (0)e^{-1000t} \text{ A} \tag{7}$$

$$= 500te^{-1000t}$$

```
F(S)=K(AS**2+BS+C)/S(S**2+DS+E)
ENTER K,A,B,C,D,E
 500    0    1    0    40000    100000000
ENTER T1,T2,N
 0    2.00000E-04    20
THE INVERSE IS:
 0+(-1.44338E-02)EXP(-37320.5)T+( 1.44338E-02)EXP(-2679.49)T

TIME,SEC           INVERSE
 0                 0
 1.00000E-05       4.11415E-03
 2.00000E-05       6.83807E-03
 3.00000E-05       8.60766E-03
 4.00000E-05       9.72296E-03
 5.00000E-05       1.03905E-02
 6.00000E-05       1.07524E-02
 7.00000E-05       1.09064E-02
 8.00000E-05       1.09199E-02
 9.00000E-05       1.08390E-02
 1.00000E-04       1.06955E-02
 1.10000E-04       1.05112E-02
 1.20000E-04       1.03011E-02
 1.30000E-04       1.00755E-02
 1.40000E-04       9.84122E-03
 1.50000E-04       9.60316E-03
 1.60000E-04       9.36451E-03
 1.70000E-04       9.12741E-03
 1.80000E-04       8.89332E-03
 1.90000E-04       8.66316E-03
 2.00000E-04       8.43754E-03
CHANGE TIME? (Y OR N).
N

!
```

Figure 9.5(a). The results of a run of the program in Figure 9.1 for the current in Figure 9.4.   R=400Ω, L=10mH, C=1μF, E=5V.

$$= 500 \, te^{-1000t}$$

Values of i(t) are shown from t = 0 to t = 0.3 ms and Figure 9.6 (b) shows a plot of i(t) based on these values. We note that the transient reaches its maximum of 18.4 mA at t = 0.1 ms. This is the critically damped case, since R = 200 = $2\sqrt{L/C}$, and it can be shown in this case that i(t) always reaches its maximum value in one time-constant of the exponential (1/10,000 = .1 ms, in this example).

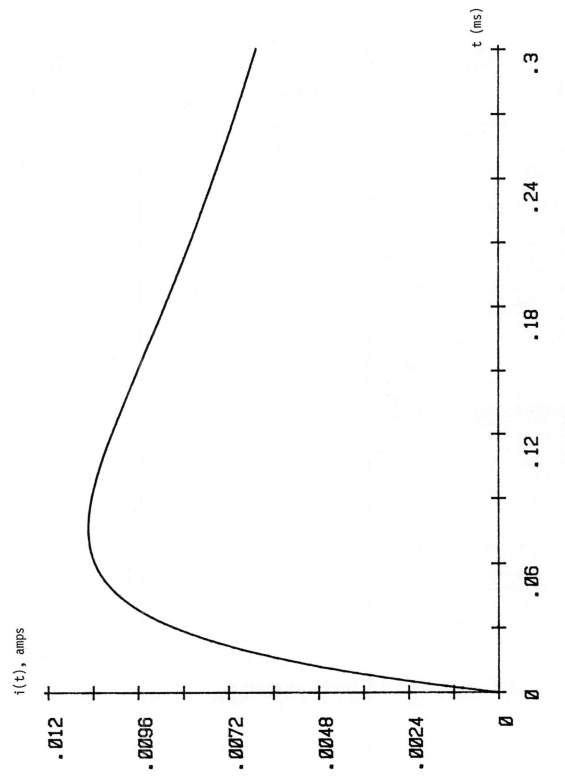

Figure 9.5(b). A plot of $i(t) = -1.44 \times 10^{-2} e^{-3.73 \times 10^4 t} + 1.44 \times 10^{-2} e^{-2.68 \times 10^3 t}$ A, based on the results shown in Figure 9.5(a). This is an overdamped response.

```
F(S)=K(AS**2+BS+C)/S(S**2+DS+E)
ENTER K,A,B,C,D,E
 500   0   1   0    20000    100000000
ENTER T1,T2,N
 0    3.00000E-04    30
THE INVERSE IS:
 0+( 500T)EXP(-10000T)+( 0)EXP(-10000T)

TIME,SEC          INVERSE
 0                0
 1.00000E-05      4.52419E-03
 2.00000E-05      8.18731E-03
 3.00000E-05      1.11123E-02
 4.00000E-05      1.34064E-02
 5.00000E-05      1.51633E-02
 6.00000E-05      1.64643E-02
 7.00000E-05      1.73805E-02
 8.00000E-05      1.79732E-02
 9.00000E-05      1.82956E-02
 1.00000E-04      1.83940E-02
 1.10000E-04      1.83079E-02
 1.20000E-04      1.80717E-02
 1.30000E-04      1.77146E-02
 1.40000E-04      1.72618E-02
 1.50000E-04      1.67348E-02
 1.60000E-04      1.61517E-02
 1.70000E-04      1.55281E-02
 1.80000E-04      1.48769E-02
 1.90000E-04      1.42090E-02
 2.00000E-04      1.35335E-02
 2.10000E-04      1.28579E-02
 2.20000E-04      1.21883E-02
 2.30000E-04      1.15298E-02
 2.40000E-04      1.08862E-02
 2.50000E-04      1.02606E-02
 2.60000E-04      9.65557E-03
 2.70000E-04      9.07274E-03
 2.80000E-04      8.51341E-03
 2.90000E-04      7.97837E-03
 3.00000E-04      7.46806E-03
CHANGE TIME? (Y OR N).
N

!
```

Figure 9.6(a). The results of a run of the program in Figure 9.1 for the current in Figure 9.4. R=200Ω, L=10mH, C=1μF, E=5V.

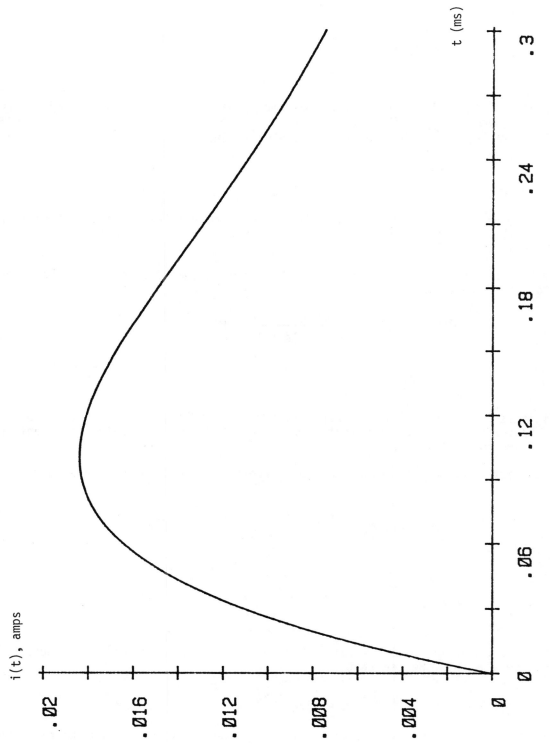

i(t), amps

Figure 9.6(b) A plot of i(t) = 500te^{-1000t}A, based on the results shown in Figure 9.6(a).
This is a critically damped response.

3.   R = 50 Ω.

In this case,

$$d = R/L = 50/10^{-2} = 5 \times 10^3$$

and the values for K, a, b, c, and e are the same as before. Results of a computer run are shown in Figure 9.7 (a). The transient response is typical of the underdamped case (note that R = 50 Ω < $\sqrt{L/C}$), namely, a <u>damped oscillation</u>.

We see that

$$i(t) \approx 5.16 \times 10^{-2} \ e^{-2500t} \sin(9682.46t) \ A \tag{8}$$

The oscillatory values are evident in the table of Figure 9.7 (a) and are plotted in Figure 9.7 (b). The response values reach a maximum of 35.35 mA at t = 0.125 ms and a minimum of -15.72 mA at t = 0.45 ms.

We may use the same transform (equation 1) to compute the voltage $v_C(t)$ across the 1 μF capacitor in Figure 9.4.

$$V_C(s) = \left(\frac{1}{Cs}\right)I(s) = \frac{1}{Cs}\left(\frac{V/L}{s^2 + (R/L)s + 1/LC}\right)$$

$$= \frac{V/LC}{s\{s^2 + (R/L)s + 1/LC\}} \tag{8}$$

The coefficients in equation (1) are therefore chosen as follows: K = V/LC, a = 0, b = 0, c = 1, d = R/L, and e = 1/LC. Note that choosing b = 0 and c = 1 results in retention of the s in the denominator of (1).

For the first case of the previous example, where R = 400 Ω, we now have

$$K = V/LC = \frac{5}{(10^{-2})(10^{-6})} = 5 \times 10^8$$

$$a = b = 0$$

$$c = 1$$

$$d = R/L = 4 \times 10^4$$

$$e = 1/LC = 10^8$$

The results of a computer run are shown in Figure 9.8 (a) and a plot of the response is shown in Figure 9.8 (b). We see that

$$v_C(t) = 5 + .387e^{-37320t} - 5.387e^{-2679t} \ V$$

As expected the transient rises towards + 5 V, the steady-state value, as the capacitor charges.

```
F(S)=K(AS**2+BS+C)/S(S**2+DS+E)
ENTER K,A,B,C,D,E
 500    0    1    0    5000     100000000
ENTER T1,T2,N
 0    1.00000E-03    40
THE INVERSE IS:
 0+( 5.16398E-02)EXP(-2500T)SIN( 9682.46T+( 0))

TIME,SEC          INVERSE
 0                0
 2.50000E-05      1.16283E-02
 5.00000E-05      2.12107E-02
 7.50000E-05      2.84273E-02
 1.00000E-04      3.31346E-02
 1.25000E-04      3.53521E-02
 1.50000E-04      3.52429E-02
 1.75000E-04      3.30867E-02
 2.00000E-04      2.92500E-02
 2.25000E-04      2.41546E-02
 2.50000E-04      1.82462E-02
 2.75000E-04      1.19656E-02
 3.00000E-04      5.72372E-03
 3.25000E-04     -1.19302E-04
 3.50000E-04     -5.26877E-03
 3.75000E-04     -9.50523E-03
 4.00000E-04     -1.26883E-02
 4.25000E-04     -1.47558E-02
 4.50000E-04     -1.57180E-02
 4.75000E-04     -1.56484E-02
 5.00000E-04     -1.46724E-02
 5.25000E-04     -1.29536E-02
 5.50000E-04     -1.06796E-02
 5.75000E-04     -8.04864E-03
 6.00000E-04     -5.25641E-03
 6.25000E-04     -2.48507E-03
 6.50000E-04      1.05879E-04
 6.75000E-04      2.38619E-03
 7.00000E-04      4.25910E-03
 7.25000E-04      5.66300E-03
 7.50000E-04      6.57096E-03
 7.75000E-04      6.98819E-03
 8.00000E-04      6.94795E-03
 8.25000E-04      6.50637E-03
 8.50000E-04      5.73639E-03
 8.75000E-04      4.72162E-03
 9.00000E-04      3.55013E-03
 9.25000E-04      2.30880E-03
 9.50000E-04      1.07839E-03
 9.75000E-04     -7.04735E-05
 1.00000E-03     -1.08022E-03
CHANGE TIME? (Y OR N).
N
!
```

Figure 9.7(a)   The results of a run of the program in Figure 9.1
                 for the current in Figure 9.4.   R=50Ω, L=10mH,
                 C=1μF, E=5V.

134

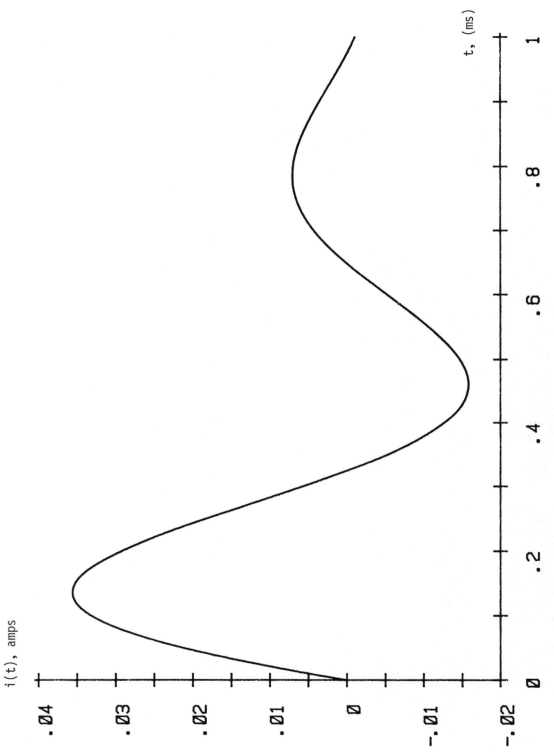

i(t), amps

.04

.03

.02

.01

0

-.01

-.02

0   .2   .4   .6   .8   1

t, (ms)

Figure 9.7(b). A plot of $i(t) = 5.16 \times 10^{-2} e^{-2500t} \sin(9682.46t)$ based on the results shown in Figure 9.7(a).
This is an underdamped response.

```
F(S)=K(AS**2+BS+C)/S(S**2+DS+E)
ENTER K,A,B,C,D,E
 500000000   0   0   1   40000   100000000
ENTER T1,T2,N
 0   1.50000E-03   30
THE INVERSE IS:
 5+( .386751)EXP(-37320.5)T+(-5.38675)EXP(-2679.49)T

TIME,SEC        INVERSE
 0              -2.08167E-16
 5.00000E-05    .348526
 1.00000E-04    .888683
 1.50000E-04    1.39753
 2.00000E-04    1.84820
 2.50000E-04    2.24324
 3.00000E-04    2.58888
 3.50000E-04    2.89120
 4.00000E-04    3.15562
 4.50000E-04    3.38688
 5.00000E-04    3.58914
 5.50000E-04    3.76605
 6.00000E-04    3.92077
 6.50000E-04    4.05609
 7.00000E-04    4.17445
 7.50000E-04    4.27796
 8.00000E-04    4.36850
 8.50000E-04    4.44768
 9.00000E-04    4.51693
 9.50000E-04    4.57750
 1.00000E-03    4.63048
 1.05000E-03    4.67681
 1.10000E-03    4.71734
 1.15000E-03    4.75278
 1.20000E-03    4.78378
 1.25000E-03    4.81089
 1.30000E-03    4.83460
 1.35000E-03    4.85534
 1.40000E-03    4.87348
 1.45000E-03    4.88934
 1.50000E-03    4.90322
CHANGE TIME? (Y OR N).
N
!
```

Figure 9.8(a). The results of a run of the program in Figure 9.1
for $v_C(t)$ in Figure 9.4.   R=400Ω.

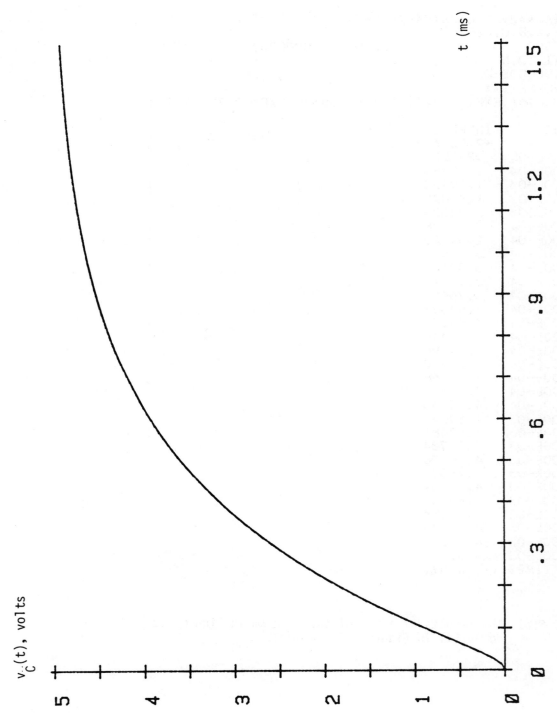

$v_C(t)$, volts

t (ms)

Figure 9.8(b). A plot of $v_C(t) = 5 + .387e^{-37320t} - 5.387e^{-2679t}$ V based on the results shown in Figure 9.8(a).

For the critically damped case, R = 200 Ω, d = R/L = 2 x 10^3, and the other coefficients are the same as before. The results of a run using these values are shown in Figure 9.9 (a) and a plot in Figure 9.9 (b). The critically damped response is seen to be

$$v_C(t) = 5 - 50000te^{-10000t} - 5e^{-10000t} \text{ V}$$

The transient again rises towards the steady-state value of 5 V, but notice how much faster it rises in comparison to the overdamped case. Compare values of $v_C(t)$ in Figure 9.8 with corresponding points in Figure 9.9.

```
F(S)=K(AS**2+BS+C)/S(S**2+DS+E)
ENTER K,A,B,C,D,E
 500000000   0   0   1   20000   100000000
ENTER T1,T2,N
 0   1.00000E-03   20
THE INVERSE IS:
 5.00000+(-50000.0T)EXP(-10000T)+(-5.00000)EXP(-10000T)


TIME,SEC          INVERSE
 0                 0
 5.00000E-05       .451020
 1.00000E-04       1.32121
 1.50000E-04       2.21087
 2.00000E-04       2.96997
 2.50000E-04       3.56351
 3.00000E-04       4.00426
 3.50000E-04       4.32056
 4.00000E-04       4.54211
 4.50000E-04       4.69450
 5.00000E-04       4.79786
 5.50000E-04       4.86718
 6.00000E-04       4.91324
 6.50000E-04       4.94362
 7.00000E-04       4.96352
 7.50000E-04       4.97649
 8.00000E-04       4.98490
 8.50000E-04       4.99034
 9.00000E-04       4.99383
 9.50000E-04       4.99607
 1.00000E-03       4.99750
CHANGE TIME? (Y OR N).
N
!
```

Figure 9.9(a). The results of a run of the program in Figure 9.1
           for $v_C(t)$ in Figure 9.4.   R=200Ω.

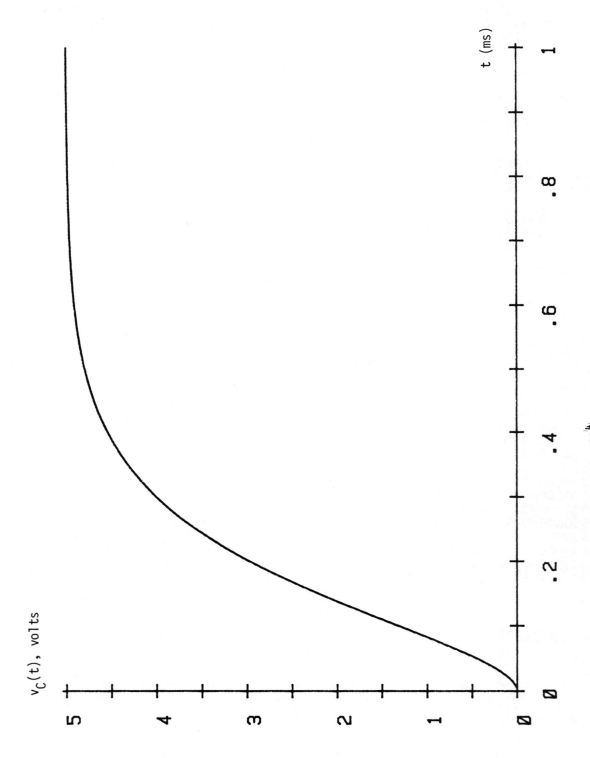

Figure 9.9(b). A plot of $v_C(t) = 5 - 50000te^{-10^4 t} - 5e^{-10^4 t}$ V based on the results shown in Figure 9.9(a).

Figure 9.10 (a) shows the print-out for the underdamped case, $R = 50 \, \Omega$, and Figure 9.10 (b) shows the plot of the response for the underdamped case, $R = 50 \, \Omega$. We see that

$$v_C(t) = 5 + 5.16e^{-2500t}\sin(9682t - 104.48^\circ) \text{ V}$$

It is clear that the transient values oscillate about the steady-state value of 5 V. The peak overshoot is 7.22 V at t = 0.325 ms (44.4%), while the peak undershoot is 4.013 V at t = 0.65 ms. The time interval between these two peaks is 0.30 ms, which is one-half the period of the oscillation frequency given by the response equation above (9682 rad/sec.).

Consider now the parallel RLC (tank) circuit shown in Figure 9.11.

Let $Z_1(s) = (Ls)||(1/Cs) = \dfrac{L/C}{Ls + 1/Cs} = \dfrac{(1/C)s}{s^2 + 1/LC}$

The total impedance of the network is then

$$Z(s) = R + Z_1(s) = R + \frac{(1/C)s}{s^2 + 1/LC} = \frac{Rs^2 + (1/C)s + R/LC}{s^2 + 1/Lc}$$

The current that flows after the switch is closed is

$$I(s) = \frac{V/s}{Z(s)} = \frac{V/s}{\dfrac{Rs^2 + (1/C)s + R/LC}{s^2 + 1/LC}}$$

$$= \frac{(V/R)(s^2 + 1/LC)}{s\{s^2 + (1/RC)s + 1/LC\}}$$

From this result, it is clear that our choice of values for the coefficients in equation (1) must be

K = V/R	c = 1/LC
a = 1	d = 1/RC
b = 0	e = 1/LC

The criterion for determining whether the response is over, under, or critically damped is now based on

$$(1/RC)^2 - 4/LC$$

Critical damping occurs for

$$(1/RC)^2 = 4/LC, \text{ or } R = \tfrac{1}{2}\sqrt{L/C}.$$

```
F(S)=K(AS**2+BS+C)/S(S**2+DS+E)
ENTER K,A,B,C,D,E
 500000000   0   0   I   5000    I00000000
ENTER TI,T2,N
 0   1.00000E-03   40
THE INVERSE IS:
 5+( 5.16398)EXP(-2500T)SIN( 9682.46T+(-I04.478))

TIME,SEC          INVERSE
 0                9.48431E-06
 2.50000E-05      .149166
 5.00000E-05      .564309
 7.50000E-05      1.18992
 1.00000E-04      1.96471
 1.25000E-04      2.82585
 1.50000E-04      3.71288
 1.75000E-04      4.57091
 2.00000E-04      5.35320
 2.25000E-04      6.02292
 2.50000E-04      6.55416
 2.75000E-04      6.93215
 3.00000E-04      7.15279
 3.25000E-04      7.22168
 3.50000E-04      7.15263
 3.75000E-04      6.96588
 4.00000E-04      6.68618
 4.25000E-04      6.34079
 4.50000E-04      5.95762
 4.75000E-04      5.56350
 5.00000E-04      5.18276
 5.25000E-04      4.83608
 5.50000E-04      4.53971
 5.75000E-04      4.30507
 6.00000E-04      4.13862
 6.25000E-04      4.04207
 6.50000E-04      4.01285
 6.75000E-04      4.04476
 7.00000E-04      4.12875
 7.25000E-04      4.25379
 7.50000E-04      4.40776
 7.75000E-04      4.57824
 8.00000E-04      4.75335
 8.25000E-04      4.92229
 8.50000E-04      5.07593
 8.75000E-04      5.20707
 9.00000E-04      5.31070
 9.25000E-04      5.38400
 9.50000E-04      5.42624
 9.75000E-04      5.43860
 1.00000E-03      5.42388
CHANGE TIME? (Y OR N).
N

!
```

Figure 9.10(a). The results of a run of the program in Figure 9.1
          for $v_C(t)$ in Figure 9.4. R=50Ω.

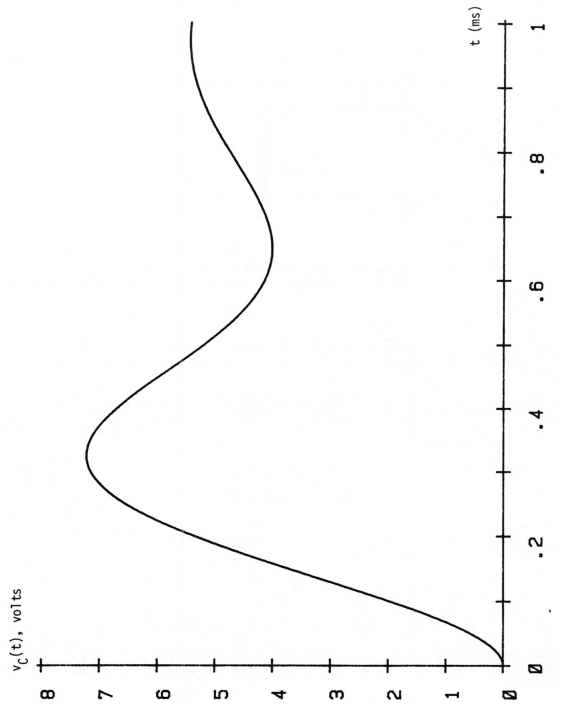

$v_C(t)$, volts

t (ms)

Figure 9.10(b). A plot of $v_C(t) + 5 + 5.16e^{-2500t}\sin(9682t - 104.48^0)$V based on the results shown in Figure 9.10(a).

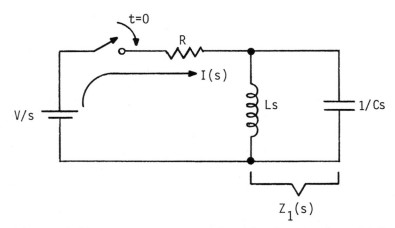

Figure 9.11. A parallel RLC (tank) circuit for which the
program of Figure 9.1 is used to compute i(t).

Underdamping occurs when $R > 1/2\sqrt{L/C}$ and overdamping when $R < 1/2\sqrt{L/C}$. In contrast with the series RLC network, the response is underdamped for <u>large</u> values of R and overdamped for small values of R.

For comparison purposes, we will use the same values of L and C that we used in the series circuit. To obtain an overdamped response, we will use a value of R that is one-half the critical value of $1/2 \ L/C = 50 \ \Omega$. Thus we let R = 25 Ω. Again using a 5 V DC excitation, our coefficients become

$$K = V/R = 5/25 = 0.2 \qquad c = 1/LC = 10^8$$

$$a = 1 \qquad\qquad d = 1/RC = 4 \times 10^4$$

$$b = 0 \qquad\qquad e = 1/LC = 10^8$$

Figure 9.12 shows the results. We see that

$$i(t) = .2 + .231e^{-37320t} - .231e^{-2679t} \text{ amps}$$

It is interesting to note that both the initial (t = 0) and steady-state values are 0.2 A. The initial value is 0.2 A because at t = 0 the capacitor is equivalent to a short-circuit and the inductor to an open-circuit. Therefore, the initial current is 5 V/25 Ω = 0.2 A. Similarly, at t = ∞, the capacitor is an open-circuit and the inductor is a short-circuit, so once again i = 5 V/25 Ω = 0.2 A.

For critical damping in the tank circuit, R = 50 Ω and K = V/R = 0.1, d = 1/RC = 2 x 10^4, while all other coefficients are the same as before. Using these values, we obtain the results shown in Figures 9.13 (a) and (b). We see that

$$i(t) = 0.1 - 2000te^{-10000t} \text{ A}$$

```
F(S)=K(AS**2+BS+C)/S(S**2+DS+E)
ENTER K,A,B,C,D,E
 .200000    1   0    100000000    40000    100000000
ENTER T1,T2,N
 0    1.50000E-03    30
THE INVERSE IS:
 .200000+(  .230940)EXP(-37320.5)T+(-.230940)EXP(-2679.49)T

TIME,SEC          INVERSE
 0                .200000
 5.00000E-05      3.37520E-02
 1.00000E-04      2.88727E-02
 1.50000E-04      4.63494E-02
 2.00000E-04      6.49993E-02
 2.50000E-04      8.18314E-02
 3.00000E-04      9.66336E-02
 3.50000E-04      .109592
 4.00000E-04      .120928
 4.50000E-04      .130842
 5.00000E-04      .139514
 5.50000E-04      .147098
 6.00000E-04      .153731
 6.50000E-04      .159533
 7.00000E-04      .164607
 7.50000E-04      .169045
 8.00000E-04      .172926
 8.50000E-04      .176321
 9.00000E-04      .179290
 9.50000E-04      .181887
 1.00000E-03      .184158
 1.05000E-03      .186144
 1.10000E-03      .187882
 1.15000E-03      .189401
 1.20000E-03      .190730
 1.25000E-03      .191892
 1.30000E-03      .192909
 1.35000E-03      .193798
 1.40000E-03      .194576
 1.45000E-03      .195256
 1.50000E-03      .195851
CHANGE TIME? (Y OR N).
N

!
```

Figure 9.12(a). The results of a run of the program in Figure 9.1 for i(t) in Figure 9.11. L=10mH, C=1μF, R=25Ω.

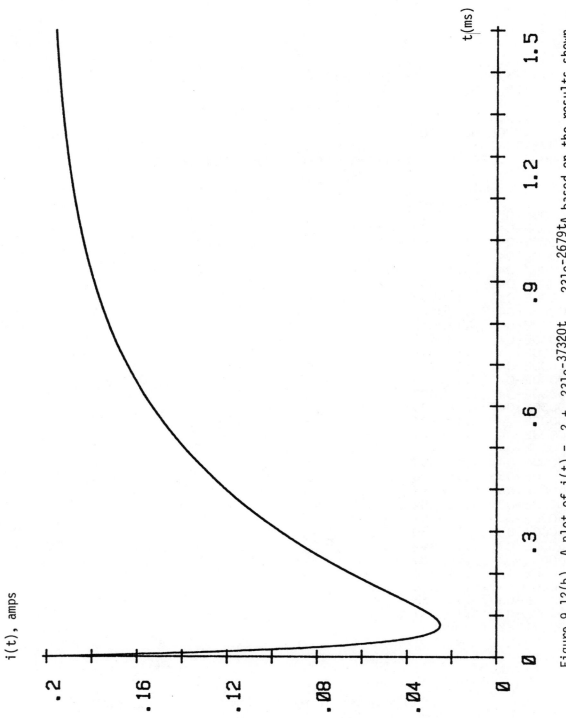

Figure 9.12(b) A plot of $i(t) = .2 + .231e^{-37320t} - .231e^{-2679t}A$ based on the results shown in Figure 9.12(a).

Once again, the initial and steady-state values are the same, 0.1 A. Note how much faster the values approach steady-state in this case compared to the previous case.

Finally, we choose R = 100 Ω to obtain an underdamped response. For this case, K = V/R = .05, d = 1/RC = 10^4 and the other coefficients are the same as before. The results are shown in Figures 9.14 (a) and (b). We see that

$$i(t) = .05 + .0577e^{-5000t} \sin(8660t-180^0)$$

or,

$$.05 - .0577e^{-5000t} \sin(8660t) \text{ A}$$

The oscillations that characterize an underdamped response are apparent in the data.

```
F(S)=K(AS**2+BS+C)/S(S**2+DS+E)
ENTER K,A,B,C,D,E
 .100000    1    0   100000000    20000    100000000
ENTER T1,T2,N
 0   1.00000E-03    20
THE INVERSE IS:
 .100000+(-2000.00T)EXP(-10000T)+( 0)EXP(-10000T)
TIME,SEC         INVERSE
 0               .100000
 5.00000E-05     3.93469E-02
 1.00000E-04     2.64241E-02
 1.50000E-04     3.30610E-02
 2.00000E-04     4.58659E-02
 2.50000E-04     5.89575E-02
 3.00000E-04     7.01278E-02
 3.50000E-04     7.88618E-02
 4.00000E-04     8.53475E-02
 4.50000E-04     9.00019E-02
 5.00000E-04     9.32621E-02
 5.50000E-04     9.55046E-02
 6.00000E-04     9.70255E-02
 6.50000E-04     9.80455E-02
 7.00000E-04     9.87234E-02
 7.50000E-04     9.91704E-02
 8.00000E-04     9.94633E-02
 8.50000E-04     9.96541E-02
 9.00000E-04     9.97779E-02
 9.50000E-04     9.98578E-02
 1.00000E-03     9.99092E-02
CHANGE TIME? (Y OR N).
N
!
```

Figure 9.13(a). The results of a run of the program in Figure 9.1
                 for i(t) in Figure 9.11. L=10mH, C=1μF, R=50Ω.

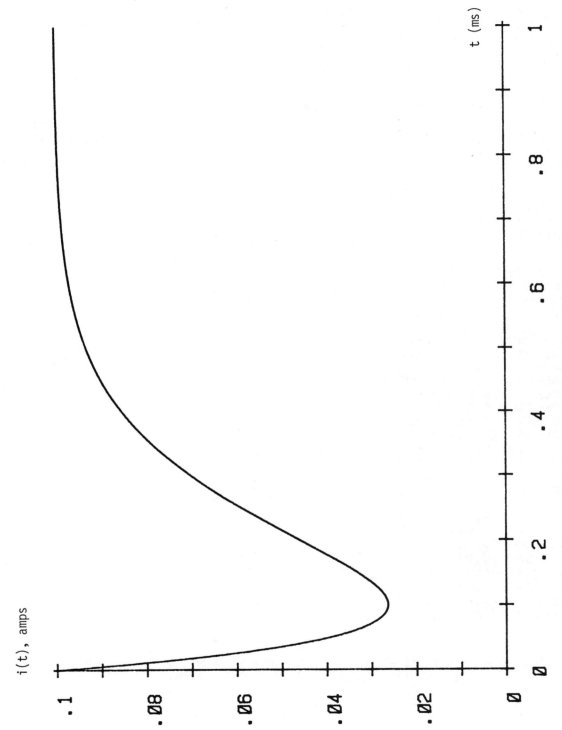

Figure 9.13(b). A plot of $i(t) = 0.1-2000e^{-10^4 t}$ A based on the results shown in Figure 9.13(a).

```
F(S)=K(AS**2+BS+C)/S(S**2+DS+E)
ENTER K,A,B,C,D,E
 5.00000E-02   1   0   100000000   10000   100000000
ENTER T1,T2,N
 0    2.00000E-03   40
THE INVERSE IS:
 5.00000E-02+( 5.77350E-02)EXP(-5000T)SIN( 8660.25T+(-180.000))

TIME,SEC         INVERSE
 0               5.00004E-02
 5.00000E-05     3.11330E-02
 1.00000E-04     2.33248E-02
 1.50000E-04     2.37288E-02
 2.00000E-04     2.90360E-02
 2.50000E-04     3.62944E-02
 3.00000E-04     4.33378E-02
 3.50000E-04     4.88935E-02
 4.00000E-04     5.24764E-02
 4.50000E-04     5.41724E-02
 5.00000E-04     5.43971E-02
 5.50000E-04     5.36861E-02
 6.00000E-04     5.25446E-02
 6.50000E-04     5.13620E-02
 7.00000E-04     5.03822E-02
 7.50000E-04     4.97143E-02
 8.00000E-04     4.93643E-02
 8.50000E-04     4.92744E-02
 9.00000E-04     4.93598E-02
 9.50000E-04     4.95349E-02
 1.00000E-03     4.97307E-02
 1.05000E-03     4.99014E-02
 1.10000E-03     5.00239E-02
 1.15000E-03     5.00936E-02
 1.20000E-03     5.01178E-02
 1.25000E-03     5.01098E-02
 1.30000E-03     5.00838E-02
 1.35000E-03     5.00519E-02
 1.40000E-03     5.00225E-02
 1.45000E-03     5.00004E-02
 1.50000E-03     4.99869E-02
 1.55000E-03     4.99812E-02
 1.60000E-03     4.99814E-02
 1.65000E-03     4.99851E-02
 1.70000E-03     4.99902E-02
 1.75000E-03     4.99952E-02
 1.80000E-03     4.99992E-02
 1.85000E-03     5.00017E-02
 1.90000E-03     5.00029E-02
 1.95000E-03     5.00031E-02
 2.00000E-03     5.00026E-02
CHANGE TIME? (Y OR N).
N

!
```

Figure 9.14(a). The results of a run of the program in Figure 9.1 for i(t) in the circuit of Figure 9.11.   L=10mH, C=1μF, R=100Ω.

148

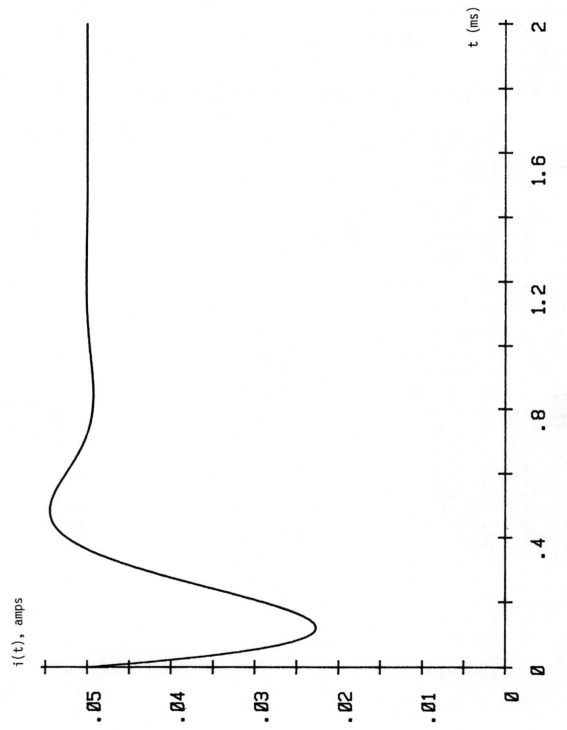

Figure 9.14(b). A plot of $i(t) = .05 - .0577e^{-5000t} \sin(8660t)$ A based on the results of Figure 9.14(a).

As a final example, consider the circuit shown in Figure 9.15.

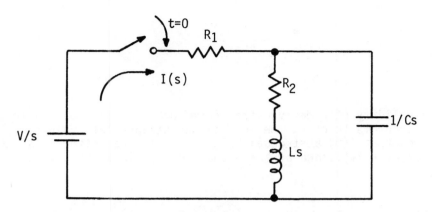

Figure 9.15. Another RLC circuit that can be solved using the program of Figure 9.1.

The equivalent impedance of the parallel branches is

$$Z_1(s) = \frac{(R_2 + Ls)1/Cs}{R_2 + Ls + 1/Cs} = \frac{R_2 + Ls}{R_2Cs + LCs^2 + 1}$$

and the total impedance is

$$Z(s) = R_1 + Z_1(s) = R_1 + \frac{R_2 + Ls}{R_2Cs + Lcs^2 + Ls}$$

$$= \frac{R_1R_2Cs + LCR_1s^2 + R_1 + R_2 + Ls}{LCs^2 + R_2Cs + 1}$$

Therefore,

$$I(s) = \frac{V/s}{Z(s)} = \frac{V(LCs^2 + R_2Cs + 1)}{s\{LCR_1s^2 + (R_1R_2C + L)s + (R_1 + R_2)\}}$$

$$= \frac{(V/LCR_1)(LCs^2 + R_2Cs + 1)}{s\left[s + \dfrac{R_1R_2C + L}{LCR_1}s + \dfrac{R_1 + R_2}{LCR_1}\right]} \tag{10}$$

With reference to our general transform (equation 1), we see that we must set

$$K = V/LCR_1$$

$$a = LC$$

$$b = R_2 C$$

$$c = 1$$

$$d = \frac{R_1 R_2 C + L}{LCR_1}$$

$$e = \frac{R_1 + R_2}{LCR_1}$$

One way to check the validity of a derived transform such as (10) above is to use the initial and final value theorems to check the initial and steady-state values. From inspection of Figure 9.15, we know that $i(0)$ must equal V/R_1, since the capacitor is a short at $t = 0$, and $i(\infty)$ must equal $V/(R_1 + R_2)$ since at $t = \infty$ the inductor is a short circuit. By the initial value theorem,

$$i(0) = \lim_{s \to \infty} sI(s) = \lim_{s \to \infty} \left[\frac{(V/LCR_1)(LCs^2 + R_2 Cs + 1)}{s^2 + \dfrac{R_1 R_2 C + L}{LCR_1} s + \dfrac{R_1 + R_2}{LCR_1}} \right]$$

$$= \{V/(LCR_1)\}LC = V/R_1$$

By the final value theorem,

$$i(\infty) = \lim_{s \to 0} sI(s) = \lim_{s \to 0} \left[\frac{(V/LCR_1)(LCs^2 + R_2 Cs + 1)}{s^2 + \dfrac{R_1 R_2 C + L}{LCR_1} s + \dfrac{R_1 + R_2}{LCR_1}} \right]$$

$$= \frac{V/(LCR_1)}{\dfrac{R_1 + R_2}{LCR_1}} = \frac{V}{R_1 + R_2}$$

These results confirm our analysis of the circuit at $t = 0$ and $t = \infty$.

III. EXERCISES

1. In the series RLC circuit of Figure 9.3, suppose R and C are fixed and L is variable. Derive an equation for the value of L that causes the circuit to be critically damped. For what values of L (in terms of R and C is the circuit overdamped? Underdamped? Using R = 1K and C = 1 µF, select values of L, based on your derivation, that cause the circuit to be under, over, and critically damped. Then use the program of Figure 9.1 to verify the types of responses obtained for the values of L you selected. Explain how your computer results confirm your predictions of the damping types.

2. A quadratic expression occurring in the denominator of a response transform is often expressed in the general form

$$s^2 + 2\zeta\omega_n s + \omega_n^2$$

where ζ is the damping factor and ω is the natural frequency, in rad/sec. It is easy to show that an underdamped response occurs for $\zeta < 1$. Use the program of Figure 9.1 to investigate the response corresponding to the inverse transformation of

$$\frac{100}{s(s^2 + 2\zeta\omega_n s + \omega_n^2)}$$

when $\omega = 10$ and for values of damping factor 0.9, 0.5, and 0.1. Compare and contrast the responses obtained for these cases, particularly in regard to the frequency of the transient oscillation, the number of cycles of the oscillation, the maximum value reached by the transient (the peak overshoot) and the length of time required for the transient to reach and stay within $\pm$ 10% of its steady-state value.

3. Derive an expression for the transform I(s) of the current in the circuit of Figure 9.16 after the switch is closed at t = 0.

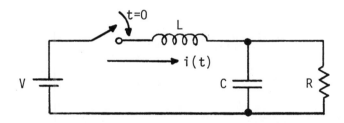

Figure 9.16

What should be the constants K, a, b, c, d, and e of equation (1), in terms of V, R, L, and C in Figure 9.16?

4. Use the program of Figure 9.1 to determine i(t) in Figure 9.16, and the peak overshoot of its transient, when L = 1H, C = 100 μF, and R = 70 Ω.

5. Modify the program of Figure 9.1 so that it can be used to find the transient response of an RLC network in which there are initial conditions, i.e., an initial inductor current I_0 and an initial capacitor voltage V_0. Then run your program to find the response of the circuit in Figure 9.4 with R = 400 Ω, V_0 = 3 V, and I_0 = 1 mA. Compare your computer results with those shown in the Discussion section for the same circuit without initial conditions. Check your program's validity by running it once with zero initial conditions and comparing results with those shown in the Discussion.

6. Write a BASIC program that can be used to find the current i(t) or voltage v(t) in an RLC network to which an AC excitation $A\sin\omega t$ is applied at t = 0. Develop a general transform, similar to equation (1), that can be applied to a variety of RLC network types (series, parallel, etc.).

7. Using the program you wrote for step 6, find i(t) in the circuit of Figure 9.4, with R = 400 Ω and V = 5sin(18 x 10³t).

8. Repeat step 7 for the circuit of Figure 9.11, using R = 50 Ω and V = 5sin(6000t).

10 Control Systems Simulation

OBJECTIVES

1. To learn how to write BASIC programs that can be used to analyze simple position control systems.

2. To learn how to perform a time-domain analysis of the response of a control system and a frequency domain analysis of its open-loop transfer function.

3. To learn how to compute the gain margin and phase margin of a stable control system.

4. To learn the effect of lead compensation on the response of a control system by computing C(t) for the same system with and without compensation.

5. To investigate the effects of the location of a zero in the transfer function on the response of a control system.

DISCUSSION

There are available today a number of large program packages that can be used to simulate complex control systems on a digital computer. One of these, CSMP, will be introduced in the next chapter. These packages are quite versatile and extremely powerful, but they require a large computer system having considerable memory capacity and, of course, the software must be purchased and must be compatible with the computer. For modeling simpler control systems, or for approximating more complex ones, the investigator may prefer to write his or her own software using BASIC and a less sophisticated computer.

Analysis of control system behavior may be performed either in the frequency (s) domain or in the time-domain. Figure 10.1 shows a generalized block diagram of a control system having forward transfer function G(s) and feedback transfer function H(s).

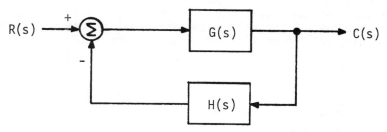

Figure 10.1. Block diagram of a control system.

The closed-loop transfer function is given by

$$\frac{C(s)}{R(s)} = \frac{G(s)}{1 + G(s)H(s)} \qquad (1)$$

Thus, if the input R(s) is known, then

$$C(s) = \frac{R(s)G(s)}{1 + G(s)H(s)} \qquad (2)$$

Time-domain analysis of the system is concerned with finding the inverse transform of (2), namely

$$C(t) = \mathscr{L}^{-1} \frac{R(s)G(s)}{1 + G(s)H(s)} \qquad (3)$$

Inverting (2) therefore produces the function C(t) that represents the response of the control system as a function of time. With this approach, we can use the computer to directly determine control system characteristics such as overshoot, settling time, natural frequency, and so forth. Frequency-domain analysis is appropriate when investigating control system stability in terms of the open-loop function G(s)H(s). The system shown in Figure 10.1 is unstable if there exists a frequency at which $|G(s)H(s)| \geqslant 1$ when $\underline{/GH} = -180°$. The computer is therefore used to determine the magnitude and phase angle of $G(s)H(s)$ as a function of frequency. For stable system, the gain margin can be computed by determining the gain at the frequency where the phase shift is -180° and the phase margin can be found by determining the phase shift at the frequency where the gain is unity.

Consider the simple position control system shown in Figure 10.2. The input Θ_{in} is an angular rotation of a potentiometer shaft. The potentiometer has transfer function $V/2\pi$ volts/radian (independent of frequency) and its output voltage applied to a differential amplifier with gain K_1, which is assumed to be independent of frequency. The differential amplifier drives a servomotor having transfer function

$$\frac{K_2}{s(s + \alpha)}$$

which in turn drives a feedback potentiometer. The angular rotation Θ_0 of the motor shaft is the output of the system, and a voltage proportional to this rotation is fed back to the differential amplifier for comparison with the input. When the output equals the input, there is no voltage applied to the servomotor and rotation ceases. The block diagram corresponding to the system of Figure 10.2 is shown in Figure 10.3.

Using equation (1), we find

$$\frac{C}{R} = \frac{K}{s^2 + \alpha s + K} \qquad (4)$$

Where $K = K_1 K_2 V/2\pi$. The open-loop transfer function is

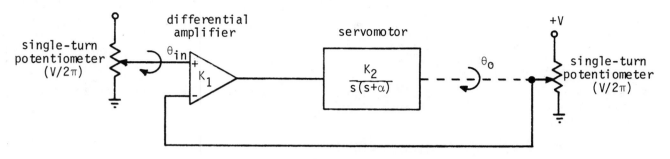

Figure 10.2 A simple position control system.

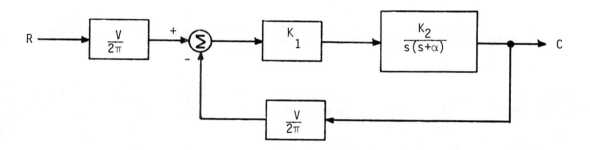

Figure 10.3 A block diagram of the position control system shown in
            Figure 10.2.

$$GH = \frac{K}{s(s + \alpha)} \tag{5}$$

Theoretically, there are no parameter values that would cause this system to be unstable.
Note from (5) that

$$\underline{/GH} = -90^\circ - \arctan(\omega/a)$$

Only as ω approaches infinity does this angle approach -180°. Therefore, we have no need
to perform a stability analysis in the frequency domain.

Suppose the input to the system is a unit step, $R(s) = 1/s$. Then, from
(4),

$$C(s) = \frac{K}{s(s^2 + \alpha s + K)}$$

and

$$C(t) = \mathscr{L}^{-1} \left. \frac{K}{s(s^2 + \alpha s + K)} \right| \tag{6}$$

In Chapter 9, we developed a BASIC program that can be used to find the inverse transform of

$$F(s) = \frac{K(as^2 + bs + c)}{s(s^2 + ds + e)} \qquad (7)$$

By setting a = 0, b = 0, c = 1, d = α, and e = K, we see that (7) can be used to solve (6). In the control system shown in Figure 10.2, suppose V = 10 volts, K_1 = 1000, K_2 = 6.28, and α = 140. Then,

$$K = K_1 K_2 V/2\pi = (10^3)(6.28)(10)/2\pi = 10^4$$

$$C(s) = \frac{10^4}{s(s^2 + 140s + 10^4)}$$

Figure 10.4 shows a result of the run of the program in Figure 9.1 using the values K = 10^4, a = 0, b = 0, c = 1, d = 140, and e = 10^4. We see that

$$C(t) = 1 + 1.4e^{-70t}\sin(71.4t-134.4^0)$$

Twenty values of C(t) are listed for t between 0 and 0.2 seconds. The output of the system is seen to overshoot its steady-state value (1.00) and oscillate slightly before settling down.

```
F(S)=K(AS**2+BS+C)/S(S**2+DS+E)
ENTER K,A,B,C,D,E
 10000   0   0   1   140   10000
ENTER T1,T2,N
 0   .200000   20
THE INVERSE IS:
 1+( 1.40028)EXP(-70T)SIN( 71.4143T+(-134.427))

TIME,SEC        INVERSE
 0              7.20095E-06
 1.00000E-02    .305946
 2.00000E-02    .725712
 3.00000E-02    .965300
 4.00000E-02    1.04160
 5.00000E-02    1.03977
 6.00000E-02    1.01959
 7.00000E-02    1.00490
 8.00000E-02    .998843
 9.00000E-02    .997924
 .100000        .998727
 .110000        .999557
 .120000        .999981
 .130000        1.00010
 .140000        1.00008
 .150000        1.00003
 .160000        1.00001
 .170000        .999997
 .180000        .999996
 .190000        .999998
 .200000        .999999
CHANGE TIME? (Y OR N).
N
!
```

Figure 10.4 The results of a run of the program in Figure 9.1 for C(t) in Figure 10.2. V = 10, K_1 = 1000, K_2 = 6.28, α = 140.

Consider now the control system whose block diagram is shown in Figure 10.5.

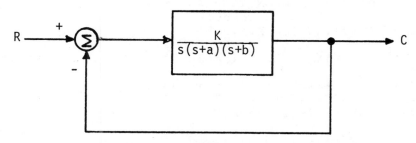

Figure 10.5 Block diagram of a control system for which a stability analysis is performed.

The open-loop transfer function of Figure 10.5 is G = K/s(s + a)(s + b) and

$$\frac{C}{R} = \frac{G}{1 + G} = \frac{K}{s\{s^2 + (a + b)\ s + ab\} + K} \tag{8}$$

In this case, the system has a potential for being unstable. If the value of K is so large that the magnitude of G is greater than or equal to one at the frequency where the phase of G is -180°, then instability will result. In Chapter 5, we developed a BASIC program that performed automatic iterative computations to determine the frequency at which the phase angle of a transfer function having the form of G above is -180°. Suppose a = 5 and b = 20 in Figure 10.5. The result of a run of th program of Figure 5.5 is shown in Figure 10.6. We see that the phase angle of G is -180° ± 0.5° at ω = 10.076 rad/sec.

```
G=K/S(S+A)(S+B). ENTER A AND B.
A=   5  B=   20
AT   10.0760  RAD/SEC, THE ANGLE IS    -180.347

!
```

Figure 10.6   A run of the program in Figure 5.5 to determine the frequency at which the open-loop gain of Figure 10.5 has angle -180° ± .5°.

Figure 10.7 shows a BASIC program that computes the magnitude and phase of G over a user-selected frequency range. Since we determined that the frequency at which the phase of G is -180° is approximately 10 rad/sec, we run the program of Figure 10.7 over a range of frequencies that includes ω = 10. The results of the run for the case K = 1000 are shown in Figure 10.8. We see from Figure 10.8 that |G| = 0.4 at ω = 10 rad/sec, where the phase shift is -180 degrees. The system is therefore stable and has a gain margin of 1/.4 = 2.5 ≈ 8 dB. We also see that |G| ≃ 1 at ω = 6 rad/sec, where the phase angle is -156.894 degrees. The phase margin is therefore 180 - 156.894 = 23.1 degrees.

When the input to the system in Figure 10.5 is a unit step, R(s) = 1/s, then from equation (8)

$$C(s) = \frac{K}{s\{s\{s^2 + (a + b)s + ab\} + K\}} \tag{9}$$

Inversion of equation (9) for time-domain analysis of the control system response C(t) is not a simple task, in the general case. It requires finding the roots of the cubic in the denominator of (9), a somewhat lengthy procedure. Programming techniques for finding the

```
10 REM THIS PROGRAM FINDS THE MAGNITUDE AND PHASE
20 REM OF G=K/S(S+A)(S+B) AT USER-SELECTED FREQUENCIES.
30 PRINT "G=K/S(S+A)(S+B). ENTER K,A,B."
40 INPUT K,A,B
50 PRINT "ENTER MIN AND MAX FREQUENCIES IN RAD/SEC AND NO. OF INTERVALS"
60 INPUT W1,W2,N
70 DEF FNM(W)=K/(W*((W**2+A**2)*(W**2+B**2))**.5)
80 DEF FNA(W)=-90-57.29578*(ATN(W/A)+ATN(W/B))
90 PRINT "FREQ,RAD/SEC","GAIN","PHASE,DEG."
100 PRINT
110 FOR W=W1 TO W2 STEP (W2-W1)/N
120    PRINT W, FNM(W), FNA(W)
130 NEXT W
140 PRINT "CHANGE FREQUENCIES? (Y OR N)"
150 INPUT A$
160 IF A$="Y" THEN 50
170 END
!
```

Figure 10.7   A BASIC program that computes the magnitude and angle of G(s)=K/s(s+a)(s+b)
over a user-selected frequency range.

```
G=K/S(S+A)(S+B). ENTER K,A,B.
 1000           5                   20
ENTER MIN AND MAX FREQUENCIES IN RAD/SEC AND NO. OF INTERVALS
 1              11                  20
FREQ,RAD/SEC   GAIN                PHASE,DEG.

 1             9.79357            -104.172
 1.50000       6.36762            -110.988
 2             4.61934            -117.512
 2.50000       3.55008            -123.690
 3             2.82669            -129.495
 3.50000       2.30562            -134.918
 4             1.91426            -139.970
 4.50000       1.61148            -144.668
 5             1.37199            -149.036
 5.50000       1.17926            -153.103
 6             1.02198            -156.894
 6.50000       .892086            -160.436
 7             .783724            -163.752
 7.50000       .692509            -166.866
 8             .615115            -169.796
 8.50000       .548972            -172.560
 9             .492076            -175.173
 9.50000       .442840            -177.649
 10            .400000            -180.000
 10.5000       .362536            -182.236
 11            .329619            -184.367
CHANGE FREQUENCIES? (Y OR N)

N
!
```

Figure 10.8   The results of a run of the program in Figure 10.7 for
G(s)=1000/s(s+5)(s+20).

roots of polynomials are a part of the field known as <u>numerical analysis</u> and are beyond the scope of this book. In any event, the frequency-domain analysis provides all the vital information needed by the designer to determine a control system's behavior.

Consider now the <u>lead-compensated</u> control system whose block diagram is shown in Figure 10.9.

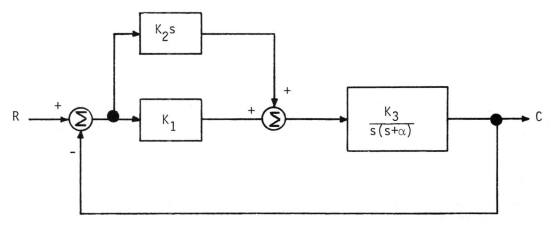

For the block diagram in Figure 10.9,

Figure 10.9 Block diagram of a lead-compensated control system.

$$\frac{C}{R} = \frac{K_1 K_3 + K_2 K_3 s}{s^2 + (\alpha + K_2 K_3)s + K_1 K_3} \tag{10}$$

Again, we see that the system is theoretically stable for any choice of parameter values. For a unit-step input $R(s) = 1/s$, we have

$$C(s) = \frac{K_1 K_3 + K_2 K_3 s}{s\{s^2 + (\alpha + K_2 K_3)s + K_1 K_3\}} \tag{11}$$

$$= \frac{K_3 K_2 (s + K_1/K_2)}{s\{s^2 + (\alpha + K_2 K_3)s + K_1 K_3\}} \tag{12}$$

We write C/R in the form of (12) so that the zero introduced into the transfer function by the lead compensation is clearly apparent. It can be seen that the zero is located at s = $-K_1/K_2$. With reference to equation (7), we see that (11) can be inverted using the program of Figure 9.1 by setting $K = K_3$, $a = 0$, $b = K_2$, $c = K_1$, $d = \alpha + K_2 K_3$, and $e = K_1 K_3$.

Of interest to the control systems designer is the effect of the location of the zero in (11) on the response C(t) of the control system. Let us first compute C(t) without any lead compensation in the system, i.e., for the case $K_2 = 0$. For this special case, we will use C/R in the form of equation (10), so we can fit the form of equation (7) by setting $K = K_1 K_3$, $a = 0$, $b = 0$, $c = 1$, $d = \alpha$ and $e = K_1 K_3$. Suppose in Figure 10.9 that $\alpha = 140$, $K_1 = 12$, and $K_3 = 10,000$. Then $K = K_1 K_3 = 120,000$ a = 0, b = 0, c = 1, d = 140, and e = $K_1 K_3 = 120,000$. Figure 10.10 shows the results of a run of the program of Figure 9.1 using these values. We see that the response is quite underdamped, exhibiting several oscillations about its steady-state value of .05 seconds.

```
F(S)=K(AS**2+BS+C)/S(S**2+DS+E)
ENTER K,A,B,C,D,E
 120000    0   0   1    140    120000
ENTER T1,T2,N
 0    5.00000E-02    20
THE INVERSE IS:
 1+( 1.02106)EXP(-70T)SIN( 339.264T+(-101.659))

TIME,SEC          INVERSE
 0                1.51580E-06
 2.50000E-03      .314895
 5.00000E-03      .943964
 7.50000E-03      1.42056
 1.00000E-02      1.50647
 1.25000E-02      1.26601
 1.50000E-02      .938462
 1.75000E-02      .744218
 2.00000E-02      .759352
 2.25000E-02      .913036
 2.50000E-02      1.07302
 2.75000E-02      1.14236
 3.00000E-02      1.10662
 3.25000E-02      1.01807
 3.50000E-02      .944927
 3.75000E-02      .926118
 4.00000E-02      .956772
 4.25000E-02      1.00406
 4.50000E-02      1.03498
 4.75000E-02      1.03597
 5.00000E-02      1.01529
CHANGE TIME? (Y OR N).
N

!
```

Figure 10.10   Results of a run of the program in Figure 9.1
              for C(t) in Figure 10.9. α=140, K_1=12, K_2=0,
              K_3=10,000.

Let us now restore the lead compensation and examine its effect by computing the inverse of (11). We begin by letting K_2 = .012, with all other constants the same as before. Figure 10.11 shows the results of a run using

$$K = K_3 K_2 = 10,000(.012) = 120$$

$$a = 0$$

$$b = 1$$

$$c = K_1/K_2 = 12/.012 = 1000$$

$$d = \alpha + K_2 K_3 = 140 + .012(10,000) = 260$$

$$e = K_1 K_3 = 120,000$$

We see that the response C(t) is still underdamped, but the inclusion of the compensation has clearly improved it. The oscilations are less severe and dampen out faster. At t = .05 sec, the response is within .00143 of its steady-state value.

```
F(S)=K(AS**2+BS+C)/S(S**2+DS+E)
ENTER K,A,B,C,D,E
 120   0   1   1000     260     120000
ENTER T1,T2,N
 0    5.00000E-02    20
THE INVERSE IS:
 1+( 1.00048)EXP(-130T)SIN( 321.092T+(-91.7842))

TIME,SEC           INVERSE
 0                 2.28822E-07
 2.50000E-03        .481839
 5.00000E-03       1.00184
 7.50000E-03       1.27235
 1.00000E-02       1.27247
 1.25000E-02       1.13136
 1.50000E-02        .989640
 1.75000E-02        .921023
 2.00000E-02        .926119
 2.25000E-02        .967058
 2.50000E-02       1.00550
 2.75000E-02       1.02272
 3.00000E-02       1.01994
 3.25000E-02       1.00816
 3.50000E-02        .997781
 3.75000E-02        .993514
 4.00000E-02        .994647
 4.25000E-02        .998012
 4.50000E-02       1.00080
 4.75000E-02       1.00184
 5.00000E-02       1.00143
CHANGE TIME? (Y OR N).
N
!
```

Figure 10.11 Results of a run of the program of Figure 9.1
for C(t) in Figure 10.9. $\alpha=140$, $K_1=12$, $K_2=.012$,
$K_3=10,000$.

In the previous run, we chose $K_2 = .012$, which resulted in adding a zero to C(s) at s = $-K_1/K_2 = -12/.012 = -1000$. Let us now move the zero closer to the origin by setting $K_2 = .12$, so $-K_1/K_2 = -12/.12 = -100$. Figure 10.12 shows the results of a run using

$$K = K_3 K_2 = (10,000)(.12) = 1200$$

$$a = 0$$

$$b = 1$$

$$c = K_1/K_2 = 12/.12 = 100$$

$$d = \alpha + K_2 K_3 = 140 + 1200 = 1340$$

$$e = K_1 K_3 = 120,000$$

We see that the response C(t) now rises rapidly towards its steady-state value and that all overshoots and oscillations have been eliminated. Moving the zero towards the origin has clearly improved the response significantly.

```
F(S)=K(AS**2+BS+C)/S(S**2+DS+E)
ENTER K,A,B,C,D,E
 1200    0    1    100    1340       120000
ENTER T1,T2,N
 0    5.00000E-02    20
THE INVERSE IS:
 1.00000+(-.962077)EXP(-1243.50)T+(-3.79234E-02)EXP(-96.5020)T

TIME,SEC          INVERSE
 0                6.93889E-17
 2.50000E-03      .927242
 5.00000E-03      .974674
 7.50000E-03      .981524
 1.00000E-02      .985548
 1.25000E-02      .988649
 1.50000E-02      .991082
 1.75000E-02      .992994
 2.00000E-02      .994496
 2.25000E-02      .995676
 2.50000E-02      .996603
 2.75000E-02      .997331
 3.00000E-02      .997903
 3.25000E-02      .998353
 3.50000E-02      .998706
 3.75000E-02      .998983
 4.00000E-02      .999201
 4.25000E-02      .999372
 4.50000E-02      .999507
 4.75000E-02      .999613
 5.00000E-02      .999696
CHANGE TIME? (Y OR N).
 N
!
```

Figure 10.12   Results of a run of the program of Figure 9.1 for C(t) in
Figure 10.9 $\alpha=140$, $K_1=12$, $K_2=0.12$, $K_3=10,000$.

Figure 10.13 shows plots of C(t) for the three cases we computed: no compensation, $K_2 = .012$, and $K_2 = .12$.   The desirable effects of lead compensation are especially apparent in this graphical comparison.   The quickened response and reduction in oscillation as the zero is placed closer to the origin are evident.

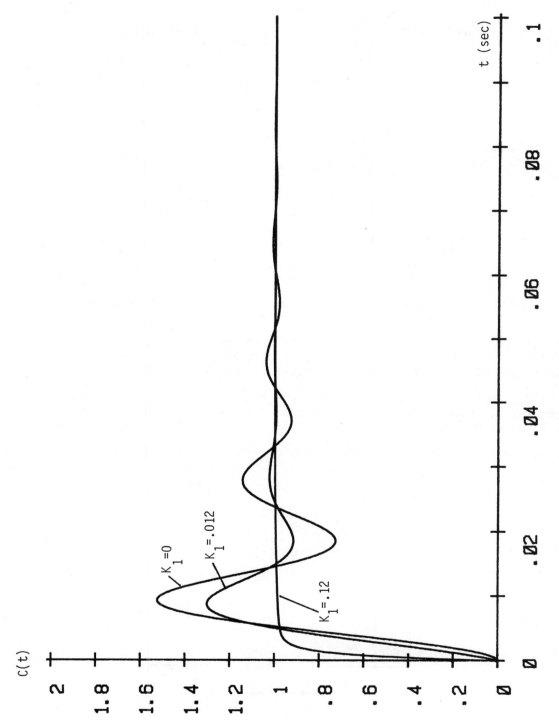

Figure 10.13 Plots showing C(t) in Figure 10.9 for three different values of K_1. These plots are based on the results shown in Figures 10.10, 10.11, and 10.12.

EXERCISES

1. Given the control system whose block diagram is shown in Figure 10.14:

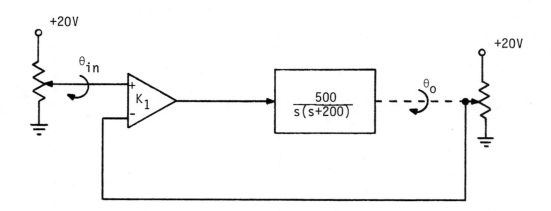

Figure 10.14

Compute the response of this system to a unit-step input for different values of amplifier gain K_1. Choose at least one value of gain K_1 that results in an underdamped response and at least one value that results in an overdamped response.

2. With K_1 = 6.28 in Figure 10.14, perform a computer analysis to determine the effect on the control system response of changes in the location of the pole at s = -200. In particular, compare results when the pole is moved to s = -100 and to s = -400.

3. Write a BASIC program that can be used to perform a frequency-domain analysis (magnitude and phase of the open-loop transfer function) for the control system whose block diagram is shown in Figure 10.15. User enters values of K.

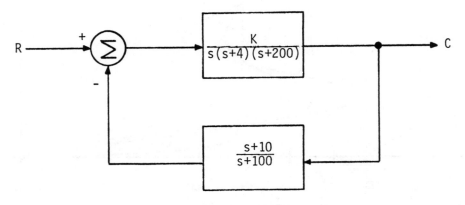

Figure 10.15

4. Use the program you wrote in step 3 to determine the value of gain K that causes the control system to become unstable. (Hint: run the program for K = 1 and determine the magnitude of GH at the frequency where the phase shift is -180°. Use this value to

determine the required gain.)

5. Run your program to determine the phase margin of the control system when K has one-half the value found in step 4.

6. According to the <u>Nyquist stability criterion,</u> a polar plot of the open-loop transfer function GH should not enclose the point -1 + j0 for a stable system. Use the program you wrote in step 3 to generate data points for a polar plot of the control system in Figure 10.15, when K is one-half the value determined in step 4. Construct the polar plot and verify the Nyquist criterion for this case.

7. Given the control system whose block diagram is shown in Figure 10.16:

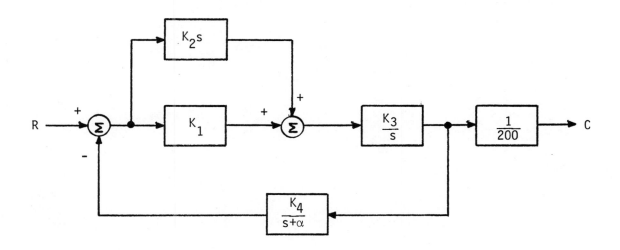

Figure 10.16

Find C/R for the system and determine what values should be substituted for K, a, b, c, d, and e in equation (6) in order to compute the response of the system to a unit-step input.

8. Compute $C(t)$ for the system shown in Figure 10.16 when the input is a unit step and K_1 = 0, K_2 = .001, K_3 = 10,000, K_4 = 5, and α = 100.

9. Investigate the effect of changes in the value of K_2 on the response of the control system shown in Figure 10.16 by computing $C(t)$ for the values given in step 8, except change K_2 to .001 and other values in that vicinity.

11 Introduction to the Continuous System Modeling Program (CSMP)

OBJECTIVES

1. To learn the basic syntax and structure of CSMP.

2. To learn how to model linear circuits and excitations using CSMP.

3. To investigate the response of simple networks when parameters and excitations are varied, and to learn how these quantities can be made to vary in automatic successive CSMP simulations.

DISCUSSION

The Continuous System Modeling Program (CSMP) is an example of a large programming package that is especially valuable for analyzing linear systems having a large number of components and/or complex transfer functions. Developed by IBM, the program utilizes a language whose statements are oriented to linear systems terminology, including Laplace transforms. It is a very easy language to learn and demands little or no programming ex-experience from a user. However, like other large program packages, it requires a large, high-speed computer with considerable memory capacity, such as the IBM System/360, for which it was developed.

Each statement written by a CSMP user is either a <u>data</u> statement, a <u>structure</u> statement, or a <u>control</u> statement. Data statements are used to assign numeric values to system parameters, constants, and/or initial conditions. Each data statement is preceded by a keyword: CONSTANT, PARAMETER, or INCON, according to the type of assignment. If, for example, we wish to assign the value 3.1416 to the name PI, then we write

    CONSTANT PI = 3.1415926

The name PI may then be used in subsequent portions of the program and will be treated by the computer in exactly the same way as the constant 3.1415926. The syntax for the specification of constants, variables, and expressions is the same as that of FORTRAN, except it is not necessary to distinguish between integer and real variables. Parameters and initial conditions for a given problem may be assigned in such a way that their values are <u>automatically</u> changed in repeated runs of the simulation. The values which these quantities are assigned in automatic reruns of the program are specified by inserting them in parentheses. For example, the statement

    PARAMETER   GAIN = (50,100,500)

will cause a simulation run to be performed first with the parameter GAIN equal to 50, then again with GAIN = 100, and a third time with GAIN = 500. Multiple value assignments of the same type may be made on one line, using commas to separate the assignments, for example:

    CONSTANT PI = 3.1415926, K = 125.04

168

Structure statements <u>define</u> the system being simulated. These statements are written in terms of the transfer function of each component in the system and tell what the name of the input to the component is, the transfer function itself, and the name of the output. The user must assign variable names to the input and output of every component. When every component has been assigned an input name, an output name, and a transfer function, then the system is completely defined. As an example, a component whose function is 1/s (an integrator) is specified in CSMP by writing

y = INTGRL (ic,x)

where x is a variable name assigned to the input of the integrator, y is a variable name assigned to the output, and ic is the initial condition, y(0). This statement illustrates the format of every structure statement: the output variable name = transfer function and specification of the input variable name. Consider the two blocks with transfer functions shown in Figure 11.1. Assume input and output variable names have been assigned as shown.

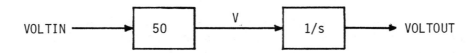

Figure 11.1   Block diagram of an amplifier and an integrator in a CSMP model.

The system shown in Figure 11.1 would be defined in CSMP by writing the following two structure statements:

V = 50*VOLTIN

VOLTOUT = INTGRL(0,V)

The first of these statements defines the first block as an amplifier, with (frequency-independent) gain 50, having an input named VOLTIN and an output named V. (These variable names are arbitrary; we could have used V1 and V2, for example.) The second structure statement defines the second block to be an integrator with zero initial condition, having input V and output VOLTOUT. The sequence in which the structure statements are written is <u>irrelevant</u>; we could, for example, reverse the order of the two statements above without affecting their meaning in any way. So long as all components in a system are identified, along with their input and output names, it makes no difference in what order the structure statements are written.

Table 11.1 shows the CSMP structure statements corresponding to the transforms that we will be using in future discussion.

Note that it may be necessary in some cases to manipulate a given transfer function to make it fit the form of one of those listed in Table 11.1. Suppose, for example, that we want to write the structure statement corresponding to a component having transfer function 1/(s + 10). In this case, we fit entry 3 in the table by writing

$$\frac{1}{s + 10} = \frac{1}{10(s/10 + 1)} = \frac{.1}{.1s + 1}$$

Table 11.1

Transfer Function	Format
1. $1/s$	$y = \text{INTGRL}(ic,x)$ y = output x = input ic = initial condition = $y(0)$
2. s	$y = \text{DERIV}(ic,x)$ y = output x = input ic = initial condition = $x(0)$
3. $1/(ps + 1)$	$y = \text{REALPL}(ic,p,x)$ y = output x = input ic = initial condition = $y(0)$
4. $(p_1s + 1)/(p_2s + 1)$	$y = \text{LEDLAG}(p_1,p_2,x)$ y = output x = input
5. $1/(s^2 + 2p_1p_2s + p_2^2)$	$y = \text{CMPXPL}(ic_1,ic_2,p_1,p_2,x)$ y = output x = input ic_1 = $y(0)$ ic_2 = $\dot{y}(0)$

A complete definition of $1/(s + 10)$ therefore requires two structure statements, as illustrated in Figure 11.2

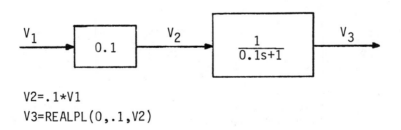

```
V2=.1*V1
V3=REALPL(0,.1,V2)
```

Figure 11.2   Block diagram and structure statements used to
model the transfer function $1/(s + 10)$.

As another example, suppose we want to write the structure statements for a component having transfer function

$$\frac{20(s + 1)}{(s + 5)(s^2 + 10s + 100)}$$

With reference to entry 5 in the table, we see that $2p_1p_2 = 10$ and $p_2^2 = 100$. Therefore, $p_2 = 10$ and $2p_1(10) = 10$, so $p_1 = .5$. Since $20/(s + 5) = \dfrac{20}{5(.2s + 1)} = \dfrac{4}{.2s + 1}$, we can perform the modeling as shown in Figure 11.3 (assuming zero initial conditions).

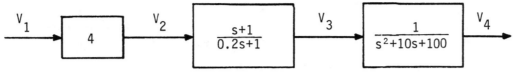

V2=4*V1
V3=LEDLAG(1,.2,V2)
V4=CMPXPL(0,0,.5,10,V3)

Figure 11.3 Block diagram and structure statements used to model the transfer function $20(s + 1)/(s + 5)(s^2 + 10s + 100)$.

There are a number of different driving functions (excitations) that can be generated using CSMP statements. The statements that produce the most commonly used functions are shown in Table 11.2.

Table 11.2

Function	Format
1. Step occurring at $t = p$	$y = \text{STEP}(p)$
$y = \begin{cases} 0 & t < p \\ 1 & t \geq p \end{cases}$	
2. Ramp with unity slope beginning at $t = p$	$y = \text{RAMP}(p)$
$y = \begin{cases} 0 & t < p \\ t - p & t \geq p \end{cases}$	
3. Impulse function	$y = \text{IMPULS}(p_1, p_2)$
$y = \delta(t - p_1) + \delta(t - p_1 - p_2) + \delta(t - p_1 - 2p_2) + \delta(t - p_1 - 3p_2) + \cdots$	
$=$ a sequence of unity-weight impulse functions beginning at $t = p_1$ sec and separated by p_2 sec.	
4. Pulse functions (triggered one shot)	$y = \text{PULSE}(p, x)$
$y =$ unity-height pulse with minimum width p sec triggered when $x > 0$ and remaining high while $x > 0$.	
5. Sine wave	$y = \text{SINE}(p_1, p_2, p_3)$
$y = \sin[p_2(t - p_1) + p_3]$	
$=$ sine wave beginning at $t = p_1$, frequency p_2 rad/sec, and phase angle p_3 rad.	

As an example, suppose we want to express the excitation E = 20sin(50t + 60°). Assuming this excitation is to be applied at t = 0, we see from entry 5 in Table 11.2 that $p_1 = 0$, $p_2 = 50$, and $p_3 = (60)(\pi/180) = \pi/3$ rad. Thus E = 20*SINE(0,50,1.0472).

Other excitations can be expressed by writing statements that combine functions from Table 11.2. For example, if we want to generate a 2 Hz square wave that alternates between + 5 V, we can first generate a 2 Hz sine wave V = sin4πt using the SINE function. We then use this sine wave to trigger the pulse generator (entry 4 in the table) by writing V1 = PULSE(0,V). The latter produces a unity height pulse each time the sine wave goes positive and returns to zero each time the sine wave goes negative. Multiplying V1 by 10 will thus produce a 2 Hz square wave that alternates between 0 and + 10 V. We then generate the required wave by adding a -5 V DC level to the square wave. The CSMP statements that implement these operations are as follows:

        V = SINE(0,12.566,0)

        V1 = PULSE(0,V)

        V2 = 10*V1

        V3 = STEP(0)

        V4 = -5*V3

        SQ = V2 + V4

Control statements are used to specify options related to the execution and input/output procedures of a CSMP run. The solution of a simulation run is presented as a set of values of one of the variables versus time, that is, a set of time-points with the corresponding values that the variable assumed at those time points. In other words, the solution is a set of discrete values of the inverse transform of a variable, just like the computer solutions we obtained in previous chapters when we wrote BASIC programs to invert Laplace transforms. We must therefore specify the size of the time intervals between which computations are performed and the total time over which they are performed (the total length of the problem-variable time, not the total time that the computer is allowed to run). The time interval is called the OUTDEL and the total time is called the FINTIM. Thus if OUTDEL = .1 and FINTIM = 10, then 101 values of the solution will be computed between t = 0 and t = 10 seconds. The values of OUTDEL and FINTIM and specified by the programmer on a line beginning with the keyword TIMER, as in the following example:

        TIMER OUTDEL = .1, FINTIM = 10

The order in which the specifications occur is not important, and they may be written on different TIMER lines if desired, anywhere in the program.

The choice of values for OUTDEL and FINTIM is often a matter of trial and error, particularly if the user has no previous knowledge of the behavior of the system being simulated. Suppose, for example, that the solution to a certain problem turned out to be $y(t) = e^{-10t}$. If we knew this solution in advance, we might choose FINTIM = .5 sec (five time-constants) and OUTDEL = .01 seconds. These choices would give good resolution, since we would obtain 51 values of y(t) between virtually the entire range of values of $y(t) = e^{-10t}$. On the other hand, if we had chosen FINTIM = 100 and OUTDEL = 1, then all the computed values would be essentially zero, since $y(t) = e^{-10t}$ goes from 1 to zero in approximately .5 seconds.

The best way to view the solution is to use the built-in plotting capability of CSMP. The control statement PRTPLOT y will cause the computer to print values of t at which y(t) is computed, the corresponding values of y(t), and a bar-chart type of plot of y(t) versus t.

The plot is developed on a conventional line printer (and/or displayed on the screen of a terminal) so no special x-y plotter or graphics terminal is required. Scaling of the plotted values is automatic.

A CSMP program may be divided into three segments, called the INITIAL, DYNAMIC, and TERMINAL segments. Each segment begins with a line containing only one of these keywords. The initial and terminal segments are optional and are used only for operations that are performed before and after an actual simulation run. We will not need either of these segments yet, so for now all our CSMP statements will be written in the dynamic segment. The first line in each program will therefore contain the single word DYNAMIC.

As a first example of a CSMP simulation, we will find the voltage $\dot{v}(t)$ across the 1 µF capacitor in Figure 11.4, after the switch is closed at t = 0.

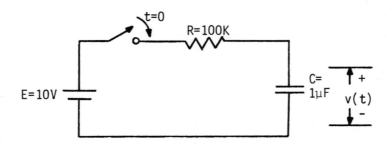

Figure 11.4 An RC network that is modeled by CSMP to determine v(t).

By the voltage divider rule,

$$V(s) = \left(\frac{1/Cs}{R + \frac{1}{Cs}} \right) E(s)$$

$$\frac{V(s)}{E(s)} = \frac{\frac{1/Cs}{RCs + 1}}{Cs} = \frac{1}{RCs + 1}$$

The transfer function is therefore

$$\frac{V}{E} = \frac{1}{10^5 \times 10^{-6} + 1} = \frac{1}{.1s + 1} \tag{1}$$

Assuming zero initial condition, the CSMP program for finding v(t), given that E(t) is a 10 volt step, is shown in Figure 11.5. Note that the last two lines in a CSMP program must be END followed by STOP. The program listed in Figure 11.5 does not show the job control language (JCL) statements that are normally required to run a program. These of course will depend upon the user's computer facility.

Figure 11.6 shows the results of the PRTPLOT V statement in a run of the program of Figure 11.5. Note that the time points and the computed values of V at those points are printed in adjacent columns. The values of V(t) are plotted horizontally, with time t increasing vertically downward.

```
***CONTINUOUS SYSTEM MODELING PROGRAM***

*** VERSION 1.3 ***

DYNAMIC
TIMER FINTIM=.5, OUTDEL=.025
E=10*STEP(0)
V=REALPL(0,.1,E)
PRTPLOT V
END
STOP
```

Figure 11.5 The CSMP program that finds v(t) in Figure 11.4.

The minimum and maximum values of V are printed at the top of the display. We see that V increases from zero towards its final value of 10 V, as we would expect, knowing that the solution is $v(t) = 10(1-e^{-10t})$.

```
                        MINIMUM              V     VERSUS TIME              MAXIMUM
                        .0000E 00                                          9.9326E 00
   TIME          V                I                                            I
  .0000E 00    .0000E 00          +
 2.5000E-02   2.2120E 00          ---------------+
 5.0000E-02   3.9347E 00          ----------------------+
 7.5000E-02   5.2763E 00          ------------------------------+
 1.0000E-01   6.3212E 00          -----------------------------------+
 1.2500E-01   7.1349E 00          ---------------------------------------+
 1.5000E-01   7.7687E 00          -----------------------------------------+
 1.7500E-01   8.2622E 00          --------------------------------------------+
 2.0000E-01   8.6466E 00          ----------------------------------------------+
 2.2500E-01   8.9460E 00          -----------------------------------------------+
 2.5000E-01   9.1791E 00          ------------------------------------------------+
 2.7500E-01   9.3607E 00          -------------------------------------------------+
 3.0000E-01   9.5021E 00          --------------------------------------------------+
 3.2500E-01   9.6122E 00          --------------------------------------------------+
 3.5000E-01   9.6980E 00          ---------------------------------------------------+
 3.7500E-01   9.7648E 00          ---------------------------------------------------+
 4.0000E-01   9.8168E 00          ---------------------------------------------------+
 4.2500E-01   9.8574E 00          ----------------------------------------------------+
 4.5000E-01   9.8889E 00          ----------------------------------------------------+
 4.7500E-01   9.9135E 00          ----------------------------------------------------+
 5.0000E-01   9.9326E 00          ----------------------------------------------------+
```

Figure 11.6 The results of a run of the CSMP program in Figure 11.5.

$$v(t) = 10(1-e^{-10t}) \text{ volts.}$$

To illustrate the use of the PARAMETER statement, let us modify the program of Figure 11.5 so that v(t) is computed first for the initial condition v(0) = + 5 V and then automatically recomputed for the initial condition v(0) = + 20 V. The modified program is shown in Figure 11.7, where the initial condition voltage is designated VO.

****CONTINUOUS SYSTEM MODELING PROGRAM****

*** VERSION 1.3 ***

```
DYNAMIC
PARAMETER VO=(5,20)
TIMER FINTIM=.5, OUTDEL=.025
E=10*STEP(0)
V=REALPL(VO,.1,E)
PRTPLOT V
END
STOP
```

Figure 11.7   The CSMP program of Figure 11.5 modified to illustrate the use of a PARAMETER statement. Computations are performed for v(0) = + 5 V and v(0) = + 20 V.

The two plots resulting from a run of the program in Figure 11.7 are shown in Figure 11.8. We see in the first case, with VO = 5, that the voltage rises from 5 towards its final value 10, while in the second case, with VO = 20, the voltage decays from this initial value towards 10. Both of these results are as expected. Note carefully that the minimum and maximum values printed at the top of each plot do NOT necessarily refer to the minimum and maximum values reached in the plot over which the values are printed. The minimum is the minimum value reached in all the plots (the minimum of the minimums), and the maximum is the maximum value reached in all the plots. In this example, the minimum value, 5, occurs in the first plot and the maximum value, 20, occurs in the second plot.

Consider now the series RLC circuit shown in Figure 11.9. We will write a CSMP program to compute v(t) for different values of R. By the voltage divider rule,

$$\frac{V(s)}{E(s)} = \frac{R}{R + Ls + 1/Cs} = \frac{RCs}{LCs^2 + RCs + 1}$$

$$= \frac{(R/L)s}{s^2 + (R/L)s + 1/LC} \tag{2}$$

Before writing CSMP statements, the programmer should construct a block diagram showing the breakdown of a system or transfer function into component parts, each of which can be represented by a single structure statement. The block diagram showing the breakdown of the transfer function in (2) is shown in Figure 11.10 (a).

	MINIMUM 5.0000E 00	V V0	VERSUS TIME = 5.0000E 00	MAXIMUM 2.0000E 01
TIME	V	I		I
.0000E 00	5.0000E 00	+		
2.5000E-02	6.1060E 00	===+		
5.0000E-02	6.9673E 00	======+		
7.5000E-02	7.6382E 00	========+		
1.0000E-01	8.1606E 00	===========+		
1.2500E-01	8.5675E 00	============+		
1.5000E-01	8.8843E 00	=============+		
1.7500E-01	9.1311E 00	==============+		
2.0000E-01	9.3233E 00	===============+		
2.2500E-01	9.4730E 00	================+		
2.5000E-01	9.5896E 00	================+		
2.7500E-01	9.6804E 00	=================+		
3.0000E-01	9.7511E 00	=================+		
3.2500E-01	9.8061E 00	==================+		
3.5000E-01	9.8490E 00	==================+		
3.7500E-01	9.8824E 00	==================+		
4.0000E-01	9.9084E 00	==================+		
4.2500E-01	9.9287E 00	==================+		
4.5000E-01	9.9445E 00	==================+		
4.7500E-01	9.9567E 00	==================+		
5.0000E-01	9.9663E 00	===================+		

	MINIMUM 5.0000E 00	V V0	VERSUS TIME = 2.0000E 01	MAXIMUM 2.0000E 01
TIME	V	I		I
.0000E 00	2.0000E 01	==+		
2.5000E-02	1.7788E 01	======================================+		
5.0000E-02	1.6065E 01	=================================+		
7.5000E-02	1.4724E 01	=============================+		
1.0000E-01	1.3679E 01	==========================+		
1.2500E-01	1.2865E 01	========================+		
1.5000E-01	1.2231E 01	======================+		
1.7500E-01	1.1738E 01	====================+		
2.0000E-01	1.1353E 01	===================+		
2.2500E-01	1.1054E 01	==================+		
2.5000E-01	1.0821E 01	=================+		
2.7500E-01	1.0639E 01	================+		
3.0000E-01	1.0498E 01	================+		
3.2500E-01	1.0388E 01	===============+		
3.5000E-01	1.0302E 01	===============+		
3.7500E-01	1.0235E 01	==============+		
4.0000E-01	1.0183E 01	==============+		
4.2500E-01	1.0143E 01	==============+		
4.5000E-01	1.0111E 01	==============+		
4.7500E-01	1.0087E 01	==============+		
5.0000E-01	1.0067E 01	=============+		

Figure 11.8   The results of a run of the program in Figure 11.7.
$v(0) = + 5$ V (top) and $v(0) = + 20$ V (bottom).

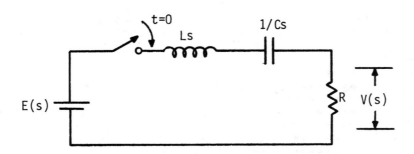

Figure 11.9 A series RLC circuit that is modeled
by CSMP to find v(t).

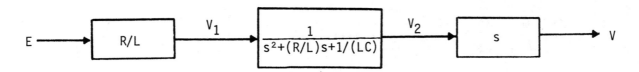

Figure 11.10 (a)   Block diagram showing the transfer functions used in modeling
Figure 11.9.

Note in Figure 11.10 that we assigned input and output variable names to each block.   Suppose $L = 0.4$ H and $C = 0.1$ μF.   Then

$$K = R/.4 = 2.5 R$$

$$R/L = 2.5 R$$

and $$1/(LC) = 2.5 \times 10^7$$

With reference to entry 5 in Table 11.2, we write

$$\frac{1}{s^2 + 2p_1 p_2 s + p_2^2} = \frac{1}{s^2 + 2.5Rs + 2.5 \times 10^7}$$

and therefore,

$$p_2 = \sqrt{2.5 \times 10^7} = 5 \times 10^3$$

$$2p_1 p_2 = 2p_1(5 \times 10^3) = 2.5R$$

so,

$$p_1 = \frac{2.5R}{2(5 \times 10^3)} = 2.5 \times 10^{-4} R$$

Using these values, the block diagram of Figure 11.10 (a) is redrawn as shown in Figure
11.10 (b), in which R is a variable parameter.

$$p_1 = 2.5 \times 10^{-4} R$$

$$p_2 = 5 \times 10^3$$

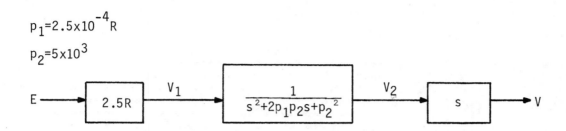

Figure 11.10(b)   Figure 11.10(a) redrawn in CSMP format with R as a parameter.

A CSMP program that computes V for three values of R, R = 3K, 4K, and 5K, is shown in Figure 11.11.

```
****CONTINUOUS SYSTEM MODELING PROGRAM****

*** VERSION 1.3 ***

DYNAMIC
TIMER FINTIM=.002, OUTDEL=.4E-4
PARAMETER R=(3.0E3,4.0E3,5.0E3)
E=10*STEP(0)
K=2.5*R
P1=R*2.5E-4
V1=E*K
V2=CMPXPL(0,0,P1,5.0E3,V1)
V=DERIV(0,V2)
PRTPLOT V
END
STOP
```

Figure 11.11   A CSMP program for modeling the circuit in Figure 11.9.   R is a parameter.

The results of a run of the program in Figure 11.11 are shown in Figure 11.12(a), (b), and (c). Figure 11.12(a) shows V for the case R = 3K. A careful examination of the values reveals that the response is slightly underdamped. Note that V goes negative (undershoots) at t = .96 ms and goes positive again at t = 1.92 ms. This result is confirmed by the fact that the critical value of R is

$$R_C = 2\sqrt{L/C} = 2\sqrt{\frac{0.4}{0.1 \times 10^{-6}}} = 4K$$

and 3K < 4K. Figure 11.12(b) shows the response for R = 4K, i.e., the critically damped case, and Figure 11.12(c) shows the overdamped response corresponding to R = 5K.

```
                          MINIMUM              V     VERSUS TIME           MAXIMUM
                         -1.9067E-01           R     = 3.0000E 03         8.0118E 00
  TIME          V                              I                                I
  .0000E 00      .0000E 00      -+
 4.0000E-05     2.6358E 00      -=-=-=-=-=-=-=-=-=+
 8.0000E-05     4.5771E 00      -=-=-=-=-=-=-=-=-=-=-=-=-=-=+
 1.2000E-04     5.7862E 00      -=-=-=-=-=-=-=-=-=-=-=-=-=-=-=-=-=-=+
 1.6000E-04     6.4408E 00      -=-=-=-=-=-=-=-=-=-=-=-=-=-=-=-=-=-=-=-=-=+
 2.0000E-04     6.7039E 00      -=-=-=-=-=-=-=-=-=-=-=-=-=-=-=-=-=-=-=-=-=-=+
 2.4000E-04     6.6678E 00      -=-=-=-=-=-=-=-=-=-=-=-=-=-=-=-=-=-=-=-=-=-=+
 2.8000E-04     6.4116E 00      -=-=-=-=-=-=-=-=-=-=-=-=-=-=-=-=-=-=-=-=-=+
 3.2000E-04     6.0008E 00      -=-=-=-=-=-=-=-=-=-=-=-=-=-=-=-=-=-=-=-=+
 3.6000E-04     5.4898E 00      -=-=-=-=-=-=-=-=-=-=-=-=-=-=-=-=-=-=+
 4.0000E-04     4.9222E 00      -=-=-=-=-=-=-=-=-=-=-=-=-=-=-=-=+
 4.4000E-04     4.3323E 00      -=-=-=-=-=-=-=-=-=-=-=-=-=-=+
 4.8000E-04     3.7458E 00      -=-=-=-=-=-=-=-=-=-=-=-=+
 5.2000E-04     3.1824E 00      -=-=-=-=-=-=-=-=-=-=+
 5.6000E-04     2.6555E 00      -=-=-=-=-=-=-=-=-=+
 6.0000E-04     2.1737E 00      -=-=-=-=-=-=-=+
 6.4000E-04     1.7418E 00      -=-=-=-=-=-=+
 6.8000E-04     1.3619E 00      -=-=-=-=-=+
 7.2000E-04     1.0336E 00      -=-=-=-=+
 7.6000E-04     7.5471E-01      -=-=-=+
 8.0000E-04     5.2216E-01      -=-=-+
 8.4000E-04     3.3189E-01      -=-=+
 8.8000E-04     1.7946E-01      -=-+
 9.2000E-04     6.0394E-02      -=+
 9.6000E-04    -2.9907E-02       +
 1.0000E-03    -9.5764E-02       +
 1.0400E-03    -1.4124E-01       +
 1.0800E-03    -1.7007E-01       +
 1.1200E-03    -1.8556E-01       +
 1.1600E-03    -1.9067E-01       +
 1.2000E-03    -1.8793E-01       +
 1.2400E-03    -1.7932E-01       +
 1.2800E-03    -1.6687E-01       +
 1.3200E-03    -1.5179E-01       +
 1.3600E-03    -1.3548E-01       +
 1.4000E-03    -1.1870E-01       +
 1.4400E-03    -1.0220E-01       +
 1.4800E-03    -8.6441E-02       +
 1.5200E-03    -7.1793E-02       +
 1.5600E-03    -5.8472E-02       +
 1.6000E-03    -4.6600E-02       +
 1.6400E-03    -3.6179E-02       +
 1.6800E-03    -2.7191E-02       +
 1.7200E-03    -1.9623E-02      -=+
 1.7600E-03    -1.3367E-02      -=+
 1.8000E-03    -8.2397E-03      -=+
 1.8400E-03    -4.1809E-03      -=+
 1.8800E-03    -9.9182E-04      -=+
 1.9200E-03     1.3580E-03      -=+
 1.9600E-03     3.0975E-03      -=+
 2.0000E-03     4.2267E-03      -=+
```

Figure 11.12(a)   The results of a run of the CSMP program in Figure 11.11, showing an underdamped response when R=3K.

```
                              MINIMUM              V      VERSUS TIME         MAXIMUM
                             =1.9067E=01           R     = 4.0000E 03        8.0118E 00
     TIME             V        I                                                 I
    .0000E 00       .0000E 00  =+
   4.0000E=05      1.7524E 00  ==========+
   8.0000E=05      5.7282E 00  ==============================+
   1.2000E=04      6.8510E 00  ===================================+
   1.6000E=04      7.3785E 00  ========================================+
   2.0000E=04      7.4897E 00  ========================================+
   2.4000E=04      7.3181E 00  =======================================+
   2.8000E=04      6.9627E 00  =====================================+
   3.2000E=04      6.4956E 00  ==================================+
   3.6000E=04      5.9690E 00  ===============================+
   4.0000E=04      5.4199E 00  ============================+
   4.4000E=04      4.8739E 00  =========================+
   4.8000E=04      4.3476E 00  ======================+
   5.2000E=04      3.8519E 00  ===================+
   5.6000E=04      3.3932E 00  =================+
   6.0000E=04      2.9741E 00  ===============+
   6.4000E=04      2.5955E 00  =============+
   6.8000E=04      2.2565E 00  ============+
   7.2000E=04      1.9551E 00  ==========+
   7.6000E=04      1.6887E 00  =========+
   8.0000E=04      1.4547E 00  ========+
   8.4000E=04      1.2501E 00  =======+
   8.8000E=04      1.0718E 00  ======+
   9.2000E=04      9.1711E=01  ======+
   9.6000E=04      7.8331E=01  =====+
   1.0000E=03      6.6783E=01  ====+
   1.0400E=03      5.6848E=01  ====+
   1.0800E=03      4.8326E=01  ===+
   1.1200E=03      4.1016E=01  ===+
   1.1600E=03      3.4760E=01  ==+
   1.2000E=03      2.9445E=01  ==+
   1.2400E=03      2.4907E=01  ==+
   1.2800E=03      2.1031E=01  ==+
   1.3200E=03      1.7773E=01  ==+
   1.3600E=03      1.4984E=01  ==+
   1.4000E=03      1.2616E=01  =+
   1.4400E=03      1.0631E=01  =+
   1.4800E=03      8.9447E=02  =+
   1.5200E=03      7.5104E=02  =+
   1.5600E=03      6.3126E=02  =+
   1.6000E=03      5.2933E=02  =+
   1.6400E=03      4.4601E=02  =+
   1.6800E=03      3.7231E=02  =+
   1.7200E=03      3.1342E=02  =+
   1.7600E=03      2.6230E=02  =+
   1.8000E=03      2.1912E=02  =+
   1.8400E=03      1.8295E=02  =+
   1.8800E=03      1.5244E=02  =+
   1.9200E=03      1.2909E=02  =+
   1.9600E=03      1.0712E=02  =+
   2.0000E=03      8.9874E=03  =+
```

Figure 11.12(b)   The results of a run of the CSMP program in Figure 11.11, showing a critically damped response when R=4K.

```
                         MINIMUM          V      VERSUS TIME         MAXIMUM
                        -1.9067E-01       R     = 5.0000E 03        8.0118E 00
    TIME            V              I                                    I
    .0000E 00       .0000E 00    -+
   4.0000E-05      2.1239E 00    -=-=-=-=-=-=-=-=+
   8.0000E-05      6.6528E 00    -=-=-=-=-=-=-=-=-=-=-=-=-=-=-=-=-=-=-=-=+
   1.2000E-04      7.6481E 00    -=-=-=-=-=-=-=-=-=-=-=-=-=-=-=-=-=-=-=-=-=-=-=+
   1.6000E-04      8.0118E 00    -=-=-=-=-=-=-=-=-=-=-=-=-=-=-=-=-=-=-=-=-=-=-=-=+
   2.0000E-04      7.9811E 00    -=-=-=-=-=-=-=-=-=-=-=-=-=-=-=-=-=-=-=-=-=-=-=+
   2.4000E-04      7.7121E 00    -=-=-=-=-=-=-=-=-=-=-=-=-=-=-=-=-=-=-=-=-=+
   2.8000E-04      7.3070E 00    -=-=-=-=-=-=-=-=-=-=-=-=-=-=-=-=-=-=-=-=+
   3.2000E-04      6.8320E 00    -=-=-=-=-=-=-=-=-=-=-=-=-=-=-=-=-=-=+
   3.6000E-04      6.3295E 00    -=-=-=-=-=-=-=-=-=-=-=-=-=-=-=-=+
   4.0000E-04      5.8262E 00    -=-=-=-=-=-=-=-=-=-=-=-=-=-=+
   4.4000E-04      5.3383E 00    -=-=-=-=-=-=-=-=-=-=-=-=+
   4.8000E-04      4.8746E 00    -=-=-=-=-=-=-=-=-=-=-+
   5.2000E-04      4.4406E 00    -=-=-=-=-=-=-=-=-=-+
   5.6000E-04      4.0381E 00    -=-=-=-=-=-=-=-=-+
   6.0000E-04      3.6671E 00    -=-=-=-=-=-=-=-+
   6.4000E-04      3.3271E 00    -=-=-=-=-=-=-+
   6.8000E-04      3.0165E 00    -=-=-=-=-=-=+
   7.2000E-04      2.7336E 00    -=-=-=-=-=-+
   7.6000E-04      2.4760E 00    -=-=-=-=-+
   8.0000E-04      2.2422E 00    -=-=-=-=+
   8.4000E-04      2.0300E 00    -=-=-=-+
   8.8000E-04      1.8376E 00    -=-=-=+
   9.2000E-04      1.6634E 00    -=-=-=+
   9.6000E-04      1.5055E 00    -=-=-+
   1.0000E-03      1.3624E 00    -=-=+
   1.0400E-03      1.2329E 00    -=-=+
   1.0800E-03      1.1157E 00    -=-+
   1.1200E-03      1.0096E 00    -=-+
   1.1600E-03      9.1347E-01    -=-+
   1.2000E-03      8.2657E-01    -=-+
   1.2400E-03      7.4811E-01    -=-+
   1.2800E-03      6.7683E-01    -=-+
   1.3200E-03      6.1243E-01    -=-+
   1.3600E-03      5.5420E-01    -=-+
   1.4000E-03      5.0157E-01    -=-+
   1.4400E-03      4.5363E-01    -=+
   1.4800E-03      4.1057E-01    -=+
   1.5200E-03      3.7143E-01    -=+
   1.5600E-03      3.3604E-01    -=+
   1.6000E-03      3.0417E-01    -=+
   1.6400E-03      2.7522E-01    -+
   1.6800E-03      2.4898E-01    -+
   1.7200E-03      2.2539E-01    -+
   1.7600E-03      2.0375E-01    -+
   1.8000E-03      1.8439E-01    -+
   1.8400E-03      1.6699E-01    -+
   1.8800E-03      1.5105E-01    -+
   1.9200E-03      1.3666E-01    -+
   1.9600E-03      1.2358E-01    -+
   2.0000E-03      1.1189E-01    -+
```

Figure 11.12(c) The results of a run of the CSMP program in Figure 11.11, showing an overdamped response when R=5K.

We should note that CSMP plots are automatically scaled for a range of values between the smallest minimum and largest maximum computed in a given run. Therefore, when a PARA-METER statement is used, all plots resulting from different values of the parameter will be scaled according to the largest range of values generated. Note that the "maximum" printed at the top of each of the three plots in Figures 11.12(a), (b), and (c) is 8.0118, but only the plot corresponding to R = 5K actually reaches that maximum. If the parameter values used in a particular problem generate some results that have a much smaller range than others, then those with the smaller range will be plotted with very poor resolution. Better resolution can be obtained by running the program a second time, using only the parameter value(s) that generate the smaller range(s) of values.

Figures 11.13(a) and (b) show the results of another run of the CSMP program, with the parameter statement changed to

PARAMETER R = (1.0E3,1.0E4)

corresponding to R = 1K and R = 10K. In this case, we see that the maximum voltage is 9.2747 V and that this maximum is reached when R = 10K. Note also that the response when R = 1K is noticeably underdamped, i.e., the voltage exhibits considerable oscillation, due to the decrease in resistance.

182

```
                          MINIMUM                V      VERSUS TIME              MAXIMUM
                         -1.6032E 00             R    = 1.0000E 03             9.2747E 00
      TIME          V                 I                                             I
     .0000E 00         .0000E 00      =------+
    4.0000E-05       9.5429E-01       =-----------+
    8.0000E-05       1.7996E 00       =--------------+
    1.2000E-04       2.4889E 00       =-----------------+
    1.6000E-04       3.0100E 00       =--------------------+
    2.0000E-04       3.3673E 00       =----------------------+
    2.4000E-04       3.5629E 00       =-----------------------+
    2.8000E-04       3.6048E 00       =-----------------------+
    3.2000E-04       3.5058E 00       =-----------------------+
    3.6000E-04       3.2833E 00       =----------------------+
    4.0000E-04       2.9574E 00       =--------------------+
    4.4000E-04       2.5503E 00       =------------------+
    4.8000E-04       2.0852E 00       =---------------+
    5.2000E-04       1.5852E 00       =------------+
    5.6000E-04       1.0728E 00       =---------+
    6.0000E-04       5.6830E-01       =------+
    6.4000E-04       9.0271E-02       =----+
    6.8000E-04      -3.4563E-01       =---+
    7.2000E-04      -7.2699E-01       =--+
    7.6000E-04      -1.0444E 00       =-+
    8.0000E-04      -1.2921E 00       =+
    8.4000E-04      -1.4671E 00        +
    8.8000E-04      -1.5699E 00        +
    9.2000E-04      -1.6032E 00        +
    9.6000E-04      -1.5727E 00        +
    1.0000E-03      -1.4853E 00        +
    1.0400E-03      -1.3499E 00       =+
    1.0800E-03      -1.1762E 00       =+
    1.1200E-03      -9.7435E-01       =-+
    1.1600E-03      -7.5476E-01       =--+
    1.2000E-03      -5.2746E-01       =---+
    1.2400E-03      -3.0176E-01       =----+
    1.2800E-03      -8.6097E-02       =-----+
    1.3200E-03       1.1228E-01       =------+
    1.3600E-03       2.8755E-01       =-------+
    1.4000E-03       4.3523E-01       =--------+
    1.4400E-03       5.5234E-01       =--------+
    1.4800E-03       6.3738E-01       =---------+
    1.5200E-03       6.9010E-01       =---------+
    1.5600E-03       7.1167E-01       =---------+
    1.6000E-03       7.0416E-01       =---------+
    1.6400E-03       6.7064E-01       =---------+
    1.6800E-03       6.1486E-01       =---------+
    1.7200E-03       5.4109E-01       =--------+
    1.7600E-03       4.5383E-01       =-------+
    1.8000E-03       3.5761E-01       =-------+
    1.8400E-03       2.5702E-01       =------+
    1.8800E-03       1.5623E-01       =------+
    1.9200E-03       5.9087E-02       =------+
    1.9600E-03      -3.1019E-02       =------+
    2.0000E-03      -1.1140E-01       =------+
```

Figure 11.13(a) The results of a run of the CSMP program in Figure 11.11, showing an
underdamped response when R=1K. Compare with 11.12(a).

```
                        MINIMUM              V     VERSUS TIME        MAXIMUM
                       =1.6032E 00           R    = 1.0000E 04       9.2747E 00
    TIME           V                         I                                 I
   .0000E 00      .0000E 00      -------+
  4.0000E-05     6.7444E 00      ---------------------------------------+
  8.0000E-05     8.6090E 00      --------------------------------------------------+
  1.2000E-04     9.2747E 00      ------------------------------------------------------+
  1.6000E-04     9.1494E 00      -----------------------------------------------------+
  2.0000E-04     8.8203E 00      --------------------------------------------------+
  2.4000E-04     8.4770E 00      ------------------------------------------------+
  2.8000E-04     8.1371E 00      ----------------------------------------------+
  3.2000E-04     7.8069E 00      --------------------------------------------+
  3.6000E-04     7.4886E 00      ------------------------------------------+
  4.0000E-04     7.1828E 00      ----------------------------------------+
  4.4000E-04     6.8894E 00      --------------------------------------+
  4.8000E-04     6.6078E 00      -------------------------------------+
  5.2000E-04     6.3376E 00      -----------------------------------+
  5.6000E-04     6.0785E 00      ---------------------------------+
  6.0000E-04     5.8299E 00      --------------------------------+
  6.4000E-04     5.5916E 00      -------------------------------+
  6.8000E-04     5.3629E 00      ------------------------------+
  7.2000E-04     5.1438E 00      -----------------------------+
  7.6000E-04     4.9335E 00      ----------------------------+
  8.0000E-04     4.7318E 00      ---------------------------+
  8.4000E-04     4.5384E 00      --------------------------+
  8.8000E-04     4.3530E 00      -------------------------+
  9.2000E-04     4.1747E 00      ------------------------+
  9.6000E-04     4.0043E 00      -----------------------+
  1.0000E-03     3.8405E 00      ----------------------+
  1.0400E-03     3.6836E 00      ---------------------+
  1.0800E-03     3.5330E 00      --------------------+
  1.1200E-03     3.3887E 00      -------------------+
  1.1600E-03     3.2501E 00      ------------------+
  1.2000E-03     3.1170E 00      -----------------+
  1.2400E-03     2.9898E 00      ----------------+
  1.2800E-03     2.8673E 00      ---------------+
  1.3200E-03     2.7502E 00      ---------------+
  1.3600E-03     2.6376E 00      --------------+
  1.4000E-03     2.5301E 00      -------------+
  1.4400E-03     2.4263E 00      ------------+
  1.4800E-03     2.3272E 00      ------------+
  1.5200E-03     2.2320E 00      -----------+
  1.5600E-03     2.1406E 00      ----------+
  1.6000E-03     2.0531E 00      ---------+
  1.6400E-03     1.9693E 00      ---------+
  1.6800E-03     1.8887E 00      --------+
  1.7200E-03     1.8115E 00      -------+
  1.7600E-03     1.7374E 00      -------+
  1.8000E-03     1.6665E 00      ------+
  1.8400E-03     1.5985E 00      -----+
  1.8800E-03     1.5329E 00      -----+
  1.9200E-03     1.4704E 00      ----+
  1.9600E-03     1.4101E 00      ---+
  2.0000E-03     1.3524E 00      ---+
```

Figure 11.13(b)   The results of a run of the CSMP program in Figure 11.11, showing an overdamped response when R=10K.   Compare with 11.12(c).

As a final example, consider the <u>active filter</u> circuit shown in Figure 11.14.

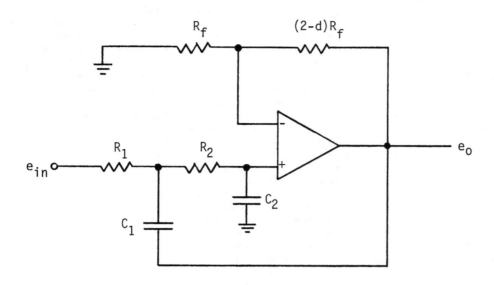

Figure 11.14   An active filter circuit that is modeled
by CSMP.

The transfer function for this second-order, low-pass filter can be shown to be

$$\frac{E_0}{E_{in}} = \frac{K/R_1 C_1 R_2 C_2}{s^2 + \left[\frac{1}{R_2 C_1} + \frac{1}{R_1 C_1} + (1-K)\frac{1}{R_2 C_2}\right] s + \frac{1}{R_1 C_1 R_2 C_2}} \tag{3}$$

(See Lancaster, <u>Active Filter Cookbook</u>, Howard W. Sams, Inc., Bobbs-Merrill, Inc., 1975, pps 121-125.)

If $R_1 = R_2 = R$ and $C_1 = C_2 = C$, then $K = 3-d$. For the unity gain case, $K = 1$, so $d = 2$, $1-K = 0$, and (3) reduces to

$$\frac{E_0}{E_{in}} = \frac{1/(RC)^2}{s^2 + (2/RC)s + (1/RC)^2}$$

$$= \frac{1/(RC)^2}{(s + 1/RC)^2} \tag{4}$$

A unity-gain low-pass filter with cutoff frequency 1 kHz can be realized by setting $R_1 = R_2 = R = 10K$, $C_1 = C_2 = C = .016$ μF, $R_f = 39K$, and $(2-d)R_f = 0$ (a short-circuit, since $d = 2$). With these values, (4) becomes

$$\frac{E_0}{E_{in}} = \frac{3.9063 \times 10^7}{(s + 6.25 \times 10^3)^2}$$

$$= \left(\frac{6.25 \times 10^3}{s + 6.25 \times 10^3}\right) \left(\frac{6.25 \times 10^3}{s + 6.25 \times 10^3}\right) \tag{5}$$

For a CSMP simulation we rewrite (5) in the equivalent form

$$\frac{E_0}{E_{in}} = \left(\frac{6.25 \times 10^3}{6.25 \times 10^3(.16 \times 10^{-3}s + 1)}\right) \left(\frac{6.25 \times 10^3}{6.25 \times 10^3(.16 \times 10^{-3}s + 1)}\right)$$

$$= \left(\frac{1}{.16 \times 10^{-3}s + 1}\right) \left(\frac{1}{.16 \times 10^{-3}s + 1}\right) \tag{6}$$

Each of the factors in (6) can now be represented by a CSMP structure statement using entry 3 in Table 11.1, with $p = .16 \times 10^{-3}$. A block diagram breakdown of the transfer function is shown in Figure 11.15.

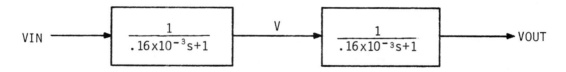

Figure 11.15 Block diagram representation for the transfer function of the active filter.

Figure 11.16 shows a CSMP program that computes the output of the filter at its cutoff frequency, 1 kHz, at one octave below cutoff, 500 Hz, and at one octave above cutoff, 2 kHz. Note that the input to the filter is a one-volt peak sine wave whose frequency is $W = 2\pi F$, where F is the variable parameter.

```
****CONTINUOUS SYSTEM MODELING PROGRAM****

*** VERSION 1.3 ***

DYNAMIC
TIMER FINTIM=2.5E-3, OUTDEL=.05E-3
PARAMETER F=(500,1000,2000)
W=6.2831853*F
VIN=SINE(0,W,0)
V=REALPL(0,.16E-3,VIN)
VOUT=REALPL(0,.16E-3,V)
PRTPLOT VOUT
END
STOP
```

Figure 11.16 A CSMP program that models the active filter at three different frequencies.

Figures 11.17(a), (b), and (c) show the results of a run of the program of Figure 11.16. Note carefully the location of the zero level in each plot. Since the same scaling is used for all three plots, there appears at first glance to be a DC offset level in the lower amplitude sine waves. This, of course, is not the case, and only appears that way because the zero level is located "higher" (displaced further to the right) to accommodate the total voltage swing of the large amplitude sine wave.

The presence of a transient component in each response is evident. Note the non-sinusoidal curvature of each output immediately after t = 0; note also that the peaks do not reach the same values in the time interval (2.5 ms) shown. Nevertheless, the low-pass filter action is apparent in the decreased peak-to-peak amplitudes of the sine waves with increasing frequency.

```
                        MINIMUM              VOUT   VERSUS TIME              MAXIMUM
                       -7.9819E-01           F    = 5.0000E 02            8.1609E-01
  TIME        VOUT         I                                                   I
 .0000E 00    .0000E 00   ----------------------------+
5.0000E-05   2.1892E-03   ----------------------------+
1.0000E-04   1.5027E-02   -----------------------------+
1.5000E-04   4.3587E-02   ------------------------------+
2.0000E-04   8.8891E-02   -------------------------------+
2.5000E-04   1.4946E-01   ---------------------------------+
3.0000E-04   2.2236E-01   -----------------------------------+
3.5000E-04   3.0386E-01   -------------------------------------+
4.0000E-04   3.8991E-01   ---------------------------------------+
4.5000E-04   4.7643E-01   -----------------------------------------+
5.0000E-04   5.5951E-01   -------------------------------------------+
5.5000E-04   6.3556E-01   ---------------------------------------------+
6.0000E-04   7.0139E-01   -----------------------------------------------+
6.5000E-04   7.5429E-01   ------------------------------------------------+
7.0000E-04   7.9205E-01   -------------------------------------------------+
7.5000E-04   8.1302E-01   --------------------------------------------------+
8.0000E-04   8.1609E-01   --------------------------------------------------+
8.5000E-04   8.0073E-01   -------------------------------------------------+
9.0000E-04   7.6694E-01   ------------------------------------------------+
9.5000E-04   7.1526E-01   ----------------------------------------------+
1.0000E-03   6.4675E-01   --------------------------------------------+
1.0500E-03   5.6290E-01   -------------------------------------------+
1.1000E-03   4.6565E-01   ----------------------------------------+
1.1500E-03   3.5728E-01   -------------------------------------+
1.2000E-03   2.4039E-01   -----------------------------------+
1.2500E-03   1.1778E-01   -------------------------------+
1.3000E-03  -7.5770E-03   ---------------------------+
1.3500E-03  -1.3263E-01   -----------------------+
1.4000E-03  -2.5432E-01   ------------------+
1.4500E-03  -3.6968E-01   --------------+
1.5000E-03  -4.7589E-01   ----------+
1.5500E-03  -5.7034E-01   -------+
1.6000E-03  -6.5072E-01   ----+
1.6500E-03  -7.1505E-01   --+
1.7000E-03  -7.6176E-01   -+
1.7500E-03  -7.8970E-01   +
1.8000E-03  -7.9819E-01   +
1.8500E-03  -7.8701E-01   +
1.9000E-03  -7.5645E-01   -+
1.9500E-03  -7.0726E-01   --+
2.0000E-03  -6.4065E-01   ----+
2.0500E-03  -5.5826E-01   -------+
2.1000E-03  -4.6213E-01   ----------+
2.1500E-03  -3.5461E-01   --------------+
2.2000E-03  -2.3836E-01   ------------------+
2.2500E-03  -1.1625E-01   -----------------------+
2.3000E-03   8.7346E-03   ---------------------------+
2.3500E-03   1.3350E-01   -------------------------------+
2.4000E-03   2.5498E-01   -----------------------------------+
2.4500E-03   3.7018E-01   -------------------------------------+
2.5000E-03   4.7627E-01   -----------------------------------------+
```

Figure 11.17(a) Response of the active filter at 500 Hz.

```
                         MINIMUM            VOUT   VERSUS TIME              MAXIMUM
                        -7.9819E-01         F    = 1.0000E 03             8.1609E-01
   TIME         VOUT                         I                                 I
 .0000E 00      .0000E 00    +------------------------+
5.0000E-05     4.3582E-03    +------------------------+
1.0000E-04     2.9564E-02    +-------------------------+
1.5000E-04     8.3860E-02    +----------------------------+
2.0000E-04     1.6536E-01    +-------------------------------+
2.5000E-04     2.6537E-01    +-----------------------------------+
3.0000E-04     3.7122E-01    +---------------------------------------+
3.5000E-04     4.6872E-01    +------------------------------------------+
4.0000E-04     5.4425E-01    +---------------------------------------------+
4.5000E-04     5.8651E-01    +-----------------------------------------------+
5.0000E-04     5.8785E-01    +-----------------------------------------------+
5.5000E-04     5.4506E-01    +---------------------------------------------+
6.0000E-04     4.5970E-01    +------------------------------------------+
6.5000E-04     3.3797E-01    +--------------------------------------+
7.0000E-04     1.8999E-01    +---------------------------------+
7.5000E-04     2.8798E-02    +-------------------------+
8.0000E-04    -1.3099E-01    +------------------+
8.5000E-04    -2.7466E-01    +-------------+
9.0000E-04    -3.8888E-01    +---------+
9.5000E-04    -4.6305E-01    +------+
1.0000E-03    -4.9036E-01    +-----+
1.0500E-03    -4.6849E-01    +------+
1.1000E-03    -3.9985E-01    +---------+
1.1500E-03    -2.9137E-01    +-------------+
1.2000E-03    -1.5384E-01    +-----------------+
1.2500E-03    -8.5133E-04    +-----------------------+
1.3000E-03     1.5254E-01    +-------------------------------+
1.3500E-03     2.9123E-01    +-----------------------------------+
1.4000E-03     4.0159E-01    +----------------------------------------+
1.4500E-03     4.7278E-01    +------------------------------------------+
1.5000E-03     4.9779E-01    +-------------------------------------------+
1.5500E-03     4.7415E-01    +------------------------------------------+
1.6000E-03     4.0416E-01    +----------------------------------------+
1.6500E-03     2.9465E-01    +-----------------------------------+
1.7000E-03     1.5634E-01    +-------------------------------+
1.7500E-03     2.7401E-03    +------------------------+
1.8000E-03    -1.5111E-01    +-----------------+
1.8500E-03    -2.9015E-01    +-------------+
1.9000E-03    -4.0077E-01    +---------+
1.9500E-03    -4.7216E-01    +------+
2.0000E-03    -4.9733E-01    +-----+
2.0500E-03    -4.7380E-01    +------+
2.1000E-03    -4.0390E-01    +---------+
2.1500E-03    -2.9446E-01    +-------------+
2.2000E-03    -1.5619E-01    +-----------------+
2.2500E-03    -2.6283E-03    +-----------------------+
2.3000E-03     1.5119E-01    +-------------------------------+
2.3500E-03     2.9021E-01    +-----------------------------------+
2.4000E-03     4.0082E-01    +----------------------------------------+
2.4500E-03     4.7220E-01    +------------------------------------------+
2.5000E-03     4.9735E-01    +-------------------------------------------+
```

Figure 11.17 (b)   Response of the active filter at 1 kHz.

```
                              MINIMUM              VOUT   VERSUS TIME            MAXIMUM
                             -7.9819E-01           F    = 2.0000E 03           8.1609E-01
   TIME          VOUT         I                                                     I
  .0000E 00      .0000E 00    =====================-----------=+
 5.0000E-05     8.5834E-03    ===========================----=+
 1.0000E-04     5.5366E-02    =============================---==+
 1.5000E-04     1.4339E-01    =================================+
 2.0000E-04     2.4572E-01    ========================================+
 2.5000E-04     3.2189E-01    ==========================================+
 3.0000E-04     3.3719E-01    ===========================================+
 3.5000E-04     2.7828E-01    =========================================+
 4.0000E-04     1.5973E-01    =================================+
 4.5000E-04     1.9226E-02    ==========================+
 5.0000E-04    -9.6462E-02    ================+
 5.5000E-04    -1.4914E-01    ==============+
 6.0000E-04    -1.2379E-01    ================+
 6.5000E-04    -3.4338E-02    =====================+
 7.0000E-04     8.1567E-02    ============================+
 7.5000E-04     1.7683E-01    ===============================+
 8.0000E-04     2.1278E-01    =====================================+
 8.5000E-04     1.7390E-01    ===============================+
 9.0000E-04     7.3589E-02    ===========================+
 9.5000E-04    -5.0952E-02    ===================+
 1.0000E-03    -1.5304E-01    ===============+
 1.0500E-03    -1.9437E-01    ============+
 1.1000E-03    -1.5968E-01    ==============+
 1.1500E-03    -6.2644E-02    ===================+
 1.2000E-03     5.9358E-02    ==========================+
 1.2500E-03     1.5948E-01    ==============================+
 1.3000E-03     1.9929E-01    ==================================+
 1.3500E-03     1.6344E-01    ==============================+
 1.4000E-03     6.5509E-02    ==========================+
 1.4500E-03    -5.7179E-02    ==================+
 1.5000E-03    -1.5782E-01    ==============+
 1.5500E-03    -1.9804E-01    ============+
 1.6000E-03    -1.6249E-01    ==============+
 1.6500E-03    -6.4791E-02    ==================+
 1.7000E-03     5.7721E-02    ==========================+
 1.7500E-03     1.5823E-01    ==============================+
 1.8000E-03     1.9834E-01    =================================+
 1.8500E-03     1.6272E-01    ==============================+
 1.9000E-03     6.4967E-02    ==========================+
 1.9500E-03    -5.7589E-02    ==================+
 2.0000E-03    -1.5813E-01    ==============+
 2.0500E-03    -1.9827E-01    ============+
 2.1000E-03    -1.6267E-01    =============+
 2.1500E-03    -6.4924E-02    ==================+
 2.2000E-03     5.7620E-02    ==========================+
 2.2500E-03     1.5816E-01    ==============================+
 2.3000E-03     1.9829E-01    =================================+
 2.3500E-03     1.6268E-01    ==============================+
 2.4000E-03     6.4935E-02    ==========================+
 2.4500E-03    -5.7612E-02    ==================+
 2.5000E-03    -1.5815E-01    ==============+
```

Figure 11.17(c) Response of the active filter at 2 kHz.

EXERCISES

1. Write a CSMP program that can be used to determine the voltage v(t) across the resistor in Figure 11.18 after the switch is closed at t = 0. Choose values for FINTIM and OUTDEL so that at least 10 values of v(t) are computed between v(t) = 20 V and v(t) = 2 V. Run your program and obtain a CSMP plot of v(t).

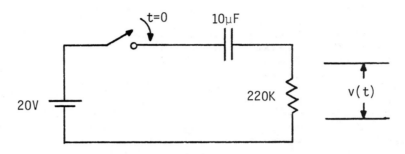

Figure 11.18

2. Repeat step 1 when the 20 V DC source is replaced by a square wave that alternates between 0 V and + 20 V at a frequency of 0.1 Hz. Run your program and obtain a plot of v(t) for at least two complete cycles of the square wave.

3. Repeat step 2 using R as a variable parameter. Write your program so that 3 plots of v(t) are obtained from one run, corresponding to values of R equal to 100 K, 220 K, and 820 K. Compare and explain your results for each case.

4. Write a CSMP program that can be used to find the voltage (t) across the tank circuit in Figure 11.19 after the switch is closed at t = 0. Write your program using R as a variable parameter and run it to obtain plots of v(t) corresponding to R = 350 Ω, 500 Ω, and 750 Ω. Compare and explain your results for each case.

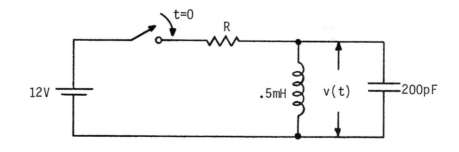

Figure 11.19

5. Write a CSMP program that can be used to generate a triangular wave that rises to 10 V in 0.5 seconds and then falls to zero volts in the next 0.5 seconds. Run your program and obtain a plot of the wave showing at least two complete cycles. (Hint: how can a triangular wave be obtained from a square wave?)

6. Write a CSMP program that can be used to find and plot values of the inverse transform of

$$F(s) = \frac{500(s + 10)}{s(s + 50)(s^2 + 40s + 100)}$$

(Hint: apply a unit step to a system having transfer function $sF(s)$.)

7. The transfer function of the operational amplifier circuit shown in Figure 11.20 is $E_0/E_{in} = -Z_f/Z_1$.

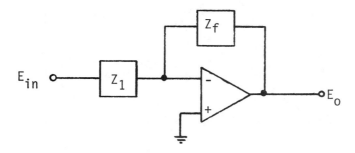

Figure 11.20

Write a CSMP program that can be used to find and plot values of the output $e_0(t)$ of the circuit shown in Figure 11.21 when the input is a 10 V step.

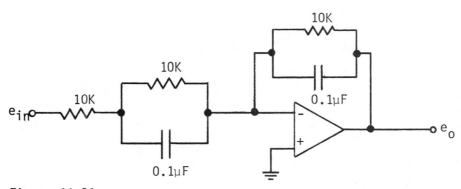

Figure 11.21

12 Modeling Control Systems and Non-linearities with CSMP

OBJECTIVES

1. To learn how control systems can be modeled using CSMP.

2. To investigate the effect of changes in gain on the performance of a position control system.

3. To learn how deadspace (backlash) can be introduced in a CSMP model, and how it affects control system performance.

4. To learn how limiting can be used in a model, including rectification.

5. To model an AM modulator/demodulator system and demonstrate the effect of multiplication of variables in a CSMP model.

DISCUSSION

CSMP is especially well-suited for control systems simulation. In particular, it relieves us of the necessity for reducing the original configuration of blocks representing individual components to a single equivalent transfer function. As we have seen, it is only necessary to define the transfer function and name the input and output of each component in the system. Signal summing junctions are represented in a similar way, except it is only necessary to write the output of such a junction as the sum (or difference) of its inputs.

Consider the simple position control system shown in Figure 12.1.

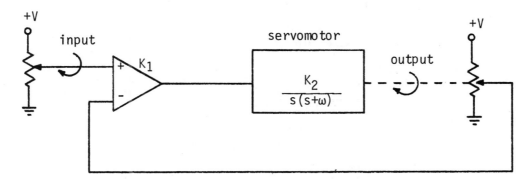

Figure 12.1 A position control system for which a CSMP model can be constructed.

The block diagram corresponding to Figure 12.1 is shown in Figure 12.2.

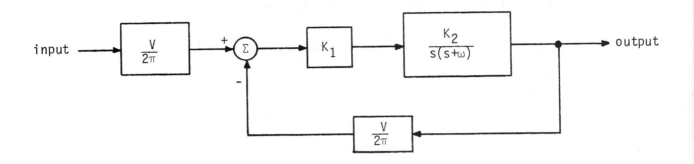

Figure 12.2 Block diagram of the control system shown in Figure 12.1

Letting $T = 1/\omega$, and recognizing that

$$\frac{1}{s + \omega} = \frac{1}{\omega\left(\frac{1}{\omega}s + 1\right)} = T\left(\frac{1}{Ts + 1}\right)$$

we redraw the block diagram of 12.2 in a form suitable for CSMP modeling, as shown in Figure 12.3. In this diagram, the constant gain terms K1, K2, and T are shown in separate blocks to make it convenient to perform simulation runs using different values of any one of these parameters. It would, of course, be permissible to combine these factors together in a single block having gain $K_1 K_2 T$.

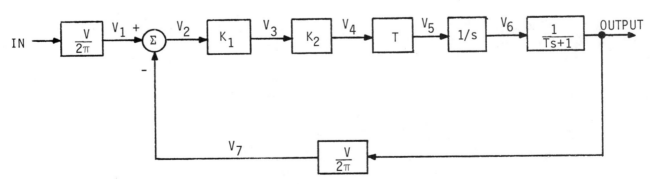

Figure 12.3 A block diagram for the CSMP model of the control system.

As a specific example, suppose $V = 10$ volts, $\omega = 10$ (so $T = .1$), and $K_2 = .8$. Figure 12.4 shows a CSMP program that will perform a simulation run for the case $K_1 = 4$, when the input is a unit step.

```
***CONTINUOUS SYSTEM MODELING PROGRAM***

*** VERSION 1.3 ***

DYNAMIC
TIMER FINTIM=1.0, OUTDEL=.02
CONSTANT TWOPI=6.2831852, K1=4
IN=STEP(0.0)
V1=(10/TWOPI)*IN
V2=V1-V7
V3=K1*V2
V4=8*V3
V5=.1*V4
V6=INTGRL(0.0,V5)
OUTPUT=REALPL(0.0,.1,V6)
V7=(10/TWOPI)*OUTPUT
PRTPLOT OUTPUT
END
STOP
```

Figure 12.4 CSMP program based on the model shown in Figure 12.3.

Figure 12.5(a) shows the results of a run of the model shown in Figure 12.4. We see that the control system is slightly underdamped, a small overshoot occurring at t = .48 seconds. The response then approaches its steady-state value of 1.0, reaching 1.0036 at t = 1 second.

Figures 12.5(b) and (c) show the results of runs of the model of Figure 12.4 when K_1 is increased to 8 and 40, respectively. We see that the system becomes increasingly under-damped as the gain K_1 is increased. A significant amount of oscillation about the steady-state value of 1.0 is apparent for the case K_1 = 40.

A typical non-linearity encountered in control systems is the <u>deadspace.</u> A deadspace is a region in the transfer function of a component over which an input produces no change in output. In other words, the input to such a component must reach a certain level before any change in output occurs. A good example is the backlash present in gear trains. CSMP has a built-in deadspace function generator, whose transfer characteristic and defining equations are shown in Figure 12.6.

Figure 12.7 shows the control system model of Figure 12.4 modified to include a dead-space for V2 between 0 and .5 (p_1 = 0 and p_2 = .5). This is represented by the structure statement:

VA = DEADSP(0.0,.5,V2)

Figure 12.8 shows the results of a run of the model of Figure 12.7 for the case K_1 = 8. Compare this result with that of Figure 12.5(b), we see that the deadspace has slowed the control system response considerably. The system is no longer underdamped, and the output, for example, is now only 0.59 at t = .2 sec compared to 0.86 at t = .2 sec in Figure 12.5(b).

```
                              MINIMUM           OUTPUT VERSUS TIME              MAXIMUM
                              .0000E 00                                        1.0457E 00
   TIME            OUTPUT         I                                                I
  .0000E 00       .0000E 00      +
 2.0000E-02      9.5235E-03      +
 4.0000E-02      3.5578E-02      =+
 6.0000E-02      7.4686E-02      ===+
 8.0000E-02      1.2376E-01      =====+
 1.0000E-01      1.8009E-01      ========+
 1.2000E-01      2.4132E-01      ==========+
 1.4000E-01      3.0544E-01      =============+
 1.6000E-01      3.7074E-01      ================+
 1.8000E-01      4.3580E-01      ===================+
 2.0000E-01      4.9946E-01      ======================+
 2.2000E-01      5.6082E-01      =========================+
 2.4000E-01      6.1914E-01      ===========================+
 2.6000E-01      6.7392E-01      ==============================+
 2.8000E-01      7.2477E-01      ================================+
 3.0000E-01      7.7148E-01      ==================================+
 3.2000E-01      8.1394E-01      ====================================+
 3.4000E-01      8.5212E-01      ======================================+
 3.6000E-01      8.8612E-01      ========================================+
 3.8000E-01      9.1605E-01      =========================================+
 4.0000E-01      9.4210E-01      ===========================================+
 4.2000E-01      9.6449E-01      ============================================+
 4.4000E-01      9.8348E-01      =============================================+
 4.6000E-01      9.9934E-01      ==============================================+
 4.8000E-01      1.0123E 00      ===============================================+
 5.0000E-01      1.0227E 00      ===============================================+
 5.2000E-01      1.0308E 00      ================================================+
 5.4000E-01      1.0369E 00      ================================================+
 5.6000E-01      1.0412E 00      =================================================+
 5.8000E-01      1.0439E 00      =================================================+
 6.0000E-01      1.0454E 00      =================================================+
 6.2000E-01      1.0457E 00      ==================================================+
 6.4000E-01      1.0452E 00      =================================================+
 6.6000E-01      1.0439E 00      =================================================+
 6.8000E-01      1.0420E 00      =================================================+
 7.0000E-01      1.0397E 00      =================================================+
 7.2000E-01      1.0371E 00      ================================================+
 7.4000E-01      1.0343E 00      ================================================+
 7.6000E-01      1.0313E 00      ================================================+
 7.8000E-01      1.0283E 00      ===============================================+
 8.0000E-01      1.0253E 00      ===============================================+
 8.2000E-01      1.0224E 00      ==============================================+
 8.4000E-01      1.0197E 00      ==============================================+
 8.6000E-01      1.0170E 00      ==============================================+
 8.8000E-01      1.0145E 00      =============================================+
 9.0000E-01      1.0122E 00      =============================================+
 9.2000E-01      1.0101E 00      ============================================+
 9.4000E-01      1.0082E 00      ============================================+
 9.6000E-01      1.0065E 00      ============================================+
 9.8000E-01      1.0050E 00      ===========================================+
 1.0000E 00      1.0036E 00      ===========================================+
```

Figure 12.5 (a) The results of a run of the program in Figure 12.4 when $K_1 = 4$.

```
                        MINIMUM              OUTPUT VERSUS TIME            MAXIMUM
                        .0000E 00                                         1.1666E 00
   TIME         OUTPUT      I                                                I
  .0000E 00    .0000E 00    +
 2.0000E-02   1.9015E-02    +
 4.0000E-02   7.0686E-02    ---+
 6.0000E-02   1.4719E-01    -------+
 8.0000E-02   2.4122E-01    -----------+
 1.0000E-01   3.4612E-01    ---------------+
 1.2000E-01   4.5607E-01    --------------------+
 1.4000E-01   5.6611E-01    -------------------------+
 1.6000E-01   6.7218E-01    -----------------------------+
 1.8000E-01   7.7108E-01    ---------------------------------+
 2.0000E-01   8.6047E-01    ------------------------------------+
 2.2000E-01   9.3880E-01    ----------------------------------------+
 2.4000E-01   1.0052E 00    -------------------------------------------+
 2.6000E-01   1.0593E 00    ---------------------------------------------+
 2.8000E-01   1.1015E 00    ------------------------------------------------+
 3.0000E-01   1.1323E 00    --------------------------------------------------+
 3.2000E-01   1.1526E 00    ---------------------------------------------------+
 3.4000E-01   1.1636E 00    ----------------------------------------------------+
 3.6000E-01   1.1666E 00    ----------------------------------------------------+
 3.8000E-01   1.1630E 00    ----------------------------------------------------+
 4.0000E-01   1.1540E 00    ---------------------------------------------------+
 4.2000E-01   1.1409E 00    --------------------------------------------------+
 4.4000E-01   1.1251E 00    -------------------------------------------------+
 4.6000E-01   1.1075E 00    ------------------------------------------------+
 4.8000E-01   1.0891E 00    -----------------------------------------------+
 5.0000E-01   1.0708E 00    ----------------------------------------------+
 5.2000E-01   1.0532E 00    ---------------------------------------------+
 5.4000E-01   1.0369E 00    --------------------------------------------+
 5.6000E-01   1.0221E 00    --------------------------------------------+
 5.8000E-01   1.0092E 00    -------------------------------------------+
 6.0000E-01   9.9831E-01    ------------------------------------------+
 6.2000E-01   9.8945E-01    ------------------------------------------+
 6.4000E-01   9.8259E-01    -----------------------------------------+
 6.6000E-01   9.7761E-01    -----------------------------------------+
 6.8000E-01   9.7436E-01    ----------------------------------------+
 7.0000E-01   9.7264E-01    ----------------------------------------+
 7.2000E-01   9.7224E-01    ----------------------------------------+
 7.4000E-01   9.7293E-01    ----------------------------------------+
 7.6000E-01   9.7450E-01    ----------------------------------------+
 7.8000E-01   9.7672E-01    ----------------------------------------+
 8.0000E-01   9.7939E-01    ----------------------------------------+
 8.2000E-01   9.8234E-01    -----------------------------------------+
 8.4000E-01   9.8540E-01    -----------------------------------------+
 8.6000E-01   9.8845E-01    -----------------------------------------+
 8.8000E-01   9.9136E-01    -----------------------------------------+
 9.0000E-01   9.9407E-01    -----------------------------------------+
 9.2000E-01   9.9651E-01    ------------------------------------------+
 9.4000E-01   9.9863E-01    ------------------------------------------+
 9.6000E-01   1.0004E 00    ------------------------------------------+
 9.8000E-01   1.0019E 00    ------------------------------------------+
 1.0000E 00   1.0030E 00    ------------------------------------------+
```

Figure 12.5(b) The results of a run of the program in Figure 12.4 when $K_1 = 8$.

198

TIME	OUTPUT
.0000E 00	.0000E 00
2.0000F-02	9.3807E-02
4.0000E-02	3.3510E-01
6.0000E-02	6.5335E-01
A.0000E-02	9.76A4E-01
1.0000F-01	1.2459E 00
1.2000F-01	1.4216E 00
1.4000F-01	1.4888E 00
1.6000F-01	1.4552E 00
1.8000E-01	1.3450F 00
2.0000E-01	1.1922E 00
2.2000F-01	1.0322E 00
2.4000F-01	8.9532E-01
2.6000F-01	8.0227F-01
2.8000F-01	7.6198E-01
3.0000F-01	7.7220E-01
3.2000F-01	8.2192E-01
3.4000F-01	8.9495E-01
3.6000F-01	9.7381E-01
3.8000F-01	1.0431F 00
4.0000F-01	1.0921F 00
4.2000E-01	1.1154F 00
4.4000F-01	1.1136F 00
4.6000E-01	1.0915E 00
4.8000F-01	1.0567F 00
5.0000F-01	1.0180F 00
5.2000F-01	9.8305E-01
5.4000F-01	9.5750F-01
5.6000F-01	9.4429F-01
5.8000F-01	9.4358F-01
6.0000F-01	9.5325F-01
6.2000F-01	9.6965F-01
6.4000F-01	9.8859F-01
6.6000F-01	1.0062F 00
6.8000E-01	1.0194F 00
7.0000E-01	1.0268F 00
7.2000F-01	1.0279E 00
7.4000F-01	1.0238F 00
7.6000F-01	1.0161E 00
7.8000F-01	1.0069F 00
8.0000F-01	9.9807F-01
A.2000E-01	9.9122E-01
A.4000F-01	9.8720F-01
A.6000F-01	9.8624E-01
A.8000F-01	9.8794F-01
9.0000F-01	9.9153F-01
9.2000F-01	9.9600E-01
9.4000F-01	1.0004E 00
9.6000F-01	1.0039E 00
9.8000F-01	1.0061F 00
1.0000F 00	1.0068F 00

Figure 12.5(c) The results of a run of the program in Figure 12.4 when $K_1 = 40$.

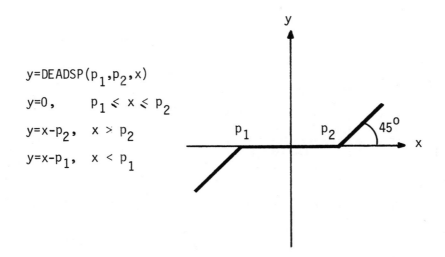

$y = \text{DEADSP}(p_1, p_2, x)$

$y = 0, \quad p_1 \leq x \leq p_2$

$y = x - p_2, \quad x > p_2$

$y = x - p_1, \quad x < p_1$

Figure 12.6 Transfer characteristics for a deadspace.

****CONTINUOUS SYSTEM MODELING PROGRAM****

*** VERSION 1.3 ***

```
DYNAMIC
TIMER FINTIM=1.0, OUTDEL=.02
CONSTANT TWOPI=6.2831852, K1=8
IN=STEP(0.0)
V1=(10/TWOPI)*IN
V2=V1-V7
VA=DEADSP(0.0,.5,V2)
V3=K1*VA
V4=8*V3
V5=.1*V4
V6=INTGRL(0.0,V5)
OUTPUT=REALPL(0.0,.1,V6)
V7=(10/TWOPI)*OUTPUT
PRTPLOT OUTPUT
END
STOP
```

Figure 12.7 A CSMP program for modeling the control system with deadspace.

```
                              MINIMUM              OUTPUT VERSUS TIME              MAXIMUM
                              .0000E 00                                           8.9603E-01
        TIME          OUTPUT        I                                                  I
       .0000E 00      .0000E 00     +
      2.0000E-02     1.3041E-02     +
      4.0000E-02     4.8479E-02     =-+
      6.0000E-02     1.0095E-01     =-=-=+
      8.0000E-02     1.6544E-01     =-=-=-=-=-+
      1.0000E-01     2.3738E-01     =-=-=-=-=-=-=-+
      1.2000E-01     3.1279E-01     =-=-=-=-=-=-=-=-=-+
      1.4000E-01     3.8826E-01     =-=-=-=-=-=-=-=-=-=-=-+
      1.6000E-01     4.6101E-01     =-=-=-=-=-=-=-=-=-=-=-=-=-+
      1.8000E-01     5.2884E-01     =-=-=-=-=-=-=-=-=-=-=-=-=-=-=-+
      2.0000E-01     5.9015E-01     =-=-=-=-=-=-=-=-=-=-=-=-=-=-=-=-=-+
      2.2000E-01     6.4387E-01     =-=-=-=-=-=-=-=-=-=-=-=-=-=-=-=-=-=-=-+
      2.4000E-01     6.8940E-01     =-=-=-=-=-=-=-=-=-=-=-=-=-=-=-=-=-=-=-=-=-+
      2.6000E-01     7.2687E-01     =-=-=-=-=-=-=-=-=-=-=-=-=-=-=-=-=-=-=-=-=-=-=-+
      2.8000E-01     7.5755E-01     =-=-=-=-=-=-=-=-=-=-=-=-=-=-=-=-=-=-=-=-=-=-=-=-=-+
      3.0000E-01     7.8268E-01     =-=-=-=-=-=-=-=-=-=-=-=-=-=-=-=-=-=-=-=-=-=-=-=-=-=-+
      3.2000E-01     8.0324E-01     =-=-=-=-=-=-=-=-=-=-=-=-=-=-=-=-=-=-=-=-=-=-=-=-=-=-=-+
      3.4000E-01     8.2008E-01     =-=-=-=-=-=-=-=-=-=-=-=-=-=-=-=-=-=-=-=-=-=-=-=-=-=-=-=-+
      3.6000E-01     8.3387E-01     =-=-=-=-=-=-=-=-=-=-=-=-=-=-=-=-=-=-=-=-=-=-=-=-=-=-=-=-=-+
      3.8000E-01     8.4516E-01     =-=-=-=-=-=-=-=-=-=-=-=-=-=-=-=-=-=-=-=-=-=-=-=-=-=-=-=-=-=-+
      4.0000E-01     8.5440E-01     =-=-=-=-=-=-=-=-=-=-=-=-=-=-=-=-=-=-=-=-=-=-=-=-=-=-=-=-=-=-=-+
      4.2000E-01     8.6196E-01     =-=-=-=-=-=-=-=-=-=-=-=-=-=-=-=-=-=-=-=-=-=-=-=-=-=-=-=-=-=-=-=-+
      4.4000E-01     8.6816E-01     =-=-=-=-=-=-=-=-=-=-=-=-=-=-=-=-=-=-=-=-=-=-=-=-=-=-=-=-=-=-=-=-+
      4.6000E-01     8.7323E-01     =-=-=-=-=-=-=-=-=-=-=-=-=-=-=-=-=-=-=-=-=-=-=-=-=-=-=-=-=-=-=-=-+
      4.8000E-01     8.7738E-01     =-=-=-=-=-=-=-=-=-=-=-=-=-=-=-=-=-=-=-=-=-=-=-=-=-=-=-=-=-=-=-=-+
      5.0000E-01     8.8078E-01     =-=-=-=-=-=-=-=-=-=-=-=-=-=-=-=-=-=-=-=-=-=-=-=-=-=-=-=-=-=-=-=-+
      5.2000E-01     8.8357E-01     =-=-=-=-=-=-=-=-=-=-=-=-=-=-=-=-=-=-=-=-=-=-=-=-=-=-=-=-=-=-=-=-+
      5.4000E-01     8.8585E-01     =-=-=-=-=-=-=-=-=-=-=-=-=-=-=-=-=-=-=-=-=-=-=-=-=-=-=-=-=-=-=-=-+
      5.6000E-01     8.8771E-01     =-=-=-=-=-=-=-=-=-=-=-=-=-=-=-=-=-=-=-=-=-=-=-=-=-=-=-=-=-=-=-=-+
      5.8000E-01     8.8924E-01     =-=-=-=-=-=-=-=-=-=-=-=-=-=-=-=-=-=-=-=-=-=-=-=-=-=-=-=-=-=-=-=-+
      6.0000E-01     8.9049E-01     =-=-=-=-=-=-=-=-=-=-=-=-=-=-=-=-=-=-=-=-=-=-=-=-=-=-=-=-=-=-=-=-+
      6.2000E-01     8.9151E-01     =-=-=-=-=-=-=-=-=-=-=-=-=-=-=-=-=-=-=-=-=-=-=-=-=-=-=-=-=-=-=-=-+
      6.4000E-01     8.9235E-01     =-=-=-=-=-=-=-=-=-=-=-=-=-=-=-=-=-=-=-=-=-=-=-=-=-=-=-=-=-=-=-=-+
      6.6000E-01     8.9304E-01     =-=-=-=-=-=-=-=-=-=-=-=-=-=-=-=-=-=-=-=-=-=-=-=-=-=-=-=-=-=-=-=-+
      6.8000E-01     8.9360E-01     =-=-=-=-=-=-=-=-=-=-=-=-=-=-=-=-=-=-=-=-=-=-=-=-=-=-=-=-=-=-=-=-+
      7.0000E-01     8.9406E-01     =-=-=-=-=-=-=-=-=-=-=-=-=-=-=-=-=-=-=-=-=-=-=-=-=-=-=-=-=-=-=-=-+
      7.2000E-01     8.9444E-01     =-=-=-=-=-=-=-=-=-=-=-=-=-=-=-=-=-=-=-=-=-=-=-=-=-=-=-=-=-=-=-=-+
      7.4000E-01     8.9475E-01     =-=-=-=-=-=-=-=-=-=-=-=-=-=-=-=-=-=-=-=-=-=-=-=-=-=-=-=-=-=-=-=-+
      7.6000E-01     8.9500E-01     =-=-=-=-=-=-=-=-=-=-=-=-=-=-=-=-=-=-=-=-=-=-=-=-=-=-=-=-=-=-=-=-+
      7.8000E-01     8.9520E-01     =-=-=-=-=-=-=-=-=-=-=-=-=-=-=-=-=-=-=-=-=-=-=-=-=-=-=-=-=-=-=-=-+
      8.0000E-01     8.9537E-01     =-=-=-=-=-=-=-=-=-=-=-=-=-=-=-=-=-=-=-=-=-=-=-=-=-=-=-=-=-=-=-=-+
      8.2000E-01     8.9551E-01     =-=-=-=-=-=-=-=-=-=-=-=-=-=-=-=-=-=-=-=-=-=-=-=-=-=-=-=-=-=-=-=-+
      8.4000E-01     8.9563E-01     =-=-=-=-=-=-=-=-=-=-=-=-=-=-=-=-=-=-=-=-=-=-=-=-=-=-=-=-=-=-=-=-+
      8.6000E-01     8.9572E-01     =-=-=-=-=-=-=-=-=-=-=-=-=-=-=-=-=-=-=-=-=-=-=-=-=-=-=-=-=-=-=-=-+
      8.8000E-01     8.9579E-01     =-=-=-=-=-=-=-=-=-=-=-=-=-=-=-=-=-=-=-=-=-=-=-=-=-=-=-=-=-=-=-=-+
      9.0000E-01     8.9586E-01     =-=-=-=-=-=-=-=-=-=-=-=-=-=-=-=-=-=-=-=-=-=-=-=-=-=-=-=-=-=-=-=-+
      9.2000E-01     8.9591E-01     =-=-=-=-=-=-=-=-=-=-=-=-=-=-=-=-=-=-=-=-=-=-=-=-=-=-=-=-=-=-=-=-+
      9.4000E-01     8.9595E-01     =-=-=-=-=-=-=-=-=-=-=-=-=-=-=-=-=-=-=-=-=-=-=-=-=-=-=-=-=-=-=-=-+
      9.6000E-01     8.9598E-01     =-=-=-=-=-=-=-=-=-=-=-=-=-=-=-=-=-=-=-=-=-=-=-=-=-=-=-=-=-=-=-=-+
      9.8000E-01     8.9601E-01     =-=-=-=-=-=-=-=-=-=-=-=-=-=-=-=-=-=-=-=-=-=-=-=-=-=-=-=-=-=-=-=-+
      1.0000E 00     8.9603E-01     =-=-=-=-=-=-=-=-=-=-=-=-=-=-=-=-=-=-=-=-=-=-=-=-=-=-=-=-=-=-=-=-+
```

Figure 12.8 Results of a run of the CSMP model for the control system with deadspace.

To illustrate further how non-linear systems can be modeled with CSMP, we will take as our last example an AM system that includes a <u>modulator</u> and a <u>demodulator</u>. In order to express the modulation process mathematically, let us define a single-frequency modulating signal by

$$e_m = A_m \sin\omega_m t$$

where A_m is the peak value and ω_m is the angular frequency, in rad/sec. Suppose this signal amplitude-modulates the carrier signal

$$e_c = A_c \cos\omega_c t$$

where A_c is the peak carrier level and ω_c is its angular frequency. (We choose to represent the carrier as a cosine wave simply for convenience in specifying OUTDEL increments later.)

In amplitude modulation, variations in the modulating signal determine the amplitude of the carrier, so the <u>envelope</u> of the composite signal is $A_c + e_m$. A double sideband, full carrier AM signal can therefore be represented mathematically as

$$e = (A_c + e_m)\cos\omega_c t$$
$$= (A_c + A_m \sin\omega_m t)\cos\omega_c t$$
$$= A_c(1 + m\sin\omega_m t)\cos\omega_c t \tag{1}$$

where $m = A_m/A_c$ is the modulation index, equal to 1 for 100 percent modulation. We note that the <u>non-linear</u> nature of this process is revealed by (1) in the multiplication of the two time-varying quantities e_m and e_c.

In the most common application of AM, e_m is an audio frequency signal used to modulate a radio frequency carrier, and the composite signal is transmitted by a broadcast station to AM receivers. <u>Demodulation</u> is the process of recovering the modulating signal from the composite signal. One way that demodulation can be accomplished is by rectifying and filtering the composite. Rectification is again a non-linear process, since it produces a constant (zero) output for negative inputs and a proportional output for positive inputs. Figure 12.9 is a diagram of the modulation/demodulation process.

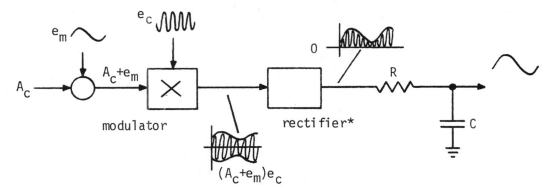

Figure 12.9 Block diagram of amplitude modulation/demodulation.

* We assume the rectifier is isolated from the filter, as by an isolation amplifier, to
  simplify the model. This is a so-called rectifier demodulator as opposed to the more common envelope detector.

The modulation process can be modeled in CSMP simply by multiplying together two SINE functions representing the modulating and carrier signals. (Actually, the carrier signal will be represented as a cosine wave, by _generating_ a sine wave with a 90⁰ phase shift.) To model rectification, we will use CSMP's built-in LIMIT function. The transfer characteristic for this function is shown in Figure 12.10, along with the defining equations.

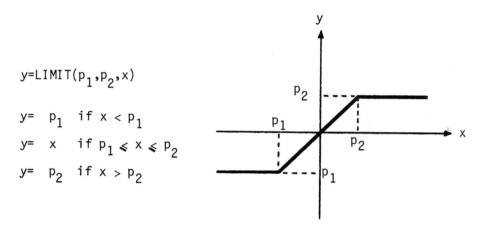

$$y = LIMIT(p_1, p_2, x)$$

$$y = p_1 \quad \text{if } x < p_1$$

$$y = x \quad \text{if } p_1 \leqslant x \leqslant p_2$$

$$y = p_2 \quad \text{if } x > p_2$$

Figure 12.10 Transfer characteristics of a limiter.

By choosing $p_1 = 0$ and p_2 equal to or greater than the maximum positive value of x, we can use the LIMIT function to model the rectification of any variable x. Figure 12.11 illustrates this fact.

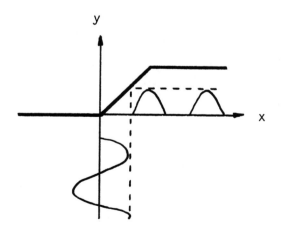

Figure 12.11 Transfer characteristic of a rectifier (based on the limiter with $p_1 = 0$).

To construct the CSMP model, we redraw Figure 12.9 in the block diagram form shown in Figure 12.12

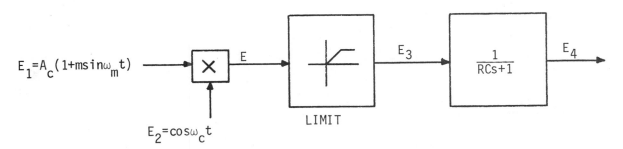

Figure 12.12   Block diagram of the AM modulator and demodulator suitable for CSMP modeling.

We will develop the model for a case in which the carrier frequency in 100 kHz, the modulating frequency is 5 kHz, A = 1 volt, and m = 1 (100 percent modulation). We will set the cutoff frequency of the low pass filter at approximately 5 kHz by choosing R = 1.5 K and C = .021 μF (f_c = 1/2πRC). Using these values we have, with reference to Figure 12.12,

$$E1 = 1 + \sin(2\pi \times 5 \times 10^3 t)$$

$$E2 = \cos(2\pi \times 10^5 t)$$

$$\frac{1}{RCs + 1} = \frac{1}{\dfrac{s}{2\pi \times 10^5} + 1}$$

We will choose a value of OUTDEL that results in only the positive and negative peaks of the carrier signal being plotted. Since the carrier is represented as a cosine wave and has period $1/10^5 = 10^{-5}$ sec, the peaks occur at 0, $.5 \times 10^{-5}$, ..., sec, in other words, at intervals of 5 μsec. The FINTIM will be chosen to equal one complete cycle of the 5 kHz modulating frequency, or 0.2 msec.

Figure 12.13 shows the CSMP model based on Figure 12.12 and the values chosen for this example. Notice that the carrier signal E2 is a cosine function by virtue of its representation as a sine function with phase angle PH = π/2 radians.

Figure 12.14 shows the results of a run of the program of Figure 12.13. Figure 12.14 (a) shows E, the 100 percent modulated waveform. Remember that only the positive and negative peaks of the carrier are plotted, so we must visualize a full cycle of carrier signal between successive positive or successive negative peaks. The amplitudes of the peaks vary in accordance with the 5 kHz modulating signal. Since CSMP places the smallest value of a plot at the "bottom" (left) and draws lines from there to the other values, the plot of E does not have the usual appearance of an AM waveform. (We are used to seeing symmetrical positive and negative excursions, above and below a zero axis.) However, the presence of the modulating signal is clearly apparent, and all computed data values are correct as listed.

Figure 12.14(b) shows E3, the waveform that results when the AM signal is rectified. The 5 kHz modulating signal is now clearly apparent. Note that all of the previously negative peaks of the carrier component are now clipped at zero. Visualize a half-wave rectified carrier, whose positive peaks are represented by the non-zero values in the plot.

```
*** VERSION 1.3 ***

DYNAMIC
TIMER FINTIM=.2E=3, OUTDEL=5.0E=6
CONSTANT PI=3.1415927
WC=PI*2.0E5
WM=PI*1.0E4
TC=1/WM
PH=PI/2
E1=1+SINE(0,WM,0)
E2=SINE(0,WC,PH)
E=E1*E2
E3=LIMIT(0.0,10.0,E)
E4=REALPL(0.0,TC,E3)
PRTPLOT E,E3,E4
END
STOP
```

Figure 12.13 A CSMP program that models the amplitude modulator/
demodulator.

Note that 100% modulation causes the modulating signal to vary through a full excursion from 0 to + 2 V, with a DC level of 1 V.

Figure 12.14(c) shows E4, the waveform that results when the rectified signal is filtered. This represents the original 5 kHz signal (with a DC component) that has been recovered as a result of the demodulation process.

EXERCISES

1. Construct a CSMP model for the control system shown in Figure 12.1 when $\omega = 40$, $V = 10$, $K_1 = 10$, $K_2 = 50$, and the input is a 5 unit step.

2. Run the program you wrote for exercise (1) to determine the frequency of the oscillation of the response about its steady-state value.

3. By performing repeated runs of the model you wrote for exercise (1), determine (approximately) the value of K_1 that causes the response of the control system to be critically damped (all other parameters remaining the same).

4. Using the parameters of exercise (1), modify the program as required and run it to determine the maximum velocity and maximum acceleration of the output. Obtain plots of these quantities and explain their behavior (shape vs. time) in terms of the behavior of the control system.

5. Modify the model of exercise (1) so that $K_2 = 5$ and the input is a 5 volt peak sine wave. By repeated runs of the model, determine the frequency at which the steady-state output of the system has peak value equal to .707 times the peak value of the input. This is the bandwidth of the system. Repeat for $K_2 = 10$. What do you conclude is the effect of K_2 on the bandwidth?

6. Write a CSMP program that models the control system whose block diagram is shown in Figure 12.15. Assume a unit step input.

```
                        MINIMUM              E     VERSUS TIME        MAXIMUM
                       -1.9877E 00                                    2.0000E 00
  TIME          E       I                                             I
  .0000E 00   1.0000E 00   ----------------------------------------+
 5.0000E-06  -1.1564E 00   ----------+
 1.0000E-05   1.3090E 00   -------------------------------------------+
 1.5000E-05  -1.4540E 00   ------+
 2.0000E-05   1.5878E 00   --------------------------------------------+
 2.5000E-05  -1.7071E 00   ---+
 3.0000E-05   1.8090E 00   ---------------------------------------------+
 3.5000E-05  -1.8910E 00   -+
 4.0000E-05   1.9511E 00   ----------------------------------------------+
 4.5000E-05  -1.9877E 00   +
 5.0000E-05   2.0000E 00   -----------------------------------------------+
 5.5000E-05  -1.9877E 00   +
 6.0000E-05   1.9511E 00   ----------------------------------------------+
 6.5000E-05  -1.8910E 00   --+
 7.0000E-05   1.8090E 00   ---------------------------------------------+
 7.5000E-05  -1.7071E 00   ----+
 8.0000E-05   1.5878E 00   --------------------------------------------+
 8.5000E-05  -1.4540E 00   -------+
 9.0000E-05   1.3090E 00   -------------------------------------------+
 9.5000E-05  -1.1564E 00   ----------+
 1.0000E-04   1.0000E 00   ----------------------------------------+
 1.0500E-04  -8.4357E-01   ------------------+
 1.1000E-04   6.9099E-01   ----------------------------------+
 1.1500E-04  -5.4601E-01   --------------------+
 1.2000E-04   4.1222E-01   -------------------------------+
 1.2500E-04  -2.9290E-01   -----------------------+
 1.3000E-04   1.9098E-01   ---------------------------+
 1.3500E-04  -1.0899E-01   ---------------------------+
 1.4000E-04   4.8944E-02   ----------------------------+
 1.4500E-04  -1.2312E-02   ---------------------------+
 1.5000E-04   .0000E 00    ----------------------------+
 1.5500E-04  -1.2311E-02   ---------------------------+
 1.6000E-04   4.8943E-02   ----------------------------+
 1.6500E-04  -1.0899E-01   ---------------------------+
 1.7000E-04   1.9098E-01   ---------------------------+
 1.7500E-04  -2.9289E-01   -----------------------+
 1.8000E-04   4.1221E-01   -------------------------------+
 1.8500E-04  -5.4601E-01   --------------------+
 1.9000E-04   6.9098E-01   ----------------------------------+
 1.9500E-04  -8.4356E-01   ------------------+
 2.0000E-04   1.0000E 00   ----------------------------------------+
```

Figure 12.14(a) Result of a run of the program in Figure 12.13 showing the AM waveform.

206

Figure 12.14(b)   Result of a run of the program in Figure 12.13 showing the AM waveform after rectification.

```
                           MINIMUM              E4      VERSUS TIME            MAXIMUM
                           .0000E 00                                          5.7316E-01
   TIME             E4        I                                                   I
   .0000E 00        .0000E 00    +
  5.0000E-06       4.5255E-02    ===+
  1.0000E-05       1.0102E-01    =========+
  1.5000E-05       1.4507E-01    ============+
  2.0000E-05       2.0002E-01    =================+
  2.5000E-05       2.4184E-01    ====================+
  3.0000E-05       2.9380E-01    ========================+
  3.5000E-05       3.3140E-01    ===========================+
  4.0000E-05       3.7760E-01    ==============================+
  4.5000E-05       4.0889E-01    =================================+
  5.0000E-05       4.4664E-01    ====================================+
  5.5000E-05       4.6965E-01    =====================================+
  6.0000E-05       4.9658E-01    =========================================+
  6.5000E-05       5.0979E-01    ==========================================+
  7.0000E-05       5.2441E-01    ===========================================+
  7.5000E-05       5.2697E-01    ============================================+
  8.0000E-05       5.2863E-01    ============================================+
  8.5000E-05       5.2057E-01    ===========================================+
  9.0000E-05       5.0981E-01    ==========================================+
  9.5000E-05       4.9205E-01    =========================================+
  1.0000E-04       4.7050E-01    ======================================+
  1.0500E-04       4.4481E-01    ====================================+
  1.1000E-04       4.1504E-01    =================================+
  1.1500E-04       3.8390E-01    ==============================+
  1.2000E-04       3.4926E-01    ===========================+
  1.2500E-04       3.1565E-01    =========================+
  1.3000E-04       2.7988E-01    ======================+
  1.3500E-04       2.4687E-01    ===================+
  1.4000E-04       2.1381E-01    =================+
  1.4500E-04       1.8452E-01    ==============+
  1.5000E-04       1.5772E-01    ============+
  1.5500E-04       1.3482E-01    ==========+
  1.6000E-04       1.1720E-01    =========+
  1.6500E-04       1.0274E-01    ========+
  1.7000E-04       9.6301E-02    ========+
  1.7500E-04       9.1469E-02    =======+
  1.8000E-04       9.7116E-02    =======+
  1.8500E-04       1.0217E-01    ========+
  1.9000E-04       1.1959E-01    =========+
  1.9500E-04       1.3376E-01    ==========+
  2.0000E-04       1.6154E-01    ============+
```

Figure 12.14(c)   Result of a run of the program in Figure 12.13 showing the demodulated
wave (after rectification and filtering).

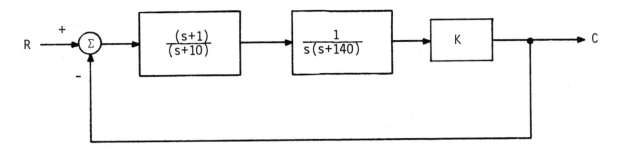

Figure 12.15

7. Run the model you wrote for exercise (6) and obtain plots of C for $K = 14 \times 10^3$ and for $K = 14 \times 10^4$. Compare and explain the responses obtained for these two cases.

8. Modify the model you wrote for exercise (6) to include a <u>deadspace</u> in the feedback loop. Assume the deadspace is such that it has zero output when its input is between 0 and 0.2. Then perform a simulation run with $K = 14 \times 10^4$ and compare the response C with that obtained in exercise (7).

9. Write a CSMP model for simulating the system shown in Figure 12.16. Assume a unit step input.

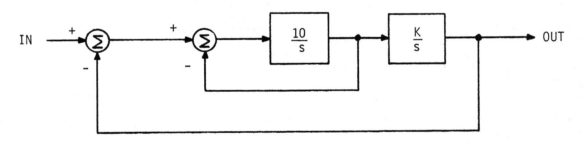

Figure 12.16

By performing repeated runs of the model, determine the approximate value of K that results in a critically damped response.

10. Write a CSMP program that can be used to simulate a modulator/demodulator system in which the carrier frequency is 100 kHz and the modulating signal is the <u>sum</u> of a 5 kHz and a 10 kHz signal:

$$e_m = A_1 \sin(2\pi \times 5 \times 10^3 t) + A_2 \sin(2\pi \times 10^4 t)$$

Run your simulation model and obtain plots of the modulated carrier, the rectified signal, and the filtered, rectified signal for the case $A_1 = A_2 = 2$ volts and a modulation index of 0.5. (Note: $m = \sqrt{m_1^2 + m_2^2}$, where m_1 is the modulation index due to A_1 and m_2 is the modulation index due to A_2).

11. Write a CSMP model for the <u>power-supply</u> shown in Figure 12.17.

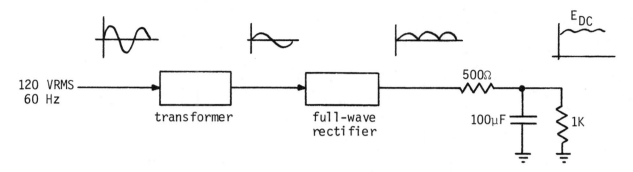

Figure 12.17

(Hint: the full wave rectifier can be modeled by summing the outputs of two half-wave rectifiers, one of which is driven by a sine wave and the other by an inverted sine wave; alternatively drive two suitably structured limiters and sum their outputs. The transfer function of the filter-load combination can be derived by considering the voltage divider formed by the parallel R_L-C combination and the series resistor.) Perform a simulation run and obtain plots of the full-wave rectified signal and the filtered output, E_{DC}. Determine the peak-to-peak ripple in the output.

13 Introduction to Analog Computation

OBJECTIVES

1. To learn how to use an analog computer to solve elementary differential equations.

2. To learn how to construct an analog computer diagram and how to wire it on an analog computer.

3. To gain familiarity with the operating controls of an analog computer.

4. To investigate the effects that changes in various component settings have on the output voltage representing the solution of a second order differential equation.

5. To investigate and verify the relationships between y, $\dot{y}$, and $\ddot{y}$ as observed during an analog computer run.

6. To verify that a solution voltage obtained from an analog computer represents the actual solution to a particular differential equation.

DISCUSSION

The principal use of analog computers is the real-time solution of differential equations. An equation is solved by using operational amplifiers to perform mathematical operations (addition, integration, etc.) on voltages that represent the variables of the equation. Recall that a solution to a differential equation is a <u>function</u> that satisfies the equation. In analog computation the independent variable is time, so solutions are obtained as functions of time. The amplifiers are connected together in such a way that the mathematical relations prescribed by the equation are performed and a time-varying voltage representing the dependent variable is then measured to obtain the solution.

In spite of the fact that differential equations contain derivatives, mathematical differentiation is almost never performed on an analog computer. Since differentiation produces voltages whose amplitudes are proportional to their frequencies, it in effect amplifies high frequency noise to an unacceptable level. The key component in an analog computation is the electronic integrator. When the input to an integrator is a voltage representing an nth-order derivative, the output represents a derivative of one lower order, i.e. of order n-1. In essence, a differential equation is solved by successive integration of its highest order derivative, each integration reducing the order, until, finally, integration of a first order derivative produces the variable itself, i.e. the solution. On an analog computer diagram, integrators are represented by the special symbol shown in Figure 13.1. Also shown is the symbol for an inverting amplifier, which is typically used to sum or scale voltages. Note in Figure 13.1 that small numbers are drawn at the inputs of the integrator and amplifier to represent voltage gains introduced by the respective devices. As usual, the operational amplifiers used for these devices also introduce phase inversions in the signals. Note also the IC input to the integrator. This must always be connected to a voltage that represents the initial condition (initial value, at t = 0) of

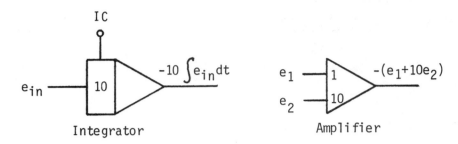

Figure 13.1 Operational amplifier symbols used in analog
computer diagrams.

the derivative or variable represented by the output of the integrator.

Before wiring an analog computer to solve a differential equation, certain procedures leading to a wiring diagram should be followed. The process is outlined as follows:

1. Algebraically manipulate the differential equation to solve for the highest order derivative present in the equation.

2. <u>Assume</u> that a voltage representing the highest order derivative is available.

3. With the assumption of step 2, we can integrate to produce a voltage representing the next lower order derivative. Draw an integrator and label its output with the next lower order derivative (including a minus sign for the phase inversion caused by the integrator).

4. Proceed to draw whatever additional integrators and amplifiers are necessary to generate all variables in the differential equation, and combine and scale them in accordance with the equation obtained in step 1.

5. When all the voltages representing all the terms on the right side of the equation in step 1 have been summed together, the result is equal to the highest order derivative that we assumed we had in step 2. Therefore, connect this sum of terms to the input of the first integrator (the one in step 3). The integrator itself may be used to perform the summation, if desired.

The procedure is best understood by way of an example. Suppose we wish to solve the differential equation

$$2\ddot{y} + 2\dot{y} + 25y = 10$$

We are using the "dot" notation, where the number of dots over a variable symbol indicates the order of the derivative of the variable. Following step 1 of the procedure, we first solve for $\ddot{y}$:
$$\ddot{y} = -\dot{y} - 12.5y + 5 \tag{1}$$

In accordance with step 2, we assume that we have $\ddot{y}$ and proceed to integrate it, thus producing $-\dot{y}$. See Figure 13.2. According to equation (1) we will need a voltage proportional to $-12.5y$. This will require another integration. We may use the scaling capability of the integrator used to generate y so that we actually generate $10y$, as shown in Figure 13.3. Since we need $-12.5y$, our next step will be to use an amplifier to provide a phase inversion. We will also use a <u>coefficient potentiometer</u> to scale the voltage by .125.

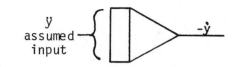

Figure 13.2   Integration of $\ddot{y}$
generates $-\dot{y}$

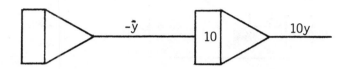

Figure 13.3   Integration and scaling of
$-\dot{y}$ generates $10y$.

Coefficient potentiometers are precision, multi-turn potentiometers that can be set very accurately (usually with a voltmeter built in to the computer) prior to problem solution. A coefficient potentiometer is shown on an analog computer diagram by a circle with its setting (the multiplicative scale factor it introduces) drawn inside the circle. Of course all potentiometer scale factors must be less than 1.00. Figure 1.34 shows the analog computer diagram as we have developed it thus far.

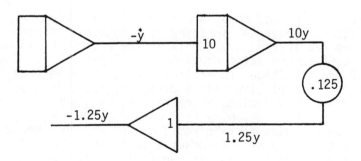

Figure 13.4   Generation of $-1.25y$ using a
coefficient potentiometer.

Our final step is to combine the voltages representing the variables of equation (1) in the same way they are combined on the right side of the equation. Notice that we have so far generated the terms $-\dot{y}$ and $-1.25y$ (see Figure 13.4) and what we need is $-\dot{y} - 12.5y + 5$. We will use the first integrator to combine the terms and to provide the extra gain needed for $-1.25y$. See Figure 13.5. Note in Figure 13.5 that the + 5 constant required by equation (1) is obtained from a coefficient potentiometer set to 0.5 and connected to a + 10 V DC source. The output of the potentiometer (+ 5) is connected to the integrator where it is combined with $-\dot{y}$ and with $10(-1.25y) = -12.5y$, the gain of 10 being supplied by the integrator. Note also that the IC inputs have been connected to 0 volts, implying that we

214

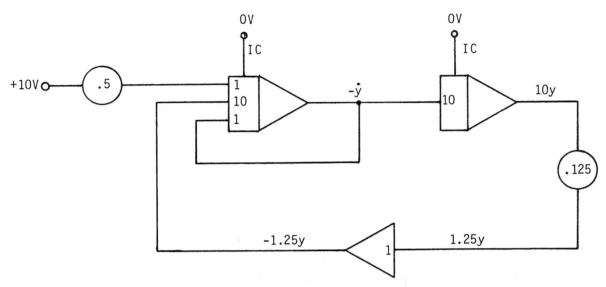

Figure 13.5 Combining voltages in the integrator to solve the equation $\ddot{y} = -\dot{y} - 12.5y + 5$.

are assuming zero initial conditions, i.e., $\dot{y}(0) = 0$ and $y(0) = 0$. Since we have summed all terms on the right side of equation 1 at the input to integrator, we know from equation 1 that the input to the integrator must equal $\ddot{y}$. In other words, we have made valid our initial assumption that we had $\ddot{y}$ available.

There is always more than one way to draw and connect an analog computer diagram for solving a particular equation. Generally speaking, the best way is the way that uses the fewest number of amplifiers and integrators. This is the reason we did not use a separate summing amplifier to combine the terms equal to $\ddot{y}$ in Figure 13.5. But note that nowhere in the circuit is there a voltage proportional to y, so if we were interested in observing this term as a function of time (as is often the case, in practice), then we would have to revise our diagram to include a separate summing amplifier for generating $\ddot{y}$.

It is only necessary now to connect the circuit on the analog computer and then to actuate the RUN control on the computer. To observe or measure the solution, we will have to make some provision for monitoring y, as with an oscilloscope or chart recorder. Note in Figure 13.5 that we will actually monitor 10y, so we will have to take this additional gain factor into account when measuring the solution voltage. When the RUN control is actuated, the computer will generate 10y as a time-varying voltage, one time only. Another identical run may be observed by using the RESET (or IC) control on the computer to restore initial conditions, and then actuating the RUN control again.

Figure 13.6 shows how the circuit is wired on a typical laboratory type analog computer, and Figure 13.7 shows 10y versus time, as viewed on an oscilloscope.

The circuit of Figure 13.5 shown wired on a typical laboratory type analog computer.

Figure 13.6

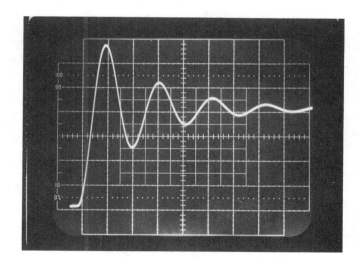

The solution 10y of the differential equation $2\ddot{y} + 2\dot{y} + 25y = 10$ computed by the computer setup of Figure 13.6 and as displayed on an oscilloscope.

Figure 13.7

PROCEDURE

NOTE: If you have a storage oscilloscope, its use will facilitate some the measurements and observations required in this experiment. Most waveforms will have very low frequencies. Alternatives include the use of a strip chart recorder, an X-Y plotter with X-axis driven by a ramp, or an oscilloscope camera. If none of this equipment is available, use a conventional oscilloscope and estimate values observed as best you can.

1. Connect the circuit shown in Figure 13.5 on an analog computer and run it. Then change the setting of the potentiometer that was originally set to 0.125 to a new setting of 0.750 and run it again. Observe the difference in the nature of the solution waveform caused by this change. Repeat for several other potentiometer settings. Also vary the setting of the potentiometer originally set to 0.5 and observe the effect this has on the solution. Observe the solution voltage when the + 10 V DC input to this potentiometer is changed to -10 V DC. Investigate the effects on the solution of connecting non-zero voltages to the IC inputs on the integrators. Be prepared to comment qualitatively on the general effect that all these changes have on the solution.

2. Restore the potentiometers to their original settings and observe or record both $-\dot{y}$ and $10y$. Be prepared to sketch the general waveforms observed and to comment on their relation to each other.

3. Redesign the circuit of Figure 13.5 so that it generates a separately available voltage proportional to $\ddot{y}$. (Be careful with your algebraic signs.) Then connect and run your circuit and observe or record voltages proportional to both $\dot{y}$ and $\ddot{y}$. Also check the voltage proportional to y to ensure that your redesigned circuit generates the same solution as the original circuit.

4. Design an analog computer circuit that can be used to solve the differential equation

$$6\ddot{y} + 3\dot{y} + 15y = 18$$

Use the minimum possible number of amplifiers and integrators. Assume zero initial conditions. It is not necessary to generate $\ddot{y}$ separately. Connect your circuit and run it. Observe or record enough data to make a sketch of the solution versus time.

5. Design an analog computer circuit that can be used to solve the differential equation

$$\ddot{y} + 900y = 0$$

Assume zero initial conditions. Connect your circuit and run it. Observe y and $\dot{y}$ simultaneously on a dual trace oscilloscope. The solution should be a low frequency oscillation. If you do not observe a sinusoidal solution, then you have an error in your circuit and it must be redesigned. Carefully measure and record the amplitudes and frequencies of y and $\dot{y}$, as observed on the oscilloscope.

6. Modify your circuit from step 5 so that it can be used to solve the slightly different equation

$$\ddot{y} + 400y = 0$$

Then repeat step 5, and compare results.

QUESTIONS

1. Describe qualitatively the changes in the observed solution voltage that were caused

by the various changes you made in the component settings and connections in step 1 of the Procedure.

2. Sketch the waveforms for $-\dot{y}$ and $10y$ that you observed in step 2 of the Procedure. How are these two waveforms related (in shape and phase)? How should they be related?

3. Repeat question 2 for the voltages proportional to $\dot{y}$ and $\ddot{y}$, based on your observations in step 3 of the Procedure.

4. Sketch the solution $y(t)$ to the differential equation you solved in step 4 of the Procedure, based on your observation of the analog computer run. Also show the computer diagram you used to solve the equation.

5. Repeat question 4 for your observations of y and $\dot{y}$ in step 5 of the Procedure. Based on your measurements, write mathematical expressions for $y(t)$ and $\dot{y}(t)$. Substitute your expression for $y(t)$ into the differential equation you solved to verify that it does satisfy the equation.

6. Repeat question 5 for y and $\dot{y}$ as observed in step 6 of the Procedure. Can you draw a conclusion that relates the constant multiplying y in the differential equation to the nature of the solution to the equation? How well do your results support this conclusion?

14 Amplitude and Time Scaling; Repetitive Operation

OBJECTIVES

1. To learn how to amplitude scale a computer diagram for maximum resolution.

2. To learn how to interpret measured voltages (machine variables) from an amplitude-scaled analog computer run in terms of actual, physical values (problem variables).

3. To learn how to interpret the results of time-scaled analog computer runs.

4. To gain experience using the repetitive operation mode of an analog computer.

DISCUSSION

Analog computers are used to solve differential equations that represent the behavior of real, physical systems. The variables in these equations, and their derivatives, therefore have the units of the quantities they represent in a physical system. For example, if a differential equation is written to determine the displacement $y(t)$ of a body in a dynamic spring-mass, damper system, then y may have the units of feet, while $\dot{y}$ has the units of ft/sec, and $\ddot{y}$ ft/sec². Depending on the system, and the forces applied to it, the magnitudes of these quantities (the <u>problem</u> variables, as opposed to the computer variables) may change over a very large or very small range of values. For example, it may be the case in some system that y ranges from 0 to 1000 ft, while $\dot{y}$ varies from -.01 to + .01 ft/sec, and $\ddot{y}$ varies from -12 to + 35 ft/sec². Clearly an analog computer simulation of this system would not be practical if we decided to let 1 volt on the computer represent 1 foot of displacement in the actual system, for then the voltage representing y would have to become 1000 volts during the course of the simulation run. Similarly, if we let 1 volt represent 1 ft/sec of velocity, then our voltage representing $\dot{y}$ would only vary from -10 mV to + 10 mV, resulting in poor resolution and possible masking by noise.

What we must do then is <u>scale</u> our computer variables so that they remain within the practical limits of the analog computer and still give us maximum resolution. We might for example let 1 volt represent 100 feet of displacement in the previous example, in which case the voltage representing y could be expected to vary from 0 to 10 volts. Similarly we might wish to scale $\dot{y}$ so that 1 volt represents .001 ft/sec, in which case this voltage would vary from -10 to + 10 volts. The process of constructing an analog computer diagram with amplifier gains and coefficient potentiometer settings adjusted to allow for the expected range of the variables is called <u>amplitude</u>, or <u>magnitude</u>, <u>scaling</u>. As a general rule, amplitude scaling should be performed so that the maximum output voltage at each amplifier is as near as possible to the maximum rated voltage of the amplifier without exceeding it. The maximum rated voltage on a given computer is called its <u>reference voltage</u>.

A number of different methods have been developed for the actual procedure of amplitude scaling. These methods lead to a variety of ways in which variable values are represented on the computer diagrams, and a corresponding variety of interpretations. We will discuss only the method that has gained the most popularity in recent years, a method that does <u>not</u> depend on a knowledge of the computer's reference voltage. It is called <u>normalized</u>, or <u>dimensionless</u> scaling, and has the advantage that diagrams produced using this method can <u>be used on any</u> machine. Whatever method is used, it must be emphasized that it is neces- sary to have some knowledge of the maximum value that each problem variable will attain during the course of a computer run. This knowledge may be based upon estimates, insight, previous experience, or trial-and-error. We will describe one method for estimating such values for one type of problem in a later experiment.

The normalized method of scaling requires that each problem variable be multiplied and divided in the original differential equation by the maximum value it might attain. Thus, for example, if it is known that $y < 4$ ft, $\dot{y} < 20$ ft/sec, and $\ddot{y} < 80$ ft/sec^2 in the dif- ferential equation: $\ddot{y} + 5\dot{y} + 25y = 50$, we would write:

$$80(\ddot{y}/80) + 5(20)(\dot{y}/20) = 25(4)(y/4) = 50$$

Any non-zero initial condition on a variable would be scaled by the same factor as the var- iable itself. Thus if $y(0) = 2$ and $\dot{y}(0) = 5$, we would calculate $y(0)/4 = .5$ and $\dot{y}(0)/20 = .25$, indicating that $.5\ V_{REF}$ and $.25 V_{REF}$ should be connected to the appropriate IC inputs (with opposite signs if the IC inputs invert). We then proceed to implement the computer solutions as described in the previous experiment, except that the variables we develop and show on the diagram are $\ddot{y}/80$, $\dot{y}/20$, and $y/4$, instead of $\ddot{y}$, $\dot{y}$, and y. Since the maxi- mum of each of the implemented quantities is <u>one</u>, we interpret actual voltages obtained on the computer as percentages of the reference voltage. Thus, for example, if we were using a computer with a 10 volt reference to solve the problem above, and we happened to read 2 volts for y, we would interpret this as $(2/10)(4) = .8$ ft. Similarly, an 8 volt reading at the output of the amplifier producing $\dot{y}$ would be interpreted as $(8/10)(20) = 16$ ft/sec. Note carefully that we do <u>NOT</u> write $\dot{y}/20 = 8 \Longrightarrow \dot{y} = 160$. Coefficient poten- tiometers are used as necessary to develop the correct multiplying factors for each of the quantities $(y/4)$, $(\dot{y}/20)$, etc. The following example illustrates the method.

Assuming that $y < 2.5$ feet, $\dot{y} < 20$ ft/sec, and $\ddot{y} < 160$ ft/sec^2, draw a magnitude- scaled analog computer diagram to solve the equation

$$\ddot{y} + 2\dot{y} + 64y = -80$$

for $\ddot{y}$, $\dot{y}$, and y. We assume zero initial conditions. Following the procedure outlined above, we first multiply and divide the computer variables by the maximum values of the problem variables:

$$160(\ddot{y}/160) + 2(20)(\dot{y}/20) + 64(2.5)(y/2.5) = -.80$$

Solving for $\ddot{y}/160$ in the usual way:

$$\ddot{y}/160 = \frac{-2(20)}{160}\left(\frac{\dot{y}}{20}\right) - \frac{64(2.5)}{160}\left(\frac{y}{2.5}\right) - \frac{80}{160}$$

$$\ddot{y}/160 = -.25(\dot{y}/20) - (y/2.5) - .5$$

The computer diagram is shown in Figure 14.1. Note in Figure 14.1 that the maximum output of each integrator will be a voltage which is near the maximum computer reference voltage. If, for example, $\dot{y}$ were actually to reach 20 ft/sec, and if $V_{REF} = 10$ V, then the output of the integrator producing $\dot{y}/20$ would be 10 volts, since

$$(10/10)(20) = 20 \text{ ft/sec.}$$

Thus we should never follow an integrator by an amplifier with a gain greater than one,

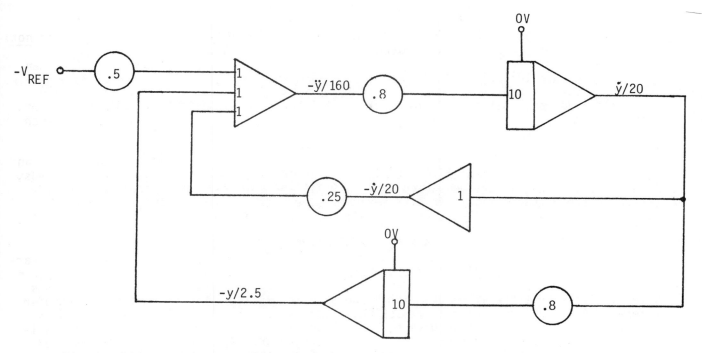

Figure 14.1   A magnitude-scaled analog computer diagram used to solve $\ddot{y} + 5\dot{y} + 25y = 50$.

unless that gain is in another integrator. An integrator following an integrator will generate another variable (derivative) which will in general have a different scale factor.
Note also in Figure 14.1 how the coefficient potentiometers are used. For example, a potentiometer set to .8 is used to multiply $\dot{y}/20$ by .8, and this result is then simultaneously
integrated and multiplied by 10 to produce:

$$-10 \int .8(\dot{y}/10)dt = -.8y = -y/2.5$$

Figure 14.2 shows an oscilloscope display of -y/2.5 versus time, as taken from a computer
run for this problem on a computer with reference voltage 10 V. In the display, 0 volts is
the bottom graticule line where the trace begins.

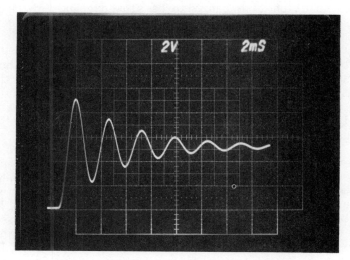

Figure 14.2   -y/2.5 versus time obtained from the computer setup of Figure 14.1

We see that the peak value reached in the display is approximately 9.5 V, and that the maximum y is therefore

$$(9.5/10)(2.5) = 2.38 \text{ ft.}$$

It is also apparent that after a long period of time the oscillation will dampen out to about 5 V or

$$(5/10)(2.5) = 1.25 \text{ ft.}$$

If a voltage corresponding to the highest order derivative of the equation to be solved is not required and is not developed explicitly in the computer setup, then it is not necessary to scale that variable for its maximum value. If in the previous example we did not wish to develop $\ddot{y}$ explicitly, then our scaling could be performed as follows:

$$\ddot{y} + 2(20)(\dot{y}/20) + 64(2.5)(y/2.5) = -80$$

$$\ddot{y}/40 = -(\dot{y}/20) - 4(y/2.5) - 2$$

Note carefully that the -2 on the right hand side is <u>not</u> -2 volts, but 2 times the negative reference voltage (-20 V on a 10 V machine). Initial conditions must be interpreted in the same way. If after scaling we have an initial condition of 1, this means the full reference voltage is applied to the IC input of an integrator. Also note that the term $4(y/2.5)$ should not appear explicitly in the computer diagram, since $(y/2.5)$ should be near the reference voltage and $4(y/2.5)$ would then be too large. Instead, use a coefficient potentiometer to produce $.4(y/2.5)$ and multiply this by 10 when integrating it in combination with other terms.

The solutions to the differential equations that govern the behavior of many practical systems are functions that change very slowly in time. It is therefore inconvenient and often difficult to observe and measure the analog computer voltage representing the solution of such a system, especially when using an oscilloscope. One remedy for this problem is the use of <u>time-scaling,</u> a technique that permits us to "speed up" time on a computer run. Using this technique, we can generate a time-varying solution that requires much less time than the <u>real time</u> that would elapse in the actual physical system being simulated. It can be shown that an analog computer solution to a differential equation can be sped up so that k seconds of real time occupies only one second of computer time, if <u>the gain of every integrator is increased by a factor of k</u> times the gain that would be used for a real time solution. (Of course, solution time can also be slowed down with respect to real time by reducing the gain of the integrators.) The voltage representing the solution to a time-scaled problem is like the real time solution in every respect except time, so it is only necessary to multiply time by the factor k when interpreting the results of a time-scaled run. To illustrate this point, consider the oscilloscope display shown in Figure 14.2. This represents the solution to the differential equation discussed in the previous example and was obtained from an analog computer run that was time-scaled by a factor of 400. A close examination of this oscilloscope display reveals that 5 cycles of the oscillation occur in approximately 13 msec. Thus in real time, 5 cycles occupy 400 x 13 msec = 5.2 seconds, and the actual frequency of the oscillation is therefore 5 cycles/5.2 seconds = .96 Hz.

To enable the user of an analog computer to view a solution on an oscilloscope, most modern analog computers have a <u>repetitive operation</u> (rep-op) mode, which, when selected, continually resets the computer and initiates another run, alternating between the run and reset modes at a high, or adjustable, rate of speed. Since the complete waveform representing the solution voltage is generated many times a second, it is possible to observe the solution on an oscilloscope. Rep-op usually incorporates time scaling, to permit each repeated solution to be generated in the short time period required. The oscilloscope display shown in Figure 14.2 was obtained from a rep-op run in which time was scaled by the factor

400. This display was made using the internal sweep of the oscilloscope, though many rep-op computers generate a sweep voltage that can be used to synchronize the oscilloscope and permit the setting of a particular time scale factor.

The rep-op mode is particularly useful when using an analog computer to investigate the effects of parameter changes on the solution to a problem. Without rep-op, a separate computer run would be required for every change made in a parameter, often a painstaking and time-consuming task. With rep-op, the investigator is able to observe immediately on an oscilloscope display the effect of any change made, for example, in the setting of a coefficient potentiometer that corresponds to a parameter of interest.

III. PROCEDURE

1. The displacement $y(t)$ of a certain spring-mass system obeys the differential equation $2\ddot{y} + 4y = -160$, where y is in feet. Draw an analog computer diagram for solving this equation. Use amplitude scaling, assuming that the maximum value of y is y_{MAX} = 40 ft. It is not necessary to develop $\dot{y}$ explicitly in the solution. Assume zero initial conditions.

2. Connect your setup and run it. Use repetitive operation if available, so that a voltage proportional to the solution (or its negative) can be observed on an oscilloscope. Be careful to note or set the time scale associated with the rep-op.

3. Record enough values of the solution waveform to enable you to reproduce it in an accurate sketch. Note particularly the initial and final values, and any other significant characteristics such as time-constants, oscillation frequency, etc. Use the DC input of the oscilloscope, and expand the horizontal and vertical sensitivities as necessary for accurate measurements. Be prepared to interpret the observed waveform in terms of the physical system being simulated, i.e. to determine actual, real-time displacements in feet, based on your scaling.

4. Now assume there is an initial displacement in the system of $y(0) = 20$ ft. (This initial displacement is in a direction opposite to the direction that y displaces in the previous step.) Scale the initial condition and modify your program to include it. Note that if you are observing an output from an integrator that is proportional to $-y$ and that if the IC input on the integrator inverts it, then you must connect a positive voltage to the IC input of the integrator. Now repeat steps 2 and 3.

5. The angular displacement $\Theta(t)$ of a certain rotational system obeys the differential equation

$$\ddot{\Theta} + \dot{\Theta} + 16\Theta = -320$$

where Θ is in radians. Assuming Θ_{MAX} = 40 rad, $\dot{\Theta}_{MAX}$ = 160 rad/sec, and $\ddot{\Theta}_{MAX}$ = 640 rad/sec², draw a scaled analog computer diagram for solving this equation. All initial conditions are zero. Include provisions for developing a voltage proportional to $\ddot{\Theta}$.

6. Repeat steps 2 and 3 for Θ, $\dot{\Theta}$, and $\ddot{\Theta}$.

7. Now assume there is an initial displacement of $\Theta(0) = 40$ radians. Revise your computer setup to include this initial condition and repeat steps 2 and 3 for Θ, $\dot{\Theta}$, and $\ddot{\Theta}$.

8. Restore all initial conditions to zero. Based on the actual measured values of Θ_{MAX}, $\dot{\Theta}_{MAX}$, and $\ddot{\Theta}_{MAX}$, as determined in step 6, rescale your diagram and run the problem

again, repeating steps 2 and 3 for Θ, $\dot{\Theta}$, and $\ddot{\Theta}$. In this case your observed voltages should have maximum values equal to the computer reference voltage.

9. Construct an analog computer circuit to solve the differential equation

$$\ddot{y} + 0.1\dot{y} + 10y = .1$$

It is not necessary to develop $\ddot{y}$ explicitly. Connect your circuit in such a way that all integrators have unity gain inputs. Run your setup and carefully record the peak value of the solution $y(t)$ and the period of one cycle of its oscillation.

10. To verify the effect of integrator gain on time scaling, change all integrator inputs so that each is now a gain 10 input. If there are an insufficient number of X10 inputs on the integrator that produces $-\dot{y}$, then simply increase the constant voltage (DC) input from 0.1 to 1.0. NOTE: you may have to reset coefficient potentiometers to their original settings, because the integrator gain changes will increase the loading of the potentiometers. Check coefficient potentiometer settings and reset them if necessary. Now repeat the measurements of peak value and period of the solution $y(t)$ that results from this setup.

11. The pressure $P(t)$ in a certain hydraulic system obeys the differential equation

$$\dddot{P} + 6\ddot{P} + 3.6\dot{P} + 7P + 3.75 = 0$$

where P is in Pascals. All initial conditions are zero. By trial and error methods construct a computer setup that results in maximum levels at the outputs of the amplifiers. That is, construct a setup that you can use to determine maximum values of $\ddot{P}$, $\dot{P}$, and P and then rescale as necessary to obtain voltage swings close to the computer reference voltage. It is not necessary to develop $\dddot{P}$ explicitly. Record the waveforms for $\ddot{P}$, $\dot{P}$, and P before and after you have achieved this goal.

QUESTIONS

1. Sketch the solution waveform you observed and recorded in step 3 of the Procedure. Show two scales on each axis of your sketch; on the horizontal axis show the measured time scale and the real-time scale; on the vertical axis show measured voltages and the values of the actual physical variable (the problem variable) to which they correspond. However, if your computer is used to produce a calibrated, horizontal sweep for the oscilloscope in the rep-op mode, then it is only necessary to label the horizontal scale in real-time units. Also show the computer diagram that you used to obtain the solution.

2. The solution to the differential equation in step 2 of the Procedure is of the form

$$y = K_1(1 - e^{-K_2 t}) \text{ ft.}$$

where K_1 and K_2 are constants. (Note that K_1 is the final value of $y(t)$ and $1/K_2$ is the time-constant.) Based on your observed data and the sketch made in question 1, what are the values of K_1 and K_2? Using these values, determine how well the observed solution satisfies the differential equation. (Calculate $\dot{y}$ and substitute $\dot{y}$ and y into the differential equation to see if it is satisfied.)

3. Repeat question 1 for the results obtained from step 4 of the Procedure. Based on your observed solution in this case, what is the initial value of the solution waveform, in volts and in actual physical units (problem variable units)?

4. Repeat question 1 for the solution waveform $\Theta(t)$ obtained in step 6 of the Procedure.

Report the measured values (in actual, physical units) of (a) the initial value of the solution; (b) the frequency of any oscillations observed; (c) the time constant of the decay of any oscillations; (d) the final value of the solution, after all oscillations have died out.

5. What were your observed maximum values of $\ddot{\Theta}$, $\dot{\Theta}$, and Θ, in volts and in actual physical units? Compare these observed values to those assumed for the scaling.

6. Sketch $\ddot{\Theta}$ and $\dot{\Theta}$ based on your measured data. Comment on the degree to which these quantities faithfully represent the derivatives of Θ. (For example, what is $\dot{\Theta}$ after Θ reaches its final value?)

7. Repeat question 1 for the results obtained from step 7 of the Procedure. Based on your observed solution in this case, what is the initial value of the solution waveform in volts and in actual physical units? How were $\dot{\Theta}$ and $\ddot{\Theta}$ affected by the inclusion of an initial condition on Θ?

8. Repeat question 1 for $\ddot{\Theta}$, $\dot{\Theta}$, and Θ using the results of step 8 in the Procedure. How successful were you in rescaling the computer run so the maximum values of each of these quantities equaled the reference voltage of the computer?

9. Compare the peak values and periods measured in steps 9 and 10 of the Procedure. Discuss how well your results confirm that time scaling can be performed by changing integrator gains.

10. Show the first computer diagram you used to solve the differential equation in step 11 of the Procedure and sketch the waveforms for $\ddot{P}$, $\dot{P}$, and P that resulted from using it. Then show your final, scaled diagram and the resulting waveforms. What are the maximum values of $\ddot{P}$, $\dot{P}$, and P in Pascals? Discuss the relationships between the $\ddot{P}$, $\dot{P}$, and P waveforms (i.e. explain how your sketches demonstrate that they are derivatives of one another). What is the advantage of using a scaled computer setup like the one you finally obtained in this step?

11. What would be one disadvantage of using a computer setup in which all amplifier outputs reached voltages near their maximum rated values? Consider, for example, a situation in which the behavior of a system is being investigated for purposes of modifying the system design.

15 Analog Simulation of Mechanical Systems

OBJECTIVES

1. To learn how to simulate mechanical systems by using an analog computer to solve their differential equations of motion.

2. To learn how to write the differential equations for simple translational and rotational mechanical systems, including those with two degrees of freedom.

3. To verify the theoretical relations pertaining to the behavior of under, over, and critically damped mechanical systems.

4. To gain experience interpreting solution waveforms obtained from analog computer simulation in terms of the physical parameters of real mechanical systems.

DISCUSSION

Analog computers are particularly valuable for studying the behavior of mechanical systems, especially in design situations, since it is far more convenient to construct and alter the characteristics of a computer model than it is to construct and modify mechanical components.

A translational mechanical system is one whose displacements occur along a straight line, while a rotational mechanical system has angular displacements. The three basic parameters of a translational mechanical system are spring constant (K), damping (B), and mass (M). The relationships between these parameters, the force F applied to them, and displacement x are as follows:

$$F = Kx \qquad (1)$$

$$F = B\dot{x} \qquad (2)$$

$$F = M\ddot{x} \qquad (3)$$

In the SI system of units, F is in Newtons (N), x in meters (m), K in N/m, B in N/m/sec, or N-sec/m, and M in kilograms. The corresponding parameters of a rotational mechanical system are rotational spring constant (K), rotational damping (B), and inertia (J). These are related to the torque T applied to them, and angular displacement Θ, as follows:

$$T = K\Theta \qquad (4)$$

$$T = B\dot{\Theta} \qquad (5)$$

$$T = J\ddot{\Theta} \qquad (6)$$

Note the similarity of equations (1) through (3) and (4) through (6). In the SI system, T is in N-m, Θ in radians, K in N-m/radian, B in N-m/rad/sec, or N-m-sec/rad, and J in N-m/rad/sec^2, or N-m-sec^2/rad.

In equations (1) through (3) and (4) through (6), we may think of the left-hand sides as the forces or torques that are developed by the mechanical components in reaction, or opposition, to an attempt to displace them, move them at a constant velocity, or accelerate them. Thus, for example, if a shaft with rotational spring constant K is twisted through Θ radians, it will resist by developing a torque of K N-m in opposition to the torque which causes the twisting. Similarly, moving a dashpot with damping constant B at a constant velocity of $\dot{x}$ m/sec will cause it to generate a force of B$\dot{x}$ N in opposition to the force creating the velocity. When writing a differential equation to describe a mechanical system, we make use of the fact that the sum of the applied forces (or torques) equals the sum of the resisting forces or torques. To illustrate, consider the translational mechanical system shown in Figure 15.1.

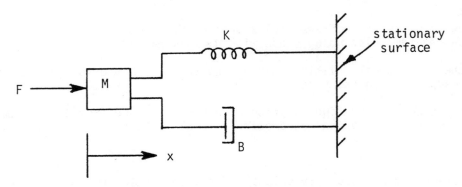

Figure 15.1 A spring-mass-damper combination in a translational mechanical system.

In Figure 15.1, we show the standard symbols for components having the parameters, K, B, and M. Also shown is the reference direction (positive direction) of the displacement x that occurs as a result of the applied force F. It is assumed that displacement occurs in a horizontal direction only, i.e. there is no vertical displacement. (Think of the mass M as resting on a frictionless surface.) The differential equation is then

$$F = M\ddot{x} + B\dot{x} + Kx \tag{7}$$

Note carefully in Figure 15.1 that all three components experience the same displacement x, velocity x, and acceleration x. Equation 7 may be written in the equivalent form:

$$\frac{F}{M} = \ddot{x} + \frac{B}{M}\dot{x} + \frac{K}{M}x \tag{8}$$

If we let $\zeta = B/2\sqrt{KM}$

and $\omega_n = \sqrt{K/M}$

then (8) may be written:

$$\frac{F}{M} = \ddot{x} + 2\zeta\omega_n\dot{x} + \omega_n^2x.$$

ζ is called the damping factor of the system, and ω_n is the natural frequency. If ζ is less than 1, the solution to the differential equation is in the form of a constant plus a damped sine wave:

$$x(t) = \frac{F}{K} - \frac{F}{K\sqrt{1-\zeta^2}} e^{-\zeta\omega_n t}\sin(\omega_n\sqrt{1-\zeta^2}t + \Theta) \qquad (9)$$

where $\Theta = \text{arc cos } \zeta$

In this case, the system is said to be underdamped, and $x(t)$ oscillates until settling down to its final value of F/K. When $\zeta = 1$, the system is critically damped and the solution to (8) is

$$x(t) = \frac{F}{K}(1 - e^{-at} - ate^{-at}) \qquad (10)$$

where $a = B/2M$.

Finally, if $\zeta > 1$ the system is overdamped and

$$x(t) = \frac{F}{K}\left(1 - \frac{b}{b-a} e^{-at} + \frac{a}{b-a} e^{-bt}\right) \qquad (11)$$

where $a = \dfrac{B/M + \sqrt{(B/M)^2 - 4K/M}}{2}$

and $b = \dfrac{B/M - \sqrt{(B/M)^2 - 4K/M}}{2}$

To illustrate how an analog computer may be used to investigate the behavior of a mechanical system, we will construct a computer diagram that will permit us to study the effects of variations in the damping B in Figure 15.1. Suppose in Figure 15.1 that M = 1 Kg, K = 400 N/m, and that a -20 N force F is applied to the system. Then equation 8 becomes:

$$-20 = \ddot{x} + B\dot{x} + 400x \qquad (12)$$

We wish to express B in terms of the damping factor ζ so that we can construct our computer diagram to permit us to change B by changing ζ. Since

$$\zeta = \frac{B}{2\sqrt{KM}} = \frac{B}{40}$$

we have B = 40ζ and equation 12 becomes:

$$-20 = \ddot{x} + 40\zeta\dot{x} + 400x$$

or, $\qquad \ddot{x} = -40\zeta\dot{x} - 400x - 20 \qquad (13)$

Figure 15.2 shows a computer diagram for solving (13), assuming zero initial conditions.

Note in Figure 15.2 that we have included a potentiometer whose setting is equal to $\zeta/2$. When this potentiometer is set to .5, we have $\zeta/2 = .5 \Longrightarrow \zeta = 1.0$, corresponding to critical damping. When the potentiometer is set to less than .5 we have the underdamped case, and a setting greater than .5 corresponds to the overdamped case. We may use this computer

230

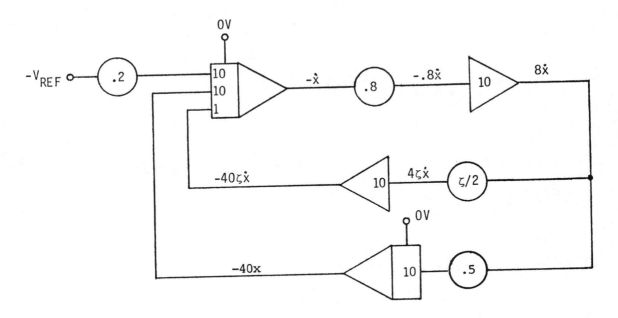

Figure 15.2 Computer diagram used for solving the spring-mass-damper equation
 $-20=\ddot{x}+40\zeta\dot{x}+400x$.

setup to investigate x(t) when various amounts of damping B are used in the system. For
example, when $\zeta = 1$, we know B = 40ζ = 40 N/m/sec. This setup will be used in the experimental Procedure that follows.

The results we have developed so far are equally applicable to rotational systems.
Equations 7 through 11 apply to the rotational system shown in Figure 15.3 when J is substituted for M, T for F and Θ for x.

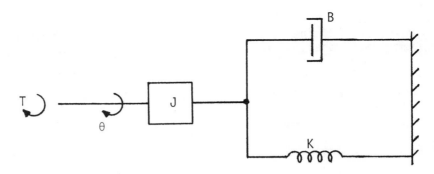

Figure 15.3 A spring-inertia-damper combination in a
rotational mechanical system.

In Figure 15.3 we can think of B as representing viscous damping caused, for example, by a
shaft rotating in a fluid, and K as representing the spring effect of a shaft that exerts
a torque in opposition to its being twisted.

In a previous chapter we learned the importance of scaling an analog computer problem. When dealing with a mechanical system such as shown in Figure 15.1 or 15.3 (a <u>second order</u> system, since the differential equations are of second order) we can make certain estimates on the maximum values of the variables, as an aid in amplitude scaling. If the system is overdamped or critically damped, then from equations 10 and 11 we can determine that $x_{MAX} = F/K$. However, both of these cases produce maximums that are less than the maximum possible x in an underdamped system. From equation 9 we see that x will always be less than $x_{MAX} = 2 F/K$, no matter what the damping factor. Furthermore, since the derivative of a sine wave has peak amplitude proportional to its frequency, and since the derivative of a constant is zero, we conclude that $\dot{x} < \omega_n(F/K) = \dot{x}_{MAX}$ and that $\ddot{x} < \omega_n^2(F/K) = \ddot{x}_{MAX}$.

(To be more precise, we should not call these maximum values of the variables, since they may not actually be reached; instead they are <u>upper bounds</u>.)

The single differential equation (7) that we wrote for the mechanical system shown in Figure 15.1 completely describes that system because the displacement (and velocity, and acceleration) of every component is the same. Consider now a system such as shown in Figure 15.4.

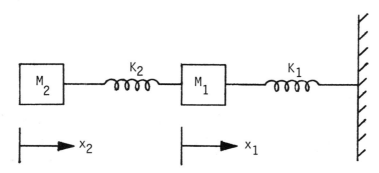

Figure 15.4 A translational mechanical system described by two simultaneous differential equations.

In Figure 15.4 there are two distinct displacement variables, x_1 and x_2. Such a system is said to have <u>two degrees of freedom</u>. Note in this idealized system that there is no damping. Consequently if one of the masses is given an initial displacement and then released, the two masses will theoretically oscillate indefinitely. Note also that the net displacement of the spring with spring constant K_2 is $x_2 - x_1$. It therefore develops a force of K_2 $(x_2 - x_1)$ and, assuming no externally applied forces, the force equation at M_2 is therefore

$$0 = M_2 \ddot{x}_2 + K (x_2 - x_1) \tag{14}$$

The force applied to M_1 is $K_2(x_2 - x_1)$ and the force equation there is

$$K_2(x_2 - x_1) = M_1 \ddot{x}_1 + K_1 x_1 \tag{15}$$

We see that we have two differential equations that we must solve simultaneously for $x_1(t)$ and $x_2(t)$. The procedure for developing an analog computer diagram for solving these equations is simular to that used for a single equation. We first solve (14) for $\ddot{x}_2$ and (15) for $\ddot{x}_1$, yielding:

232

$$\ddot{x}_2 = \left(\frac{-K_2}{M_2}\right) x_2 + \left(\frac{K_2}{M_2}\right) x_1 \tag{16}$$

$$\ddot{x}_1 = \left(\frac{K_2}{M_1}\right) x_2 - \left(\frac{K_2 + K_1}{M_1}\right) x_1 \tag{17}$$

We then use integrators and coefficient potentiometers to develop the lower order terms and combine them in accordance with the equations. To illustrate, suppose $M_1 = M_2 = 1$ Kg, and $K_1 = K_2 = 5$ N/m. Then equations (16) and (17) become

$$\ddot{x}_2 = -5x_2 + 5x_1$$

$$\ddot{x}_1 = 5x_2 - 10x_1$$

Figure 15.5 shows the computer diagram that can be used for solving these equations, when the initial conditions are $x_1(0) = 0$, $x_2(0) = 1$, $\dot{x}_1(0) = \dot{x}_2(0) = 0$, i.e., when the system starts at rest with an initial displacement of M_2.

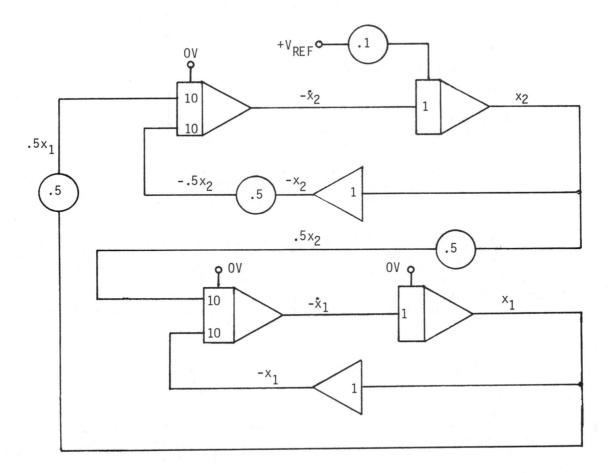

Figure 15.5   Computer diagram used for solving the differential equations
$\ddot{x}_2 = -5x_2 + 5x_1$ and $\ddot{x}_1 = 5x_2 - 10x_1$ simultaneously.

This example provides a good illustration of the value of an analog computer for investigating systems whose differential equations are difficult to solve analytically. The solutions $x_1(t)$ and $x_2(t)$ to equations 16 and 17 are quite difficult to obtain without a computer. The solutions turn out to be sums of sine waves with different frequencies and phase angles, and the waveshapes depend heavily on the initial conditions. Figure 15.6 shows an oscilloscope display of $x_1(t)$ and $x_2(t)$ obtained from a computer run of Figure 15.5. The harmonic content of the waveforms is apparent.

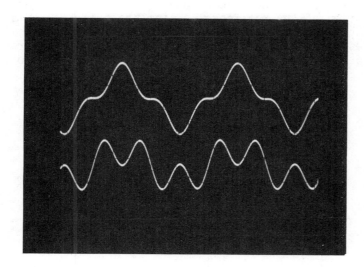

Figure 15.6   The solutions $x_1(t)$ and $x_2(t)$ obtained
from the computer setup of Figure 15.5.

PROCEDURE

1. Construct the analog computer circuit shown in Figure 15.2 of the Discussion. Monitor the voltage proportional to -x on an oscilloscope and run the problem using repetitive operation, if available.

2. Vary the $\zeta/2$ potentiometer setting back and forth and observe the effect that changes in ζ have on the solution waveform. Critical damping occurs when the $\zeta/2$ potentiometer is set to a value just slightly greater than that which causes the waveform to first overshoot, i.e., just before it rises slightly above the value it finally settles down to. Adjust the potentiometer until your observation of the waveform convinces you that you have critical damping. Then record the potentiometer setting.

3. Now set the $\zeta/2$ potentiometer to 0.1. Carefully measure and record the voltage proportional to -x at several different time points. Record the period of the damped oscillation, its peak and final values, and the time-constant of the envelope.

4. Repeat step 3 with the $\zeta/2$ potentiometer set to 0.7, except this time no oscillations should be observed. Record a sufficient number of values to enable you to reproduce the waveform accurately in a sketch and to verify the theoretical equation at several time points.

5. Now set the $\zeta/2$ potentiometer to zero. Record relevant information needed to describe the waveform that results in this case. Be prepared to describe and explain the appearance of this wave.

6. Restore the setting of the $\zeta/2$ potentiometer of 0.1. Now modify the setup so that it simulates the system of Figure 15.1 with no external force applied but with an initial displacement $x(0)$. Set, measure, and connect an initial condition voltage at an appropriate location in the circuit. Observe how this change affects the solution waveform (particularly its initial and final values).

7. Draw an analog computer diagram that can be used to solve the differential equation that describes the motion of the rotational system shown in Figure 15.7. Include provisions for developing a voltage proportional to Θ, and amplitude-scale your diagram using the criteria described in the Discussion section for second order systems. (In this system, $\omega_n^2 = K/J$.) Assume a torque of $T = 10$ N-m is applied to the inertia J.

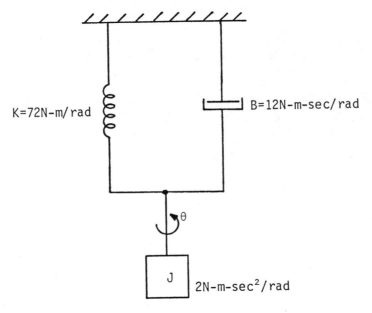

Figure 15.7

8. Run your problem setup and monitor and record voltages proportional to Θ, $\dot{\Theta}$, and $\ddot{\Theta}$, obtaining enough values to enable you to reproduce the waveforms in accurate sketches.

9. Construct and run the analog computer circuit shown in Figure 15.5 of the Discussion. Monitor and record the waveforms x_1 and x_2 using repetitive operation. It is not necessary to record a large number of values of these waveforms, but obtain sufficient data to sketch their general waveshapes.

10. Now use a coefficient potentiometer to connect an initial condition to the integrator whose output is x_1, thus simulating an initial displacement of the mass M_1 (in addition to the initial displacement of M_2). Observe the effect of changing the magnitude and polarity of this initial displacement on the waveshapes of x_1 and x_2. Experiment with different combinations of initial conditions of x_1, x_2, $\dot{x}_1$ and $\dot{x}_2$ and observe the effects these combinations have on x_1 and x_2.

11. Now restore all initial conditions to their original values. Set the horizontal sweep on the oscilloscope to "external," so there is no horizontal deflection of the trace. To gain insight into the variations of the displacements x_1 and x_2, run the problem in real-time (in the run, or operate, mode, i.e., without repetitive operation) and

observe how the amplitudes of x_1 and x_2 vary with time and with respect to each other. Try to visualize the two masses moving back and forth as you observe the display. With this setup, experiment also with the effects of initial condition inputs.

12. Add damping B_1 and B_2 to the two masses shown in Figure 15.4. Write the differential equations that describe this modified system and draw a computer diagram for solving them. Construct the computer circuit and investigate the effects of various amounts of damping on the waveshapes of the solutions.

13. Write the differential equations of motion for the system shown in Figure 15.8.

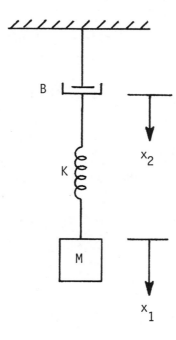

Figure 15.8

Select values for B, K, and M and draw a computer diagram for solving $x_1(t)$ and $x_2(t)$. Construct your circuit and run the problem for the case where x_1 has an initial value. Record the solution waveforms obtained and experiment to determine the effects that different values of the parameters have on the solutions.

QUESTIONS

1. Describe in general terms the effects of varying the setting of the $\zeta/2$ potentiometer in step 2 of the Procedure. Relate your discussion to the spring-mass-damping system that the computer setup simulates.

2. How close were you able to adjust the damping factor to step 2 of the Procedure to its

critical value? What was the potentiometer setting that you obtained through experimental observation of the solution waveform?

3. What actual damping B was simulated in step 3 of the Procedure? Sketch the solution waveform that you observed. Based on your observations and the measurements made in this step, write a mathematical expression for the solution $x(t)$. Convert all voltage readings to the actual physical quantities represented in the mechanical system and use these quantities in your expression for $x(t)$. Then compare your expression with the theoretical expression given in the Discussion for this case. In particular, compare significant characteristics of the theoretical and experimentally derived expressions, such as peak, initial, and final values, time constants, etc. For at least one value of t (other than t = 0), calculate the theoretical $x(t)$ and compare its value with a measurement made at that value of t, after adjusting for scaling.

4. Repeat question 3 for Procedure step 4.

5. Sketch the waveform observed in step 5 of the Procedure. What damping was in the system in this case? How do you explain the results?

6. What value of initial condition did you use in step 6 of the Procedure? Describe and explain how the changes made in this step affected the solution $x(t)$, as compared to that obtained in step 3 of the Procedure.

7. Show the computer diagram that you used to solve the differential equation describing the system in Figure 15.7. Sketch the waveforms $\Theta(t)$, $\dot{\Theta}(t)$, and $\ddot{\Theta}(t)$ that you observed when you ran your setup on the computer. Based on your experimental results, is the system under, over, or critically damped? Write the theoretical expression for $\Theta(t)$ and calculate the theoretical damping factor. How well do your observations support the theory? How successful was your amplitude scaling in this problem, in terms of the actual maximum values reached by the variables? Discuss similarities between this rotational system and the translational system investigated previously.

8. Sketch the general waveshapes of the waveforms $x_1(t)$ and $x_2(t)$ that you observed in steps 9 and 10 of the Procedure for the various combinations of initial conditions that you tried. According to theory, the solutions $x_1(t)$ and $x_2(t)$ are of the general form:

$$x_1(t) = A_1\sin(\omega_1 t + \Theta_1) + A_2\sin(\omega_2 t + \Theta_2)$$

$$x_2(t) = A_3\sin(\omega_1 t + \Theta_3) + A_4\sin(\omega_2 t + \Theta_4)$$

where the amplitudes A_1, A_2, ... , and phase angles Θ_1, Θ_2, ..., are determined by the initial conditions. Based on your observations of $x_1(t)$ and $x_2(t)$, can you determine an approximate relationship between ω_1 and ω_2? Discuss how the terms in the theoretical solutions seem to be affected by changes in the initial conditions, based on your observations.

9. Show the differential equations you wrote for the system of Figure 15.4 after the damping terms B_1 and B_2 were included. Show the computer diagram you used to solve the modified problem. Compare and contrast the solution waveforms you obtained from running this problem with those obtained in the undamped problem. Explain differences, in terms of the physical behavior of the system.

10. Show the differential equations you wrote for the system of Figure 15.8, and the computer diagram used to solve them. Describe the results of your investigation of the system. Relate your observations to the actual physical parameters that you used in your simulation and the effects that different combinations of the values of these parameters have on the solutions.

16 Forcing Functions; Electronic Multiplication

OBJECTIVES

1. To learn how to generate certain forcing functions that are commonly encountered in differential equations.

2. To verify experimentally the solutions of differential equations having nonconstant forcing functions.

3. To learn through experimental verification the principle of superposition applied to a differential equation with more than one forcing function.

4. To learn how to use an electronic multiplier in an analog computer setup, and how to generate a forcing function by multiplication of two time-varying voltages.

DISCUSSION

In previous experiments we solved differential equations that were in the form of a sum of terms involving a dependent variable and its derivatives set equal to zero or to a constant. We studied, for example, the equation of the motion x of a spring-mass-damping system:

$$M\ddot{x} + B\dot{x} + Kx = F \tag{1}$$

where F is a constant equal to the applied force. In many practical systems that are simulated on an analog computer, the right hand side of an equation such as (1) is not a constant, but rather some function of the independent variable time (t). For example, in the spring-mass-damping system the applied force might be changing with time. In that case the force would be expressed as a function of time $F(t)$, and we would have to connect computer elements to generate that function. Such a function is called a <u>forcing function</u>. Commonly encountered forcing functions include Kt, e^{-Kt}, and $K\sin\omega t$, where K and ω are constants. We should note that $F(t) = K$, a constant, is also considered a forcing function.

It is easy to generate the forcing function $F(t) = \pm Kt$, a <u>ramp</u> that increases or decreases linearly with time and that has slope $\pm K$. Recall that

$$\int_0^t K\,dt = Kt$$

Consequently, taking into account the sign inversion caused by the operational amplifier, we can generate $\pm Kt$ simply by connecting a constant voltage $\mp K$ to the input of an integrator. See for example Figure 16.1. Clearly this function will eventually reach a voltage equal to the maximum rated computer voltage. For example, if $V_{REF} = 10$ V and K = 2 then

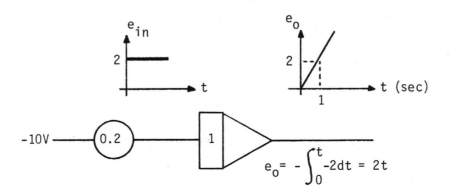

Figure 16.1 An integrator used to generate the (ramp)
forcing function F(t) = 2t.

$F(t) = Kt = 2t$ will saturate the integrator generating it in 5 seconds. Similarly, the solution $y(t)$ to most differential equations having the driving function $F(t) = Kt$ will increase indefinitely with time. For example, the theoretical solution to $\dot{y} + y = K_1 t + K_2$ is

$$y(t) = (K_1 - K_2 + y(0))e^{-t} + K_1 t + K_2 - K_1$$

and $\lim_{t \to \infty} y(t) = \infty$.

Figure 16.2 shows a computer diagram for solving this equation, assuming that K_1/V_{REF} and K_1/V_{REF} are between 0 and 1.

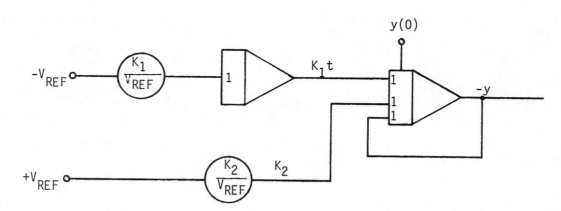

16.2 A computer diagram used to solve the differential equation $y + y = K_1 t + K_2$.

To generate the forcing function $F(t) = K_0 e^{-Kt}$, we may use the circuit shown in Figure 16.3 (assuming $0 \le K \le 1$). The circuit shown in Figure 16.3 is simply the computer implementation required to solve the differential equation $\dot{y} + Ky = 0$, or

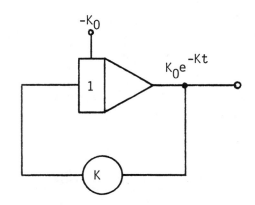

Figure 16.3 An integrator used to generate the forcing function $F(t) = K_0 e^{-Kt}$.

$$\dot{y} = -Ky, \text{ with } y(0) = K_0.$$

Note that if $y = K_0 e^{-Kt}$, then $\dot{y} = -KK_0 e^{-Kt}$ and the equation is satisfied.

An example of a differential equation with this forcing function is

$$\ddot{y} + K_1\dot{y} + K_2 y = e^{-at}.$$

If $K_1^2 < 4K_2$, then its theoretical solution is the sum of
(1) an exponentially decaying term with time constant $1/a$ seconds, and
(2) a damped oscillation with frequency $\omega\sqrt{1-\zeta^2}$, the time constant of whose envelope is $1/\zeta\omega$, where $\omega = K_2$ and $\zeta = K_1/2\sqrt{K_2}$.

That is, $y(t)$ is of the form

$$y(t) = Ae^{-at} + Be^{-\zeta\omega t}\sin(\omega\sqrt{1-\zeta^2}t + \Theta)$$

where A, B, and Θ are constants whose values depend on K_1, K_2 and a.

To generate a sinusoidal forcing function $F(t) = \sin\omega t$ on the computer, we solve the differential equation:

$$\ddot{y} + \omega^2 y = 0, \text{ or } \ddot{y} = -\omega^2 y.$$

Note that if $y = \sin\omega t$, then $\dot{y} = \omega\cos\omega t$, and $\ddot{y} = -\omega^2\sin t$, and the equation is solved. Figure 16.4 shows one computer implementation. With this setup the user can change the frequency ω by adjusting the potentiometer $(\omega^2/1000)$. Note in Figure 16.4 that the initial condition for the integrator producing $-\dot{y}$ is $-\dot{y}(0) = \omega\cos(0) = -\omega$, while that for $10y$ is $10\sin(0) = 0$. An example of a differential equation with this forcing function is

$$\ddot{y} + K_1\dot{y} + K_2 y = K_3\sin\omega t \tag{2}$$

When $K_1^2 < 4K_2$, its theoretical solution is of the form

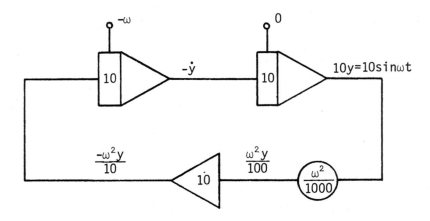

Figure 16.4 A computer diagram that generates a
sinusoidal forcing function by solving
the differential equation $\ddot{y} + \omega^2 y = 0$.

$$y(t) = Ae^{-\zeta\omega_1 t}\sin(\sqrt{1-\zeta^2}\,\omega_1 t + \Theta) + B\sin(\omega t + \phi)$$

where $\omega_1 = K_2$, $\zeta = K_1/2\sqrt{K_2}$ and A, B, Θ, and ϕ are constants. Note the presence of two
distinct frequencies, $\sqrt{1-\zeta^2}\,\omega_1$ and ω. The term with frequency $\sqrt{1-\zeta^2}\,\omega_1$ is the transient solution which eventually decays to zero with time constant $1/\zeta\omega_1$ seconds, while the term with
frequency ω is the steady-state solution, reached after a long period of time. The circuit
of Figure 16.5 illustrates a physical system which gives rise to the differential equation
of this example.

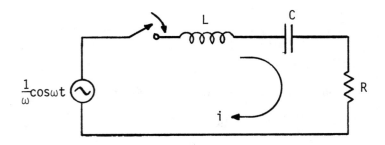

Figure 16.5 An RLC circuit whose differential
equation has a sinusoidal forcing
function.

When the switch is closed, Kirchhoff's Voltage Law requires that

$$L\frac{di}{dt} + iR + \frac{1}{C}\int i\,dt = \frac{1}{\omega}\cos\omega t$$

Differentiating both sides, we obtain

$$L \frac{d^2i}{dt^2} + R\frac{di}{dt} + \frac{i}{C} = \sin\omega t$$

or,

$$\frac{d^2i}{dt^2} + \frac{R}{L}\frac{di}{dt} + \frac{i}{LC} = \frac{1}{L}\sin\omega t \qquad (3)$$

By comparison with equation (2) we see that $K_1 = R/L$ and $K_2 = 1/LC$. The frequency $\omega_1 = \sqrt{K_2} = 1/\sqrt{LC}$ is the natural frequency of the circuit, while the damping factor is $\zeta = K_1/2\sqrt{K_2} = (R/2)(\sqrt{C/L})$. When the switch is thrown, the current exhibits an initial, transient oscillation at the damped natural frequency $\omega_1 \sqrt{1-\zeta^2}$, as determined by circuit parameters, in combination with a sinusoidal term whose frequency ω is that of the forcing function $\sin\omega t$. The latter persists after the former decays to zero. Figure 16.6 is an oscilloscope display of the solution $i(t)$ to equation (3) for a case in which ω_1 is considerably less than ω. At the beginning of the waveform the presence of both frequencies is clearly evident. Note how the transient oscillation is superimposed on the oscillation having frequency ω, and that the latter eventually persists.

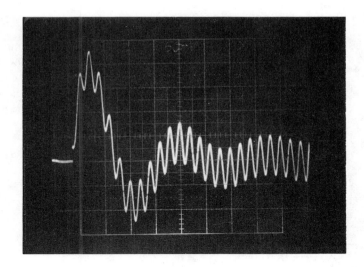

Figure 16.6 i(t) versus t in the underdamped RLC
circuit. The damped natural frequency
ω_1 is less than the frequency ω of the
forcing function.

The differential equations we have investigated thus far have all been <u>linear</u> differential equations, equations in which neither the dependent variable nor any of its derivatives are raised to a power other than unity, and in which there are no product terms of the dependent variable nor any of its derivatives with each other. Examples of <u>non-linear</u> differential equations are $\ddot{y}^2 + y = K$ and $\ddot{y}y + y = K$. If a differential equation is linear, then the <u>principle of superposition</u> may be applied to it. According to this principle, if there is more than one forcing function we may obtain the solution of the equation due to each forcing function acting alone and then add these results to obtain the actual solution due to all forcing functions acting simultaneously. For example, if the solution to $\dot{y}$ + Ky = $f_1(t)$ is $y_1(t)$ and if the solution to $\dot{y}$ + ky = $f_2(t)$, then the solution to $\dot{y}$ + ky = $f_1(t)$ + $f_2(t)$ is $y_1(t)$ + $y_2(t)$.

Most modern analog computers are equipped with electronic <u>multipliers</u>. .A multiplier can be patched into an analog setup in such a way that it produces a voltage which is proportional to the product of two time-varying voltages. This is a useful feature for generating forcing functions that can be represented as the product of two other functions, as for example F(t) = $K_1 te^{-K_2 t}$. The standard symbol for a multiplier is shown in Figure 16.7.

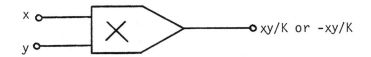

Figure 16.7 Analog computer symbol for a multiplier.

Depending on the type of analog computer used, it may be necessary to patch a multiplying network to one of the general purpose operational amplifiers in order to accomplish multiplication. Also, the output of a multiplier is typically a voltage equal to the product -xy, divided by a constant, for example -xy/10. Figure 16.8 shows the connections necessary to achieve multiplication on the Comdyna GP6 analog computer. The output E_0 of the amplifier is -xy/10.

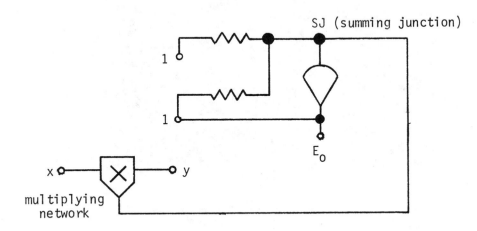

Figure 16.8 Multiplier connection on a Comdyna GP6 analog computer.

Hereafter, we will use the symbol shown in Figure 16.7 to represent multiplication, with the understanding that the user will connect whatever additional amplifier circuitry necessary to achieve multiplication on the computer being used. We will assume the output of the multiplier is $-xy/V_{REF}$.

PROCEDURE

1. Draw a computer diagram and construct the computer circuit necessary to solve the differential equation $\dot{y} + y = .5t + 5$, given that $y(0) = -10$. Construct your circuit in such a way that you can observe + $y(t)$ on an oscilloscope.

2. Monitor the voltages proportional to .5t and + $y(t)$ simultaneously on a dual trace oscilloscope while running the problem in rep-op, if available. Record a sufficient number of values to enable you to reproduce the waveforms in an accurate sketch. Note that one or more amplifiers may saturate during the course of a run, particularly if the rep-op frequency is set low. Disregard saturation voltages.

3. Experiment with the polarity and magnitude of the constant voltage applied to the integrator that generates the ramp voltage, and observe the effects that changing this voltage has on the shape of the ramp and on $y(t)$.

4. Draw a computer diagram and construct the circuit necessary to solve the differential equation $\ddot{y} + 2\dot{y} + 100y = 10e^{-.25t}$.

5. Monitor the voltages proportional to $10e^{-.25t}$ and $y(t)$ simultaneously on a dual trace oscilloscope while running the problem in rep-op, if available. Record a sufficient number of values to enable you to reproduce the waveforms in an accurate sketch.

6. Experiment with the setting of the coefficient potentiometer used to set K in the generation of $10e^{-kt}$ (initially set, in step 5, to 0.25). Observe the effects of changing K on the exponential forcing function and on $y(t)$. Record $y(t)$ when the forcing function is $10e^{-.125t}$.

7. Now remove the exponential forcing function and replace it with the constant forcing function + 7. Record the resulting $y(t)$.

8. Now connect both the constant forcing function + 7 and the exponential forcing function $10e^{-.125t}$ so that both are applied simultaneously to find the solution of

    $$\ddot{y} + 2\dot{y} + 100y = 10e^{-.125t} + 7.$$

    Again record $y(t)$.

9. Draw a computer diagram and construct the circuit necessary to solve the differential equation

    $$\ddot{y} + .5\dot{y} + y = 2.5 \sin 10t$$

    Construct your circuit so that the frequency ω of the forcing function can be changed by changing the setting of a potentiometer (see the Discussion).

10. Monitor the voltages proportional to $y(t)$ and $2.5\sin(10t)$ and record a sufficient number of values and waveform characteristics to enable you to reproduce them in an accurate sketch.

11. Experiment with the setting of the potentiometer used to set ω^2 in the forcing function generator and observe the effects that changes in this setting have on $y(t)$. Be sure to adjust initial conditions, as necessary.

12. Draw a computer diagram and construct the computer circuit necessary to generate the forcing function $F(t) = 10te^{-.4t}$. Use a multiplier to produce the product of t and $10e^{-.4t}$. Be certain to include an appropriate initial condition in the generation of the latter.

13. Run your setup using rep-op. Use a rep-op frequency that is fast enough to prevent the ramp voltage t from saturating the amplifier that generates it. Monitor and record the voltage representing F(t), obtaining enough values to reproduce it accurately in a sketch.

14. Experiment with the potentiometer used to set 0.4 in the generation of $e^{-.4t}$ and observe the effects on F(t) of changing this value.

QUESTIONS

1. Show the computer diagram you used to solve the differential equation in step 1 of the Procedure. Write the theoretical solution to this differential equation (see the Discussion section).

2. Sketch the waveforms observed in step 2 of the Procedure. Based on these sketches and the data recorded in the Procedure, write the equations for the forcing function and the solution y(t), remembering to take into account any time-scaling that may be involved. Compare these results with their theoretical counterparts.

3. Describe the effects of your experimentation in step 3 of the Procedure. Interpret these effects in light of the theory.

4. Repeat question 1 for Procedure step 4.

5. Repeat question 2 for Procedure step 5.

6. Repeat question 3 for Procedure step 6.

7. Sketch the y(t) waveform observed when the forcing function was set to $10e^{-.125t}$ in step 6 of the Procedure, and with the same set of axes (on the same graph) sketch the y(t) waveform observed when the forcing function was set to the constant + 7 in step 7 of the Procedure.

8. Now do a point-by-point (graphical) addition to these two waveforms, using the same set of axes.

9. Sketch the y(t) waveform observed in step 8 of the Procedure. Compare this waveform with that determined by graphical addition in question 8. Should these be the same? Explain. Give an example of a differential equation whose solution could not be found this way.

10. Repeat question 1 for Procedure step 9.

11. Repeat question 2 for Procedure step 10.

12. Repeat question 3 for Procedure step 11.

13. Show the computer diagram you used to generate the forcing function in step 12 of the Procedure.

14. Sketch the function F(t) observed in step 13 of the Procedure. Based on your sketch and observed data, write the expression for F(t), taking into account any time scaling that may have been involved. Compare this result with the theoretical F(t).

15. Describe the results of your experimentation in step 14 of the Procedure. Explain these results in light of the theory.

16. What is the theoretical maximum value of $F(t) = 10te^{-.4t}$, and at what value of t does it occur? (Hint: differentiate and set equal to zero.) Compare these theoretical values with those taken from your sketch in question 14.

17 Analog Simulation of Control Systems

OBJECTIVES

1. To learn how to write the differential equation describing a control system, after deriving its closed-loop transfer function C/R.

2. To learn how to simulate a control system on an analog computer using the differential equation derived from its transfer function.

3. To investigate the effect of lead compensation on the response of a control system using an analog computer simulation.

4. To investigate the stability of a control system as a function of its open loop gain K using an analog computer simulation.

DISCUSSION

Analog computers are particularly well suited for the simulation of continuous type control systems. In this role, they are a valuable aid to the control systems designer because they make it possible to observe the effects of changes in control system components on response times, overshoots, stability, and other characteristics related to system optimization. By simply changing potentiometer settings, the designer is able to observe instantly the effects of changes in such parameters as gain, damping, inertia, and so forth.

The first step in a control systems simulation is to draw a block diagram of the system using blocks that show the transfer function of each component in the system. The transfer functions should be expressed using Laplace transforms. Consider, for example, the simple position control system shown in Figure 17.1. The input Θ_{in} is an angular rotational of a potentiometer shaft. The potentiometer has transfer function $V/2\pi$ volts/radian (independent of frequency) and its output voltage is applied to a differential amplifier with gain (transfer function) K_1, which is assumed to be independent of frequency. The differential amplifier derives a servomotor having transfer function $K_2/s(s + a)$, which in turn drives a feedback potentiometer. The angular rotation Θ_0 of the motor shaft is the output of the system, and a voltage proportional to this rotation is fed back to the differential amplifier for comparison with the input. When the output equals the input, there is no voltage applied to the servomotor and rotation ceases.

The next step in the simulation is to simplify the block diagram so that the overall transfer function of the control system (C/R) is obtained. For the block diagram in Figure 17.2, we first use the simplification $G/(1 + GH)$, where G is the forward transfer function and H is the feedback transfer function, to reduce the portion of the diagram that contains the feedback loop:

248

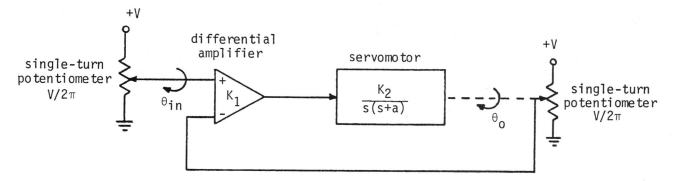

Figure 17.1 A position control system whose response can be modeled on an analog computer.

The block diagram corresponding to Figure 17.1 is shown in Figure 17.2.

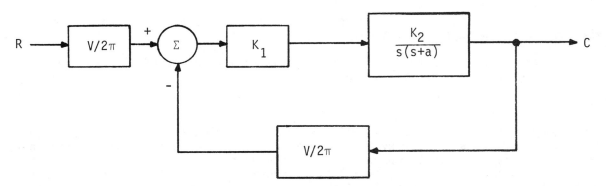

Figure 17.2 Block diagram showing the transfer functions of the control system in Figure 17.1

In Figure 17.2, the conventional symbols for the input (R) and output (C) of a control system are used, instead of Θ_{in} and Θ_0.

$$\frac{G}{1 + GH} = \frac{\dfrac{K_1 K_2}{s(s+a)}}{1 + \left[\dfrac{K_1 K_2}{s(s+a)}\right]\dfrac{V}{2\pi}} = \frac{K_1 K_2}{s(s + a) + K_1 K_2 V/2\pi}$$

The block diagram of Figure 17.2 is thus simplified to that shown in Figure 17.3.

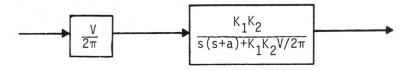

Figure 17.3 A simplified block diagram of the position control system.

From Figure 17.3, we see that

$$C/R = \frac{K_1 K_2 V/2\pi}{s(s + a) + K_1 K_2 V/2\pi}$$

$$= \frac{K}{s^2 + as + K} \tag{1}$$

where
$$K = K_1 K_2 V/2\pi$$

The next step in the simulation is to write a differential equation that is equivalent to the transfer function. "Cross-multiplying" equation (1), we have

$$C(s^2 + as + K) = KR$$

$$Cs^2 + Cas + CK = KR \tag{2}$$

Assuming zero initial conditions, the multiplication of a variable by s corresponds to differentiation of that variable in the time-domain, while multiplication by s^2 implies the second derivative with respect to time. Therefore, equation (2) may be expressed in the time-domain as

$$\ddot{C} + a\dot{C} + KC = KR$$

Equation (3) is now in a form that can be readily solved by analog computer, using the standard approach we have seen in previous experiments. We solve for the highest order derivative ($\ddot{C}$) and obtain

$$\ddot{C} = KR - a\dot{C} - KC \tag{4}$$

The analog computer solution of equation (4) for the variable C gives us a voltage which varies in the same way that the angular output Θ_0 varies in the control system of Figure 17.1. Figure 17.4 shows an analog computer diagram that can be used for this example. Of course Figure 17.4 does not reflect any magnitude or time scaling, since we do not have specific values for a and K. We have assumed that $a \leqslant 10$ and that $K \leqslant 100$ and hence use coefficient potentiometers with settings a/10 and K/100. In practice, we may have to adjust amplifier gains and potentiometer settings to accommodate different ranges for a and K and to accomplish magnitude scaling. However, the important idea that Figure 17.4 conveys is that we can examine the effect of variations in the potentiometer settings on the output C of the control system. We can therefore experimentally determine values of the control system parameters that produce a desired or optimum response. Note in particular that by varying the potentiometers set to K/100, we can determine the effects of changes in the open-loop gain of the system (recall that $K = K_1 K_2 V/2\pi$). We could, for example, find the maximum amplifier gain K_1 that the system could tolerate without having the response overshoot a prescribed value, or find the value of gain that results in a critically damped response to a step input.

Consider now the control system whose block diagram is shown in Figure 17.5. This represents a position control system that has been lead-compensated. The block diagram shown in Figure 17.5 can be simplified to obtain

$$C/R = \frac{K_1 K_3 + K_2 K_3 s}{s^2 + (a + K_2 K_3)s + K_1 K_3} \tag{5}$$

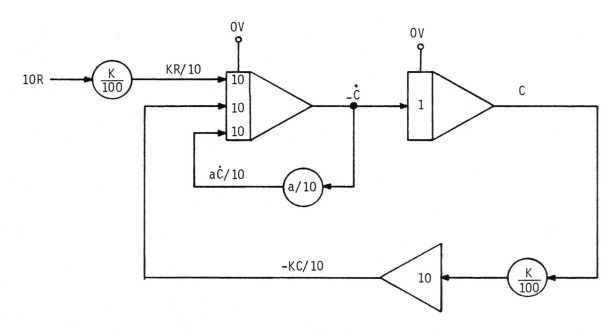

Figure 17.4 Analog computer simulation of the position control system.

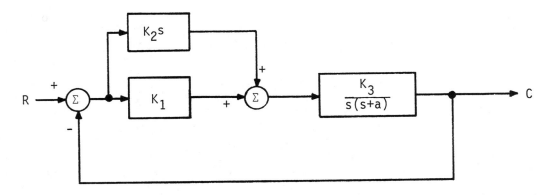

Figure 17.5 Block diagram of a lead-compensated position control system.

Equation (5) is equivalent to

$$Cs^2 + C(a + K_2K_3)s + K_1K_3C = K_1K_3R + K_2K_3Rs \qquad (6)$$

Assuming zero initial conditions, the time-domain equivalent of equation (6) is

$$\ddot{C} + (a + K_2K_3)\dot{C} + K_1K_3C = K_1K_3R + K_2K_3\dot{R} \qquad (7)$$

We note in equation (7) that there is a term $\dot{R}$, which represents the derivative of the input to the control system. Since we do not wish to perform differentiation on the analog computer (because of noise problems, as discussed in Chapter 13), we must devise a means for solving equation (7) without the use of a differentiator. This can be accomplished by first solving (7) for the quantity $\ddot{C}-K_2K_3\dot{R}$, instead of C as we usually do. From (7), then, we obtain

$$\ddot{C}-K_2K_3\dot{R} = K_1K_3R - (a + K_2K_3)\dot{C} - K_1K_3C \qquad (8)$$

Proceeding in the usual way, we assume we have the quantity $\ddot{C}-K_2K_3\dot{R}$, integrate it, and develop the other terms of the equation. Note that

$$\int(\ddot{C}-K_2K_3\dot{R})dt = \dot{C}-K_2K_3R$$

Therefore, the output of the first integrator will be $-(\dot{C}-K_2K_3R) = -\dot{C} + K_2K_3R$, and so to obtain $-\dot{C}$ we need only subtract K_2K_3R from that output. Figure 17.6 illustrates this result.

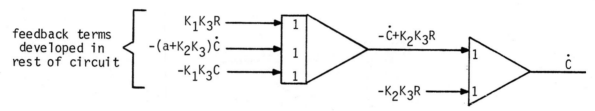

Figure 17.6   Generation of the term $\dot{C}$ from the equation $\ddot{C}-K_2K_3\dot{R} = K_1K_3R$
(a + $K_2K_3)\dot{C}-K_1K_3C$.

As a specific example, suppose $a = 10$, $K_1 = 1$, and $K_3 = 500$. We will construct an analog computer simulation of the control system and investigate the effect of the lead compensator gain K_2 on its response. With these parameter values, equation (8) becomes

$$\ddot{C} - 500K_2\dot{R} = 500R - (10 + 500K_2)\dot{C} - 500C \qquad (9)$$

Figure 17.7 shows the analog computer setup that solves equation (9).

When $K_2 = 0$, the system has no lead compensation at all, and for this case, the potentiometer having setting $(10 + 500K_2)/100$ is set equal to 0.1. Figure 17.8 is an oscilloscope photograph of the response C of the uncompensated system to a step input. We see that the system is underdamped and exhibits considerable oscillation before settling to its steady-state condition.

For $K_2 = 0.1$, the potentiometer having setting $(10 + 500 K_2)/100$ is set equal to 0.6. Figure 17.9 is an oscilloscope photograph of the response C for this case. We see that lead compensation has significantly improved the response. The rise time is essentially the same as in the uncompensated case, but the oscillations have been entirely eliminated.

Analog simulation of a control system is a useful way to investigate its <u>stability</u>. The output of a stable control system ultimately reaches and maintains some steady-state position, while the output of an unstable system <u>oscillates</u> indefinitely. If there exists some frequency at which the open-loop gain of the system has magnitude greater than or equal to 1 and phase shift 180°, then the system will oscillate at that frequency. Typically, increasing the open-loop gain K of the system makes it more vulnerable to instability and the accompanying oscillation. It is often possible to construct an analog computer circuit in which the gain K can be controlled by adjusting a single potentiometer and thus determine what value of K, if any, will cause instability.

Consider the control system whose block diagram is shown in Figure 17.10.

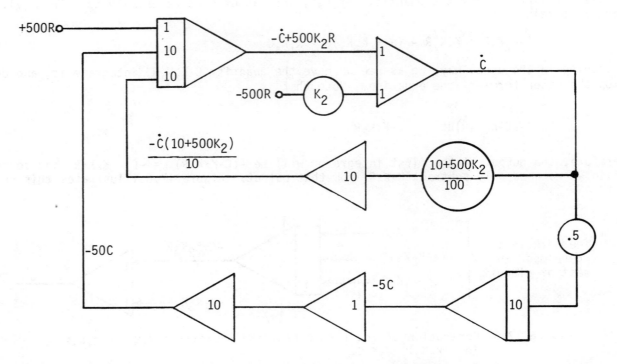

Figure 17.7   Analog computer setup for simulating the lead-compensated control system.

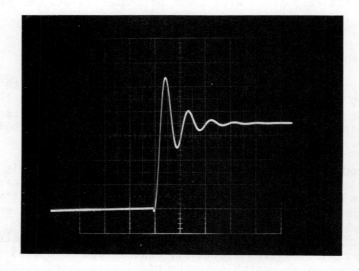

Figure 17.8   Response of the uncompensated control system ($K_2 = 0$).

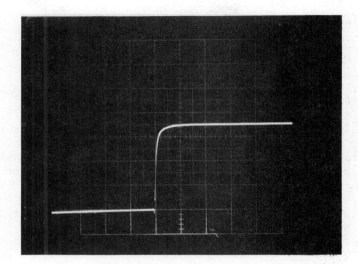

Figure 17.9 Response of the lead-compensated
control system (K_2 = 0.1).

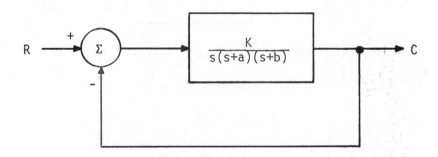

Figure 17.10 A control system whose stability is
determined by the loop-gain K.

Unlike the control systems discussed in the previous two examples, the system of Figure
17.10 has a potential for becoming unstable. Note in this case that the phase angle of the
open-loop transfer function, $K/[s(s + a)(s + b)]$, can exceed 180°, and in fact approaches
270° with increasing frequency. Thus it is possible that, for sufficiently large K, there
may exist a frequency that satisfies the oscillation criteria:

$$\left| \frac{K}{s(s + a)(s + b)} \right| > 1 \text{ and } \angle \frac{K}{s(s + a)(s + b)} = -180°$$

It can be shown* that the system will be unstable if $K \geqslant ab(a + b)$, and that the frequency of oscillation in such a case will be $f_c = \sqrt{ab}/(2\pi)$.

EXERCISES

1. Draw an analog computer diagram that can be used to simulate the control system shown in Figure 17.1 when a = 10, V = 10, K_2 = 8, and $1 \leqslant K_1 \leqslant 100$.

2. Construct the analog computer setup whose diagram you drew in exercise 1 and investigate the response C to a step input when K_1 = 4, K_1 = 8, and K_1 = 50. Sketch the response waveforms C(t) that you observe in each case. Compare your results with the results of the CSMP simulation runs that were described in Chapter 12 for the same control system.

3. Draw an analog computer diagram that can be used to simulate the control system whose block diagram is shown in Figure 17.11. Assume $1 \leqslant K \leqslant 100$.

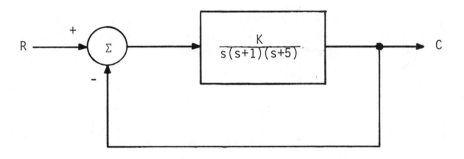

Figure 17.11

4. Construct the analog computer setup whose diagram you drew in Exercise 3. Determine experimentally the value of K that causes the system to become unstable. Measure the oscillation frequency when the system is unstable. Compare these experimentally determined values of gain and frequency with the theoretical values. Also determine experimentally the value of gain K that causes the system to be critically damped in response to a step input. (Adjust K to a value just less than that required to produce an overshoot in the response.)

5. Modify your analog computer diagram so it can be used to simulate the system of Figure 17.11 when K = 1.5 and the feedback loop contains a constant gain term H. Then repeat Exercise 4, finding values of H rather than K.

6. Draw an analog computer diagram that can be used to simulate the control system shown in Figure 17.12.

7. Construct the analog computer circuit whose diagram you drew in Exercise 6 and use it to determine the response C(t) to a step input when K_1 = 1 and K_2 = 0 (no lead compensation). Sketch the uncompensated response waveform. Then experimentally determine the effect of different values of K_2 on C(t) and sketch the response waveforms that result. Using your results, design what you consider to be an optimum system. (You

*See Bogart, <u>Laplace Transforms and Control Systems Theory for Technology</u>, Wiley, 1982, p. 223.

may experiment with different values for both K_1 and K_2.)

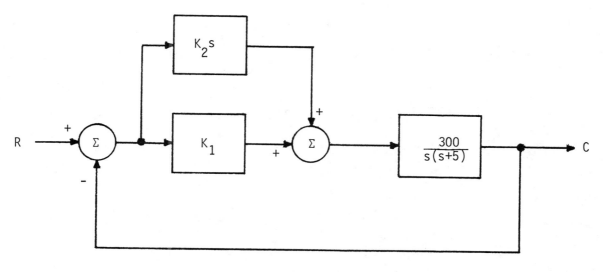

Figure 17.12